FRAMING INTERSEC

The Feminist Imagination – Europe and Beyond

Series Editors: Kathy Davis, Utrecht University, The Netherlands and Mary Evans, London School of Economics and Political Science, UK

With a specific focus on the notion of 'cultural translation' and 'travelling theory', this series operates on the assumption that ideas are shaped by the contexts in which they emerge, as well as by the ways that they 'travel' across borders and are received and re-articulated in new contexts. In demonstrating the complexity of the differences (and similarities) in feminist thought throughout Europe and between Europe and other parts of the world, the books in this series highlight the ways in which intellectual and political traditions, often read as homogeneous, are more often heterogeneous. It therefore provides a forum for the latest work that engages with the European experience, illuminating the various exchanges (from the USA as well as Europe) that have informed European feminism. The series thus allows for an international discussion about the history and imaginary of Europe from perspectives within and outside Europe, examining not only Europe's colonial legacy, but also the various forms of 'cultural imperialism' that have shaped societies outside Europe. Considering aspects of Europe 'abroad' as well as Europe 'at home', this series is committed to publishing work that reveals the central and continued importance of the genealogy of feminist ideas to feminism and all those interested in questions of gender.

Forthcoming title in the series

Transatlantic Conversations
Feminism as Travelling Theory
Edited by Kathy Davis and Mary Evans
ISBN 978-0-7546-7835-9

Framing Intersectionality
Debates on a Multi-Faceted Concept in Gender Studies

Edited by

HELMA LUTZ
MARIA TERESA HERRERA VIVAR
LINDA SUPIK
Goethe University, Frankfurt, Germany

ASHGATE

Published by
Ashgate Publishing Limited
Wey Court East
Union Road
Farnham
Surrey, GU9 7PT
England

Ashgate Publishing Company
Suite 420
101 Cherry Street
Burlington
VT 05401-4405
USA

www.ashgate.com

British Library Cataloguing in Publication Data
Framing intersectionality : debates on a multi-faceted
concept in gender studies. -- (The feminist imagination -
Europe and beyond)
1. Sex role--Research--United States. 2. Sex role--
Research--Europe. 3. Women's studies--United States.
4. Women's studies--Europe. 5. Men's studies--United
States. 6. Men's studies--Europe. 7. Feminist theory--
United States. 8. Feminist theory--Europe.
9. Discrimination--Research--United States.
10. Discrimination--Research--Europe.
I. Series II. Lutz, Helma. III. Herrera Vivar, Maria
Teresa. IV. Supik, Linda, 1975-
305.3'072-dc22

Library of Congress Cataloging-in-Publication Data
Framing intersectionality : debates on a multi-faceted concept in gender studies / [edited] by Helma Lutz, Maria Teresa Herrera Vivar and Linda Supik.
    p. cm. -- (The feminist imagination : Europe and beyond)
Includes bibliographical references and index.
ISBN 978-1-4094-1898-6 (hbk) -- ISBN 978-1-4094-1899-3 (pbk) -- ISBN 978-1-4094-1900-6 (ebook) 1. Women's studies--Research. 2. Men's studies--Research. 3. Interdisciplinary research.
I. Lutz, Helma. II. Herrera Vivar, Maria Teresa. III. Supik, Linda, 1975-

HQ1180.F686 2011
001.4--dc22
                                                                                          2010046198
ISBN 9781409418986 (hbk)
ISBN 9781409418993 (pbk)
ISBN 9781409419006 (ebook)

Printed and bound in Great Britain by the
MPG Books Group, UK

Contents

**PART III: ADVANCING INTERSECTIONALITY:
POTENTIALS, LIMITS AND CRITICAL QUERIES**

List of Contributors

Mechthild Bereswill, Prof. is Professor of Sociology at Kassel University (Department of Social Work). Her main research topics are feminist theories and research traditions; social inequalities; social control; and qualitative methodologies.

Kimberlé W. Crenshaw, Prof., B.A., J.D., LL.M., is Professor of Law at the University of California (UCLA) and Columbia School of Law, New York, USA. Her primary scholarly interests are race and the law, critical race studies, constitutional law, and civil rights.

Kathy Davis, Prof. is now senior researcher at the Institute of History and Culture at Utrecht University in the Netherlands. Her research interests include contemporary feminist approaches to the body, the beauty culture and cosmetic surgery, biography as methodology, reflexivity and critical theory, intersectionality, and transnational feminism.

Mary Evans, Prof. has taught Women's/Gender Studies in both the UK and the United States. She is now a Centennial Professor at the London School of Economics and is working on a study (with Barbara Einhorn) entitled Gender, Religion and the State.

Myra Marx Ferree, Prof. is Martindale–Bascom Professor of Sociology and Director of the Center for German and European Studies at the University of Wisconsin, Madison, USA. Her main research topics are women's movements, global feminisms, political discourse, gender equality policies, and intersectionality struggles.

Jeff Hearn, Prof. is Professor of Gender Studies (Critical Studies on Men), at Linköping University, Sweden; Professor of Management and Organization at Hanken School of Economics, Finland; and Professor of Sociology at the University of Huddersfield, UK. His main research topics include men, gender, sexuality, violence, organisations, management, transnationalisation and postcolonialism.

Maria Teresa Herrera Vivar, M.A., is researcher and lecturer at the Faculty of Social Sciences, Goethe University Frankfurt, Germany. She is preparing a doctoral thesis on the self-organisation of Latin-American domestic workers in Germany. Her further research interests are gender studies, migration, postcolonial theory, racism, intersectionality, and biographical research.

Gudrun-Axeli Knapp, Prof. was until recently Professor of Sociology and Social Psychology at the Institute of Sociology and Social Psychology, Leibniz University of Hannover, Germany. From 1999 until 2009 she was the Director of the Interdisciplinary Programme in Gender Studies at the Faculty of Philosophy. Her main research topics are feminist issues, developments in international feminist theory, social theory and interlocking structures of inequality and dominance.

Kira Kosnick, Prof. is Professor of Sociology with a special focus on Culture and Communication at the Faculty of Social Sciences, Goethe University Frankfurt, Germany. Her research interests focus on transnational migration, urban ethnicity, diversity politics and migrant media.

Helma Lutz, Prof. is Professor of Sociology with special focus on Women's and Gender Studies, Faculty of Social Sciences, Goethe University Frankfurt. Her main research topics include: women's and gender studies, migration, intersectionality, racism and ethnicity, qualitative research methods and biographical research.

Nina Lykke, Prof. is Professor of Gender Studies with special reference to Gender and Culture, Department of Thematic Studies: Gender Studies, Linköping University, Sweden. Her main research topics are feminist theories and methodologies, intersectionality, feminist cultural studies, feminist technoscience studies, and critical sexuality studies.

Anke Neuber, Dr., is researcher and lecturer at Kassel University (Department of Social Work). She is preparing her 'habilitation' on deviant behaviour and gender. Her further research interests are gender studies, feminist theories and approaches to masculinity studies, violence studies, methods of qualitative research, and biographical research.

Ann Phoenix, Prof. is Director of the Thomas Coram Research Unit, Institute of Education, at the University of London. Her research interests are psychosocial, including motherhood, social identities, young people, racialisation and gender.

Linda Supik, M.A., is researcher and lecturer at the Faculty of Social Sciences, Goethe University Frankfurt, Germany. She is preparing a doctoral thesis on the collection of ethnic data in the British census. Further research interests are racism and ethnicity, intersectionality, postcolonial theory, critique of statistics, and gender studies.

Paula-Irene Villa, Prof. holds a chair for Sociology/Gender studies at the Institute of Sociology at LMU Munich. Her main topics are social and feminist/gender theories, body and practices of embodiment, culture, and parenthood.

Nira Yuval-Davis, Prof. is Director of the Research Centre on Migration, Refugees and Belonging (CMRB) at the School of Humanities and Social Sciences, University of East London, UK. Her main research interests are theoretical and empirical aspects of intersected nationalisms, racisms, fundamentalisms, citizenships, identities, belonging/s and gender relations.

Dubravka Zarkov is Associate Professor of Gender, Conflict and Development at the International Institute of Social Studies/EUR (The Hague/Rotterdam). Her main research interests are media representations of war and violence, gender, ethnicity, sexuality and violent conflict, globalisation, development and war, intersectional analysis, and discourse analysis.

Preface

Feminism as a political movement was, and is, built around alliances that unite individual women. Yet the composition and focus of these alliances has, as the essays in this volume suggest, not always been unproblematic. A very important reason for this has been the differences in privilege and power that have always existed between women: in all the societies in which there has been a visible feminist movement there have also been hierarchies, be they of class or race. Since women do not exist in some extra-social space (although the gender of the majority of those in positions of institutional power has sometimes suggested that this is actually the case) some women have, to adapt George Orwell, been more unequal than others.

The identification of the major form of inequality between women was initially framed in different terms in different places. In the United States, the differences in civic status between African-Americans and white citizens were so marked and often so difficult to transcend that it was impossible to contest the view that women were deeply divided by race. In many parts of Europe, on the other hand, differences of social class created divisions between women that had, like those between women in the United States, long histories both of hostility and attempts at co-operation. From this, two observations are possible. The first is that the study of intersectionality, given a vibrant presence in this collection, draws on diverse histories which have different political dynamics to them. For example, the history of feminism in Britain demonstrates the efforts many women made to overcome differences of class, whilst at the same time a parallel history tells a story of the determined maintenance by other women to secure hierarchies of privilege through strategies of exclusion and marginalisation. What also becomes clear from those readings of history that recognise its complexity and contradiction is that part of the 'intersectional' history of women was a struggle both for the public space and for a democratisation of the private sphere. Yet in both cases, as much as both struggles were feminist in their identification, so the struggles related to, and had implications for, other interests of class and race.

The second observation that can be made about questions of intersectionality is that the issues that divide women can often change over time or be superseded by others. In the case of the history of Europe in the past 30 years it could be argued that both the concept and the reality of social class have changed dramatically as a result of shifts in the labour market and transformations of those cultural constructions that once underpinned rigid class and gender divisions. As women have come to make up an increasingly significant part of the labour force of many countries in the global north, feminist ideas and expectations about the possible rewards of work could be seen as an increasingly integrated and public part of the lives of all women, across lines of race and class. However, at the same time it is important to note that although feminism may have been responsible for the increasing equality of women with men in sectors of the labour market, so there is evidence of widening inequality between women.

Boundaries, therefore, whether of class or race, whilst not disappearing do not have consistent and unchanging contours. Related to this is the way in which we have become aware, in the past 20 years, of various other forms of difference, and inequality, between women. Two of the most striking instances here are the characteristics of age and ageing and various forms of disability. To grow old as a woman is, as Simone de Beauvoir pointed out, often a state in which the existing inequality of women with men is further magnified. To this verdict, we might well add that to be an old, poor woman who belongs to a marginal racial or ethnic group is even more unenviable.

However, this example serves to illuminate the ways in which a theory such as that of intersectionality, which is open to the many possible situations of human beings, has great richness. Indeed, it is also arguably a form of feminist theory that significantly advances those fundamentalist views of the social world that can only see human beings in terms of binary categories, be they of male/female or old/young. Although aspects of the history of feminism speak to the strength of the unifying force of the term 'woman', we now also recognise that this unity was sometimes formed by exclusion and the priorities of the most privileged. Yet intersectionality does not suggest that we should wholeheartedly abandon categories about ourselves, rather that we should enrich and enhance them by the recognition of the diverse, and constantly changing, circumstances in which we all live.

A commitment to learning to live with theoretical ambiguity, and the value of the possibilities of diversity, is the thread that unites the essays in this volume. It is a thread that, as well as underpinning considerable theoretical innovation, also allows us to find our way out of a politics (both within and external to explicit feminist campaigns) that maintains division through its oppositional and often all too coercive identities. It is thus that intersectionality offers us a form of politics, and political engagement, that is – paradoxically for all its emphasis on difference – a politics of the shared similarity of the diversity of human experience.

Mary Evans
Gender Institute, London School of Economics

Acknowledgements

Many people have helped us in the preparation of this volume.

We would like to thank Christine Grote for her energetic editorial assistance, and Gerard Holden for editing the contributions. Stefan Fey, Barbara Kowollik, Stefanie Mielast, AnkePtak, LieselotteRahbauer, Cecilia Scheid, Greta Wagner and Nele Zimmermann provided invaluable help with the planning, organization, and running of the conference on Celebrating Intersectionality? – Debates on a Multi-Faceted Concept in Gender Studies (http://www.cgc.uni-frankfurt.de/intersectionality/index.shtml). Raul Gschrey kindly made available the photograph of the Mikado sticks on the cover, and also designed the conference poster. We would like to thank the international conference participants for their stimulating contributions. We are also grateful to Neil Jordan of Ashgate for his work in helping us to bring the book to fruition.

Helma Lutz, Maria Teresa Herrera Vivar and Linda Supik
Frankfurt, Spring 2011

Framing Intersectionality: An Introduction

Helma Lutz, Maria Teresa Herrera Vivar and Linda Supik
[translated by Gerard Holden]

The debate about intersectionality is currently in full swing in Europe (see Grabham et al. 2008, Winker and Degele 2009, Lykke 2010, Schiek and Lawson 2010, Taylor et al. 2010). Our conference entitled 'Celebrating Intersectionality? Debates on a Multi-Faceted Concept in Gender Studies', which took place on 22–23 January 2009 at the Goethe University in Frankfurt, was based on the opinion that the concept's 20th anniversary should be celebrated in attendance of its 'mother' Kimberlé W. Crenshaw, who followed our invitation, along with other important feminist scholars from Europe and the US. At the same time, it seemed appropriate to discuss and challenge intersectionality's maturity after 20 years – therefore the title carries a question mark. Evidently, the conference came at just the right time. It was very well attended, with 300 participants of whom a third came from abroad (some of them from outside Europe). This volume is the result of the debates conducted at the conference. It attempts to take up both the agreements and the controversies that emerged, and in addition to taking stock of the debates it indicates future lines of investigation that could be followed. We therefore begin by looking back at the early stages of the debate about intersectionality, with the intention of making visible research from those early days that is usually neglected in the current debate (foundational narratives); we then present the range of different (European) locations and disciplinary fields in which intersectionality appears (the state of the debates); third, we discuss some ideas about future developments and possible trajectories of feminist intersectionality research (from women's and gender studies to feminist intersectionality studies). Our fourth section deals with one example that seems particularly challenging for the feminist research agenda in Europe, the debate about 'race' and racism (let's talk about 'race'). Our introduction ends with brief summaries of the contributions to this volume.

Foundational Narratives

The current discussion of the concept of intersectionality often fails to appreciate that the search for a satisfactory theorisation of the interlocking of and interactions between different social structures has a long history. Among the interventions that have been made on this topic, we can identify: attempts by Marxist-feminist theorists to analyse the relationship between capitalist societalisation and gender relations (see Barrett 1982, Barrett and McIntosh 1982); interventions from the perspective of (*white*[1]) lesbian feminism (see Radicalesbians 1970, Johnston 1973, Rich 1980); and publications on the connections between gender and disability (see Morris 1989, Meekosha 1990).

In view of these earlier contributions, it is open to debate how far the widespread use and acceptance of the term 'intersectionality' establishes a *new* agenda for women's and gender studies. The claim that intersectionality is just old wine in new bottles can be countered with the argument that, even though the ideas mentioned above shaped the debate at particular times and can be understood as forerunners of the concept of intersectionality, they did not yet reflect an intersectional perspective. The earlier discussions did pave the way for the debate around intersectionality in a number of different ways, but the concept of intersectionality itself, coined and substantiated by Crenshaw, released energies that made it possible to advance from an intersectionally conceived starting point. At the same time, as Nina Lykke has argued, one can distinguish within this debate between implicit, explicit, and alternative approaches to intersectionality (see Lykke 2010: 68–69; this volume).

In the analysis of the specific socio-economic situation of black women, it is possible for the first time to speak of the simultaneity and mutual co-constitution of different categories of social differentiation and to emphasise the specificity of the experiences shaped by these interactions. This premise means we can trace the roots of the intersectionality debate back to the analyses carried out by black feminists[2] in the context of the black women's rights movement in the USA. The critical consequences of this extension of the category of gender, and what this implied for feminist theory and politics, have been very well summed up by Kathy Davis: '"Intersectionality" addresses the most central theoretical and normative concern within feminist scholarship: namely, the acknowledgement of differences among women. This is because it touches on the most pressing problem facing contemporary feminism – the long and painful legacy of its exclusions' (Davis in this volume: p. 45).

At the heart of the exchanges about intersectionality was the accusation made by black feminists that *white*, bourgeois feminism had only raised the issue of *white* middle-class women's experiences of oppression and made this the measure of feminist politics, and so had ignored the needs and the reality of the lives of

---

1   The terms '*white*' and 'black' identify ascribed social-historical positions. It is important to stress that neither category relates to 'natural', visible pigmentations but rather to ideological constructions of 'skin colour' (Morrison 1992, hooks 1992, Frankenberg 1993, Ignatiev 1995, Jacobsen 1999).

2   One cannot, however, speak of black feminism as a homogeneous movement. There are very different assessments of the tensions between self-positioning as a feminist and as a protagonist of the black liberation movement (incorporating both genders), and one needs to bear in mind the criticisms of sexist tendencies that were present in that movement (see Roth 2004).

all other women, including black women. In response, they attempted to capture analytically the multidimensional nature and complexity of their own experience. Patricia Hill Collins' model of a 'matrix of domination', for example, includes an alternative conception which criticises both one-dimensional, single-axis analyses in *white* feminism and the additive conception formulated in such analyses of the combined action of different relations of oppression (for example the model of triple oppression or Francis Beale's [1979] concept of double jeopardy). Collins (1990) describes 'race',[3] class and gender instead as 'interlocking systems of oppression'. The socialist lesbian Combahee River Collective also argued that 'race', class and gender needed to be understood in terms of their mutual interactions: 'We believe that sexual politics under patriarchy is as pervasive in Black women's lives as are the politics of class and race. We also often find it difficult to separate race from class from sex oppression because in our lives they are most often experienced simultaneously' (Combahee River Collective 1981: 213). While lesbian feminist activists were criticising the marginalisation of the perspectives and concerns of lesbian women in the feminist mainstream, which they saw as dominated by heterosexuals, they were themselves being criticised on similar grounds. In *This Bridge Called My Back: Writings by radical women of color* (1981), Cherrie Moraga and Gloria Anzaldúa argued that lesbian feminism was itself unable to take into account the multiple dimensions of the social situation of women of colour and was instead perpetuating racist structures. Queer studies, which is seen as the continuation of this strand of feminist politics and theorising, is currently being subjected to similar criticism (see the contribution by Kira Kosnick in this volume).

In the European context, one can mention the fundamental contributions of Floya Anthias and Nira Yuval-Davis (1992) and of Avtar Brah (1996), who advocated the integration of other categories of social differentiation into feminist theoretical work. This led to exchanges about 'difference between women' and the category of 'women', which were framed in different ways in the various national contexts. In Germany, for example, these positions were treated as part of research on racism and migration, and were for a long time marginal in women's and gender studies (Gümen 1998, Erel et al. 2008), whereas in the UK the questions associated with these arguments were taken up as part of gender studies from the start (Davis 2008).

These strands in the development of intersectional approaches in the European context are brought together by interventions from different social movements that have emerged and identified various lines of difference (Walgenbach 2007[4]).

---

3 In this volume, the editors place the term 'race' in inverted commas to indicate that it is socially constructed. We consider the concept to be problematic, but do not at present see any way to avoid using it (see below).

4 Walgenbach's identification of a range of different genealogies can only serve here as a German example of further European contexts: the movements of Jewish German women, disabled women, migrant women, and black feminism in Germany (Oguntoye et al. 1985, Walgenbach 2007).

The task of tracing these 'diverse genealogies' is a major challenge for scholars concerned to establish a theoretical foundation for intersectionality, an approach whose strength lies in the way it makes multiple European voices (social movements) audible and European multidimensionality (of identities and social positionings) visible. We would argue that intersectionality has the potential to remain sensitive to possible new omissions, de-namings, and exclusions (see also Lutz 2001, Lutz and Wenning 2001).

At the same time, however, every effort to display invisibility and to take into consideration the perspectives of minority groups gives rise to a representational dilemma. By this we mean the problem of arriving at a non-essentialist self-representation of marginalised women and the impossibility of comprehensive representation on the basis of any identity formation that is not exclusionary (see Spivak 1988, Castro Varela and Dhawan 2005). Davis (in this volume: p. 46) observes in this connection that intersectionality offers an opportunity to reconcile with each other two currents of thought that have both played a central role in decentring the collective subject 'woman' – poststructuralist feminist theory (or anti-categorical approaches) and 'critical feminist theory on the effects of sexism, class, and racism' (for example, standpoint theory of black women or other references to categories on the basis of identity politics).

The starting point for many publications in this field was the concept of intersectionality formulated by the American legal scholar Kimberlé Crenshaw. In terms of the intellectual history of the field, it is interesting to note that Crenshaw's intersection metaphor (1989; this volume) spread quickly and was taken up in a variety of fields of research and areas of politics, whereas other (early) conceptual innovations designed for the same purpose did not enjoy the same success. Collins' term 'interlocking systems' (1990), for example, and Floya Anthias and Nira Yuval-Davis's concept of 'racialised boundaries' (1992), which they used to demonstrate the interconnections between the categories of 'race', nation, gender, skin colour, and class, were no more successful in attracting worldwide attention than Deborah King's concept of 'multiple jeopardies', which King uses to characterise multiple social, economic and political threats in the lives of black women.[5]

The State of the Debates

Within Europe the concept of intersectionality was taken up at different times in different places, resulting in a number of controversies. The concept entered the British debate quickly, since there were already lively discussions in the UK about the recognition of 'differences' between women (see Barrett and McIntosh 1982), and the question of the connections between and mutual interpenetrations of 'race',

---

5   '… racism, sexism and classism constitute three, interdependent control systems. An interactive model, which I have termed multiple jeopardy, better captures those processes' (King 1988: 42).

class and gender had already been discussed as 'intersection' (Anthias and Yuval-Davis 1983). As a result, intersectionality received considerable attention from the mid-1990s onwards in the critical debate about racism and nationalism (see Lutz et al. 1995). In continental Europe,[6] the ground had already been prepared for the concept in those places where the critical debate about migration, ethnicity and post-colonialism had been taken up, at least to some extent, as was the case for example in the Netherlands (see Wekker 2004, Prins 2006, Verloo 2006, Buitelaar 2006, Saharso 2002). The Dutch scholars Mieke Aerts and Sawitri Saharso had already provoked heated exchanges in 1994 with an article in which they argued that conceptualising *gender* as *ethnicity* would have the advantage of avoiding the essentialisation of gender, and would make it a dynamic category that could be investigated in a culture-sensitive way (Aerts and Saharso 1994). In their article one can already observe the tendency to decentre gender which was received so enthusiastically in some Scandinavian countries. The Swedish scholar Anna Bredström (2006) has drawn attention to the need to extend gender to include sexuality, paying particular attention to heteronormativity. Other Swedish scholars, most of them associated with the Department of Gender Studies at Linköping University, have analysed multiple constructions of identity, and in this way counteracted the reduction of identity to the dimensions of marginalisation and vulnerability by pointing to the use of the 'strategic advantages' (Søndergaard 2005) of multiple identities. Other scholars influenced by Judith Butler and Michel Foucault have pointed to the subversive and disruptive effects that can be produced by marginalised ethnicities; 'ethnic trouble', argues Knudsen (2006), has the potential to place in question powerful images of belonging, 'home', and so on. It was also argued that there was a need for a constant reflection on and deconstruction of power, knowledge, and self-positioning, which was seen to imply the decentring of gender (Lykke 2005, Staunæs 2003).

In France, where there are few interfaces between the racism/migration debate and the gender debate, so far only a few marginal references to intersectionality can be identified (see CIERA 2009).

This also applies to the Mediterranean countries, in the majority of which one can hitherto observe only the early stages of debates about the respective country's colonial history (Italy[7] and Spain), and where scholars are traditionally more aware of contributions from the Francophone rather than the Anglophone world. One can, however, identify initial signs of debates about *intersezionalità* (Italy) and *interseccionalidad* (Spain), even though these have not yet reached the (feminist) mainstream discourse. In both Italy and Spain, the European Anti-Discrimination Directives have served as a catalyst for the debate (Bello 2008, 2010, Bustelo et al. 2009).[8]

---

6   For an excellent overview, see Kathy Davis 2008.

7   An exception here is the work of Laura Balbo (1998).

8   The legal scholar Barbara G. Bello studies the precarious situation of Roma women in Italy and Germany from an intersectional perspective, and also works on the multiple

We have provided a brief and admittedly selective summary of European intersectionality debates; it would be quite justifiable to object that such debates, and the imparting and constitution of knowledge, cannot be accounted for in national terms alone. It is quite clear that the authors we have cited here cooperate in the European space or have been inspired by international publications (for example, Lutz et al. 1995). Nevertheless, we can see clearly from the way intersectionality has been taken up and developed further at different times within Europe that a significant division has shaped the reception of the concept: countries in which the English-language literature is more widely read have taken the debate up more quickly.

There is still a long way to go before the diverse European foundational narratives merge in a shared discursive surface, and form a 'European' intersectionality discourse – even if this only happens in such a way that new invisibilities, contradictions, and incompatibilities emerge. The multitude and divisions of languages and experiences in Europe are at present giving rise to a number of marginalising effects; therefore, we consider *language* an intersectionality dimension which needs thorough investigation. English seems to drown out all other languages, multilingualism is unequally distributed social capital, and the various languages contain very unequal symbolic currencies. There are clear hierarchies among the (academic) languages. However, while the diversity of the European academic languages is characterised by an absence of simultaneity and the demarcation of linguistic boundaries, it is noticeable that the legal space of the European Union (EU) is growing together and is also building bridges.

While, as a result of Crenshaw's intervention, the debate in the USA was strongly influenced by jurisprudence from the late 1980s onwards, in Europe a legal discussion really got going by the beginning of the new millennium. The European discourse on equal rights and the intersectionality in the anti-discrimination legislation differed from the social-scientific debate (see Phoenix in this volume) in that it was a top-down rather than a bottom-up movement. The international women's movement was successful at the supranational level in getting institutions to start thinking differently, and it achieved this via United Nations bodies which saw to it that the idea of intersectional discrimination was

---

discrimination approach of the European Anti-Discrimination Directives (Bello 2008, 2010). She notes that one cannot yet speak of an intersectionality debate in the Italian discourse (Margiotta 2008, Bonfiglioli et al. 2009, Vingelli 2009). In Spain, the question of *interseccionalidad* is usually raised in the context of the implementation of the European Anti-Discrimination Directives. For example, in the recently set up Ministry of Equality (*Ministerio de la Igualdad*, set up in April 2008), a working group has been established and tasked with working out proposals for an Equal Treatment Law. In this context, Bustelo comments that although there is genuine interest within the ministry in the intersectional perspective, there is a long way to go before intersectional approaches are institutionalised in the sphere of state anti-discrimination work. It is also the case, she argues, that although some articles on the subject have been published (Rodríguez Martinez 2006, Platero 2007), the academic debate has only just begun (Bustelo 2009).

included in various conventions (see Yuval-Davis 2006). This concern was taken up in the EU, and from this higher policy level it influenced the legislation of the individual member states.

With the consolidation of the EU's third pillar – pertaining to social and welfare state regulations– anti-discrimination policy was also anchored in the legislation of those European nation states that had, up until that time, hardly incorporated it at all (the UK is an exception in this respect). The process of the adaptation of the European Non-Discrimination Directives into national law allowed for a discussion about multiple discrimination (Schiek and Chege 2008, Schiek and Lawson 2010), and in this context the intersectionality approach was debated for the first time. As a consequence, a certain kind of multiple discrimination is now characterised as 'intersectional discrimination' (see European Commission 2007). This success in the legal sphere is striking when one considers the absence or marginality of social movements in most of the EU member states.[9] It seems to be a certain representation of the human rights discourse as 'European' which has made possible the embrace of intersectionality in the legal sphere.

Hitherto, there has been hardly any dialogue between jurisprudence and the social sciences on this issue, and it is therefore worth asking where the difficulties of translation between disciplines lie. One possibility is that legal discourse tends to see things in terms of individual cases, whereas sociology tries to grasp structural categories. However, this explanation does not seem very plausible in view of the large number of empirical intersectional studies in the field of microsociology. In addition, the case of the action brought by black women against General Motors in the 1970s, which is examined by Crenshaw in this volume, shows that a single decision on company policy taken by a firm affected all black women employees there as a category, or rather led to the non-employment of black women as a category. This can hardly be termed an individual case. Myra Marx Ferree's framework analysis (in this volume) of the differences between the connections of the women's rights discourse in the USA (with the civil rights discourse) and in Germany (with the labour movement and the social-democratic inequality discourse) may help to explain why legal scholars and social scientists (in and beyond Germany) have found fewer points of contact.

From Women's and Gender Studies to Feminist Intersectionality Studies?

In order to answer the question of whether the intersectionality approach is the future of feminist scholarship and politics, the first important step seems to be to establish that intersectionality not only challenges us to integrate marginalised perspectives but also demonstrates the necessity of understanding relations of rule

---

9   The FRA, the European Agency for Fundamental Rights, is currently investigating on behalf of the Commission the question of the precise definition of the category 'intersectional discrimination'; a number of expert groups have been set up.

and power differentials as co-constituted and co-constitutive. This is the aspect to which black feminists have drawn our attention by arguing against an exclusively deconstructive way of dealing with categories, i.e. what McCall calls an anti-categorical approach (see hooks 1992, Mohanty 2003). On the one hand, one of the insights of post-structuralism is that identity categories (gender, 'race', etc.) cannot be understood in an essentialist way, but at the same time the power effects generated by these categories are profoundly inscribed in historical and societal terms and, by virtue of the numerous overlaps between them, form the basis for the hierarchisation of groups and the formation of unequal social relations. Gayatri C. Spivak argues that political action must refer *strategically* to these categories, and calls this paradoxical movement 'strategic essentialism' (see Davis in this volume). This contradictory and contentious way of proceeding only seems to be justifiable if both elements (the strategic reference *and* the reifying effects associated with it) are treated as reflections of a fundamentally irresolvable tension. This attitude can be both an activist position and a scholarly perspective, and it resembles Stuart Hall's concept of 'decentred positioning' (see Supik 2005), which always has a provisional character ('for the time being') and makes this provisional character available 'without guarantees' of solid alliances or unchanging individual or collective identities.

This means that the intersectionality approach challenges us to look at the different social positioning of women (and men) and to reflect on the different ways in which they participate in the reproduction of these relations. As we do this, intersectionality serves as an instrument that helps us grasp the complex interplay between disadvantage and privilege, a requirement to which objections have sometimes been raised. For example, Tove Soiland's (2008) polemical comment that the intersectionality approach means that 'the relations go and the categories come' bears witness to a reception that reduces the intersectionality approach to the crossroads metaphor and so neglects the relations discussed in the development of the approach itself.

For decades now, the central positioning of the category of gender has been questioned from the margins of feminist theory and practice. The claim to represent *all* women that was once formulated by the bourgeois, *white*, Western women's movement is no longer accepted. The awareness that the reality of the lives and experiences of women is shaped not just by gender but also by other social categories now seems to be commonplace. Those who see *this* decentring as a danger for the discipline are right to the extent that intersectionality does indeed challenge feminist academic practices of exclusions and resistances to fundamental revisions. Reciting the 'race–class–gender' trinity like a mantra runs the risk of lapsing into uni-dimensionality, even if it is now informed by intersectionality. Unless it examines the processes of exclusion associated with each category and the ways they are interconnected with one another, intersectionality could lead to a rhetorically legitimised re-centring.

The need to translate intersectionality for use in the European context poses both theoretical and political problems. Raising the issue of the experiences of black women and the associated focus on the overlaps and connections between different social power relations has led to an approach praised by Leslie McCall (2005) as the most important contribution to women's studies.

There is a danger that the political impulse which led to the formulation of the concept in the first place, might fall by the wayside when it is adapted for use in Europe, and this danger seems to be at its greatest in places where the distinction between activism and scholarship has been very strictly adhered to and, up until now, it has been hard to imagine a sub-discipline such as black feminist studies being accepted as part of the canon of feminist theory. If, therefore, the present 'hype' (Villa in this volume) of the intersectionality debate leads to a situation where the approach is hastily and superficially adopted *as an import*, there is a danger that the discussion will not really get to grips with the implications of intesectionality. Although Kathy Davis argues convincingly that the unfinished quality, ambiguity, and vagueness of intersectionality should be seen as an advantage, the approach cannot be separated from its history as a political project.[10]

If these considerations were to be taken seriously, gender studies would be making a quantum leap: from the idea of difference between women, via the deconstruction of the category of gender, to the interconnections between different dimensions of inequality – from the multiple oppression of black American women to the 'multiple positioning' (Phoenix) of all human beings. It is true that these are paradigmatic statements which *simultaneously* make claims to validity and yet are hard to reconcile with one another. Are we observing a paradigm shift, even though such a claim has been contested so far (see Bührmann 2009)? One can at least say that in the (continental) European debate, there is at present a problem of non-simultaneity between existing societal contextual conditions and the state of the theoretical discussion.

One can identify a number of places where urgent and important work is going on within the intersectionality debate. Queer studies is using intersectional analysis in critical work on heteronormativity: 'We see Queer Theory and intersectionality as two perspectives which provide control mechanisms for one another, which are able to reflect each other methodologically,' in the words of Gabriele Dietze and her colleagues (2007: 136). Queer intersectionality studies add a deconstructive perspective to the reference to categories; it is an anti-categorical approach in McCall's sense, and attaches central importance to the category of sexuality, which is often neglected in intersectional analyses.

Scholars working in disability studies criticise the neglect of the category of disability in intersectionality research (Meekosha 2006, Raab 2007). However, within German-language disability studies one can observe an opening up to intersectional analyses which does not treat ableism and disability as a singular phenomenon but examines the ways in which they interact with other categories (see Raab 2007, Gummich 2010, Hutson 2010). This perspective emphasises the

---

10 Parallels with the academic reception of critical whiteness studies are notable – see Tißberger et al. 2006.

connection between queer and disability studies, and uses them in a productive way. Intersectionality is treated here as an interdisciplinary approach which makes it possible to explore the ways in which disability, heteronormativity, and gender interlock and interact with one another (see Raab 2007, 2010).

Finally, we are seeing a growing trend within gender studies towards work on masculinity (see the contributions by Hearn and by Bereswill and Neuber in this volume). In all these cases, it is noticeable that an attempt is being made to focus on the relationship between the dominant, privileged, hegemonic sides of societal structural categories and their antitheses.

In view of this diversity it is clear that no single project, no matter how broadly it may be conceived, can do justice to all dimensions of the concept of intersectionality simultaneously. We would therefore like to present in rather more detail one specific example, a central dimension of the approach and one which poses particular challenges for the German-language discourse on critical racism research and critical whiteness studies.

Let's talk about 'race'

Especially in German-speaking countries, the intersectionality discourse gets into trouble when the concept of 'race' is given more attention than just as one term listed within the mantra of 'race, class, and gender'. The German word '*Rasse*' has been naturalised by colonial and Nazi racial ideologies; for more than a century, racialisation processes provided colonial rule with representations and stereotypes which were also inscribed in/on bodies. Moreover, racialisation also *created* socioeconomic facts *and, in particular, subject positions*. It is, therefore, not easy to rise to the challenge posed by '*Rasse*' as a 'negative category' (Knapp 2009: 224), one that cannot be used in an affirmative way. Conceptualising 'Rasse' as a negative category has resulted in avoidance of the word in German social science debates. Alternatively, the English word 'race' is used by German-speakers, in order to make reference to its political genealogy. Speaking of 'racialisation' indicates our concern with the results and processes of institutional and social actions; it confirms that we consider subject positions as effects of racist exclusions and hence that 'race' is the result of racism. But is a theory of racism persuasive if it lacks a clear reference to the category of 'race'; in other words: can we speak of racism without races?

There is certainly no way to answer these questions in a general way. However, like in Germany, there are similar reservations which can be traced back to the Holocaust in many other European countries.

In the Netherlands, for example, where the concept of race was replaced by culture and ethnicity in academic and political debates after the Second World War, one consequence was that the debate about the far-reaching effects of colonialism remained marginal (Wekker 2004, Davis 2009).

In East European societies with their newly won autonomy, even raising the question of ethnic difference within the 'nation' is a provocation, something that also applies to France with its republican *citoyenneté*. In France, however, academic discourse uses the terms 'ethnicisation', 'discrimination', or 'racial discrimination', and 'racism' is heard much less frequently. However, the situation has begun to change since the protests in the *banlieues* in 2005 and some important studies have been published (Dorlin 2009, Fassin and Fassin 2006, Benelli et al. 2006a, 2006b, N'Diaye 2009).[11]

In the UK, the first Race Relations Act was passed as long ago as 1965, the first such piece of legislation anywhere in Europe. Further legislation followed, and there is a state-backed anti-discrimination policy which means that people have got used to speaking of *race* as well as *ethnicity* (Solanke 2009).

The German usage may provide the starkest contrast with the British, but we suspect that most European discourses are closer to the problematic German relationship with '*Rasse*' than to the British case. However, we do not have the linguistic competence to investigate this question more closely, so we will confine ourselves here to discussing the German case in more detail.

In Germany, the practice of referring to ethnicity rather than '*Rasse*' runs the risk of making it difficult to raise the issue of racism. An investigation like the one carried out by Ann Phoenix (in this volume) on adults' memories of their family socialisation in 'visibly ethnically different households' would be hard to conceptualise in Germany, since the translation of 'mixed race'as '*gemischt-rassig*' reactivates the colonial and fascist vocabulary of racist ideology, which is a reminder of the history of violence and extermination and therefore tends to be avoided in the social sciences. This means that German lacks the words that could provide a satisfactory translation of a term which is also used affirmatively in English as a form of self-identification. People in Germany who identify themselves by using the English term *people of colour* employ it in this positive sense.[12]

In addition, the use of 'ethnicity' or 'hybridity' rather than '*Rasse*' can serve to obscure the connection with racialised biologisation which continues to dominate the discourse of the life sciences, where the term '*Rasse*' is constantly being activated and where hardly any critical discussion of this terminology seems to

---

11 We are grateful to Elise Pape for drawing our attention to this material.

12 In the USA and the former French colonies, the term *Free People of Color* or *gens de couleur libres* was used to describe formerly enslaved persons. It was given a positive meaning for the first time in the anti-colonial writings of Frantz Fanon. The civil rights movement took up this meaning of the term and used it for purposes of self-empowerment and self-description (Ogbar 2004). 'People of Colour' was used to reject hegemonic discourses which use exclusionary terms like 'non-white' or 'coloured'. German-speaking *People of Colour* use the English expression to describe people 'who have all had the experience, which manifests itself in many variations and is experienced in *unequal* ways [emphasis in original], of being defined as "other" and "not belonging" on the basis of bodily and cultural attributions made by the dominant White society' (Ha et al. 2007: 12; Dean 2010).

have developed (AG gegen Rassismus in den Lebenswissenschaften 2009, Rose 2006).

'Ethnicity' can be used as an academically 'neutral' term, which suggests an apparently equal, multicultural juxtaposition of cultures which tolerate and respect each other, whereas the concept of '*Rasse*' is associated with the history of immanent contempt, hierarchisation, and inequality on both sides of the 'colour line', the privileging of *white* and the disadvantaging of black positions. Whiteness is a relational category here, and its meaning depends on how being black, as antithesis, is conceived of; in the process of the construction of racialised difference, white remains an unmarked position. Critical whiteness studies conceptualise this position as the unmarked place from which others are defined, at the centre of the analysis of racialisation processes and their violent consequences. Critical whiteness studies' basic insight is that racialisation processes do not just affect black people; they are also of fundamental importance for *white* people's views of themselves and their social positioning (Eggers et al. 2005, Frankenberg 1993, Ware 1992, Ware and Back 2002).

The tendency for critical racism research to concentrate on ethnicisation and culturalisation (as, for example, in the cultural racism debate of the 1990s – see Balibar and Wallerstein 1988 among others) needs to be understood in the context of the fact that a number of European societies refused to perceive of themselves as countries of factual immigration and at the same time the social and discursive heritage of colonialism disappeared behind fascism, for example in Germany and the Netherlands (see Rommelspacher 1999, Lutz and Gawarecki 2005).

There are some further elements that make up the structure of racist relations in which white and black mark positions of power differentials (including cultural-religious attributions such as anti-Semitism and anti-Islamism), and each of these elements is articulated in a different way and inscribed on the body. There is a longstanding and ongoing dispute within German social-scientific discourse as to whether racism should be considered a proper subject for academic research.[13] In the sociological mainstream the concept is considered normatively loaded, moralistic, or polemical, and is rejected. This academic attitude needs to be seen in its current political context: in June 2010 the German Institute for Human Rights, in a report that agreed with the findings of another published shortly before by Githu Muigai, the UN Special Rapporteur on Racism (Deutsches Institut für Menschenrechte 2010, UN Human Rights Council 2010), stated that because they were operating with a narrow conception of racism (restricted to extreme right-

---

13   During the 1990s and 2000s, not a single article was published in the main German sociology journals (*Kölner Zeitschrift für Soziologie und Sozialpsychologie*, *Zeitschrift für Soziologie* and *Soziale Welt*) that used the term *Rassismus*. Instead, terms that are not used outside German-language publications were employed – *Gruppenbezogene Menschenfeindlichkeit* (group-related hostility to other people), *Ausländerfeindlichkeit* (hostility to foreigners), or *Fremdenfeindlichkeit* (hostility to outsiders). We are grateful to Sonja Erkens for surveying the literature.

wing ideology and violence), the state and other public institutions in Germany were unable to meet their obligations to protect people against discrimination on grounds of 'ethnic origin or race'.

But does this mean that the term 'race' should be used in the European debates in order to make racialised positions visible and nameable? The question of whether critical whiteness studies can provide new and emancipatory insights into a form of structural privilege that has not yet been investigated sufficiently must be answered in the context of the contradictions and relations of domination we have explored here. For one thing, if 'race' is used in a strategically essentialist way, we may find ourselves caught in the trap of identity; furthermore, there is always the danger of implicitly following racist logics and reifying them.

As the editors of this volume, and as scholars who are located in different theoretical traditions, socially positioned in different ways as *of colour* or *white*, with different political orientations and belonging to different generations, we have not come up with any consensual answer to this question.

This, however, is probably a reflection of current debates rather than an accident. Lykke (2010) finds that there have not yet been any truly serious dialogues 'beyond the comfort zones', engaging with awkward questions, between feminists who position themselves differently and are positioned differently.

We do, however, agree that it is important to seize the opportunity for repositioning presented by the intersectionality perspective. This means looking at both the disadvantaging and the privileging effects of all the dimensions of inequality we investigate, and so taking consciously critical standpoints in relation to racism, sexism, heteronormativity, class oppression, and so on.

This Volume

At the risk of oversimplifying matters somewhat, we have grouped the contributions that follow into three parts. In Part I we ask who has been working with the concept of intersectionality, when and where they have been doing this, and whether these scholars have managed to establish the concept or carried it over into other contexts; in Part II we ask which research questions and issues are best suited to being investigated by means of intersectional analyses; and in Part III we ask what the future might hold for the further development of intersectionality.

In the first part of the volume, our contributors trace the *transatlantic journey* of the concept, together with its geographical and theoretical implications. We start with a somewhat shortened version of the text which, 20 years ago, introduced the concept and launched the debates that followed. Kimberlé Crenshaw criticises American jurisprudence and feminist theory, and the US anti-racism movement, for employing one-dimensional approaches with a limited explanatory capacity, arguing that each of these approaches treats either gender or 'race' as an isolated dimension of discrimination. Such conceptualisations, she argues, fail to understand the specific situation of black women whose experiences are shaped by the intersection between two dimensions of inequality. Using the intersection metaphor, she argues that all three spheres need a change of perspective and should adopt an intersectional approach that will be capable of examining the multidimensional experiences of discrimination and the diverse identities of black women. Kathy Davis analyses the successful career of the concept of intersectionality from the perspective of the sociology of science. She shows how and why intersectionality has been so well and broadly received in women's and gender studies, and argues that the very ambiguity and vagueness of the concept have contributed to its popularity and made it one that can be taken up in connection with so many issues. This, she argues, is what makes the approach a good feminist theory. On the basis of this assessment, Davis emphasises the theoretical, methodological, and political advantages of the concept for the further development of feminist theory and practice. Myra Marx Ferree presents an example of an intersectional framework analysis, which enables her to move directly to answer the question of why there are certain problems of translation between the American and German women's movements. Ferree focuses on the level of discourse, and she shows how the American women's movement was able to develop successful strategies precisely by means of its reference to and connection with the black civil rights movement, while in Germany the relationship between 'the women's movement' and 'the migrants' movement' has been complicated. On the other hand, argues Ferree, there have been and still are analogies and synergy effects in Germany between the women's movement and the labour movement with reference to the category of class.

In the second part of the book, the contributors present insights from *new research fields, intersectional research on masculinity, heteronormativity and transnationality.* Using the example of an empirical study of male prison inmates, Mechthild Bereswill and Anke Neuber discuss the connection between constellations of inequality and gender. They are particularly interested in what they identify as a change in gender relations that has been taking place at the same time as male rule has persisted. Bereswill and Neuber examine the question of the current configuration of the gender order, with special reference to the main theories of masculinity studies, and relate this to the intersectionality approach. They show how each of these theoretical perspectives poses difficult questions for the other one but can also complement it, and argue for the retention of gender as a master category in the analysis of social inequality. Jeff Hearn chooses a different starting point, and reconstructs the issues raised by intersectionality from the perspective of critical masculinity studies. He criticises the overemphasis on the concept of *hegemonic masculinity* on the grounds that it cannot capture adequately the complexity of the social category 'man'. He proposes an alternative perspective which is less narrow and which emphasises neglected intersectionalities: age, virtuality, and transnationality. It is crucial that these intersectionalities should be analysed in order to advance the project of abolishing 'men' as a category of social power. Dubravka Zarkov investigates the intersectional connections between masculinity, ethnicity and heteronormativity. Her first case study concerns the representation in the media of sexual violence towards 'ethnically other' men in wartime. Her analysis of Croatian war reporting in daily newspapers during the war in ex-Yugoslavia shows how the making visible and invisible of both perpetrators and victims constructs (hetero-) normative masculinity in combination with a new national identity. Zarkov's second example is an analysis of the voyeurism of the Western media in relation to the torture photos from Abu Ghraib prison in Baghdad. She shows that, and how, the hypervisibility of these images plays a significant role in the construction of a Christian–Islamic antagonism and military masculinity.

Kira Kosnick criticises the way mainstream migration studies ignore the intersectionality of migrant ethnicities, and identifies the heteronormative assumptions on which this research rests. She demonstrates with the help of an example how the interplay between racism and homophobia creates queer migrant subject positions that are precarious and apparently oxymoronic. Against this background, Kosnick argues that this variant of intersectionality should not be left out of the analysis of migration processes. She also argues that we need to examine the intersectional visibility of ethnicised queer subjects and to look at the contradictory effects connected with this. Ann Phoenix analyses biographical interviews with adults who differ visibly from their parents and/or siblings in respect of their skin colour. How, Phoenix asks, do they manage to lead 'normal' lives as adults after such non-normative childhood experiences? Charlene, one of Phoenix's interviewees, says: 'I think at an early age you pick up the hierarchy around skin colour.' She thus provides a clue to the way social structure and power relations are experienced and handled individually. Based on biographical narrations, Phoenix theorises everyday experience and develops an integrated analysis of structure and agency from the perspective of her interviewees.

The third and final part of the book deals with the *potential and limits* of intersectionality and poses *critical questions* to the concept. Nira Yuval-Davis sees the concept of intersectionality as one with a great deal of theoretical potential. She proposes treating the approach consistently as a theory of social stratification, thereby replacing (Marxist) class theory. Intersectionality, she argues, is better equipped to do justice to the complex relations of inequality in contemporary societies than either classical Marxism or Weberian models, and it can also capture the multidimensionality of social inequality better than Nancy Fraser's dual social-philosophical approach involving recognition and redistribution. Paula-Irene Villa's deconstructive contribution informed by discourse theory focuses on what is known as the 'etcetera' problem, and takes an anti-categorical and category-critical approach to the issue. Providing a vivid account of Argentine tango, she shows how concentrating on the 'classical triad' of 'race', class and gender runs the risk of rendering invisible what lies between these categories. Villa argues that especially at the level of embodiment, as we can see in the example of dance, the social can never be entirely accounted for in terms of the categorical. Finally, Gudrun-Axeli Knapp gives an account of some of the challenges that arise when the triad 'race', class and gender is conceptualised intersectionally. At the centre of her analysis is the concept of intersectional invisibility, which she broadens in the direction of structural theory by using sociation theories with a view to placing intersectional approaches on a sound social-theoretical footing. Nina Lykke completes this final section by presenting a re-reading of Judith Butler as an intersectionality theorist. Focusing on the intersection of sex, gender and sexuality, Lykke gives yet another challenging answer to the 'etcetera problem' – the supposedly infinite number of categories – often quoted by intersectionality's critics. Lykke argues that while intersectionality is indeed in danger of being simply used as a black box, it can also be seen as a productive rizomatic deterritorialisation.

The volume ends with a postscript by Kimberlé W. Crenshaw.

Bibliography

Aerts, M. and Saharso, S. 1994. Seks als etniciteit. Een beschouwing over collectieve identiteit en sociale ongelijkheid. *Tijdschrift voor vrouwenstudies*, 15(1), 11–26.

AG gegen Rassismus in den Lebenswissenschaften (ed.) 2009. *Gemachte Differenz. Kontinuitäten biologischer "Rasse" – Konzepte*. Münster: Unrast.

Anthias, F. and Yuval-Davis, N. 1983. Contextualising feminism: Ethnic, gender and class divisions. *Feminist Review*, 15, 62–75.

Anthias, F. and Yuval-Davis, N. 1992. *Racialized Boundaries. Race, Nation, Gender, Colour and Class and the Anti-Racist Struggle*. London, New York: Routledge.

Balbo, L. 1998. *Immigration et Racisme en Europe*. Bruxelles: Ed. Complexe.

Balibar, E. and Wallerstein, I. 1988. *Race, Nation, Classe. Les identités ambiguës*. Paris: Editions La Découverte.

Barrett, M. 1982. *Women's Oppression Today*. London: Verso.

Barrett, M. and McIntosh, M. 1982. *The Anti-Social Family*. London: Verso.

Beale, F. 1979. Double Jeopardy: To Be Black and Female, in *The Black Woman: An Anthology*, edited by T. Cade. New York: New American Library, 90–100.

Bello, B.G. 2008. *Intersectionality: an approach to empower women at the Crossroads*. [Online] Available at: http://www.salto-youth.net/tools/toolbox/find-a-tool/945.html?&search=&pagerCurrentOffset=582 [accessed: 30 July 2010].

Bello, B.G. 2010. *Multiple Discrimination between the EU Agenda and Civic Engagement: The Long Road of Intersectional Perspective*. [Online]. Available at: http://www.errc.org/cikk.php?page=2&cikk=3564 [accessed: 30 July 2010].

Benelli, N., Delphy, C., Falquet, J., Hamel, C., Hertz, E. and Roux, P. (eds) 2006a. *Nouvelles Questions Féministes, special issue: Sexisme et Racisme. Le cas francais*, 25(1).

Benelli, N., Delphy, C., Falquet, J., Hamel, C., Hertz, E. and Roux, P. (eds) 2006b. *Nouvelles Questions Féministes, special issue: Sexisme, Racisme et Postcolonialisme*, 25(3).

Bonfiglioli, C., Cirillo, L., Corradi, L., De Vivo, B., Farris, S. R. and Perilli, V. (eds) 2009. *La Straniera: informazioni, sito-bibliografie e ragionamenti su razzismo e sessismo*. Roma: Quaderni Viola nuova serie n. 2 – Edizioni Alegre.

Brah, A. 1996. *Cartographies of Diaspora: Contesting Identities*. London: Routledge.

Bredström, A. 2006. Intersectionality: A challenge for feminist HIV/AIDS research? *European Journal of Women's Studies*, 15(3), 229–44.

Bührmann, A.D. 2009. Intersectionality – ein Forschungsfeld auf dem Weg zum Paradigma? Tendenzen, Herausforderungen und Perspektiven der Forschung über Intersektionalität. *Gender. Zeitschrift für Geschlecht, Kultur und Gesellschaft*, 2, 28–44.

Buitelaar, M. 2006. 'I am the ultimate challenge': Accounts of intersectionality in the life-story of a well-known daughter of Moroccan migrant workers in the Netherlands. *European Journal of Women's Studies*, 15(3), 211–28.

Bustelo, M. and Bravo Letelier, S. 2009. Gender Politics in Spain. The Challenge of Intersectionality, in *Teaching Intersectionality. Putting Gender at the Centre*, edited by Franken, M., Woodward, A., Cabó, A. and Bagilhole, B.M. Utrecht: Athena Book Series, 121–32.

Castro Varela, M. and Dhawan, N. 2005. *Postkoloniale Theorie. Eine kritische Einführung*. Bielefeld: transcript.

Centre interdisciplinaire d'études et de recherches sur l'Allemagne (CIERA), Paris, and Ecole des hautes études en sciences sociales (EHESS), Paris, und Universität Erfurt. 2009. *Race, Class, Gender as categories of difference and inequality: Which perspectives arise from the concept of 'intersectionality' for human and cultural sciences?* International Conference for Young Academics, 10–12 September 2009. Available at: http://www.ciera.fr/ciera/spip.php?article1312 [accessed: 30 July 2010].

Collins, P.H. 1990. *Black Feminist Thought: Knowledge, Consciousness, and the Politics of Empowerment*. Boston: Unwin Hyman.

Combahee River Collective. 1981 (first published 1977). A Black Feminist Statement, in *This Bridge Called My Back: Writings by Radical Women of Color*, edited by C. Moraga and G. Anzaldúa. New York: Kitchen Table, Women of Color Press, 210–18.

Crenshaw, K. 1989. Demarginalizing the Intersection of Race and Class. A black feminist critique of antidiscrimination doctrine. *University of Chicago Legal Forum*, 139–67.

Davis, K. 2008. Intersectionality in transatlantic perspective, in *ÜberKreuzungen. Fremdheit, Ungleichheit, Differenz*, edited by Klinger, C. and Knapp, G.-A. Münster: Westfälisches Dampfboot, 19–37.

Davis, K. 2009. 'Black is beautiful' in European Perspective. Editorial. *European Journal of Women's Studies*, 16(2), 99–101.

Dean, J. 2010. Person/People of Colo(u)r, in *Wie Rassismus aus Wörtern spricht. Kerben des Kolonialismus im Wissensarchiv deutscher Sprache. Ein kritisches Nachschlagewerk*, edited by Arndt, S. and Bischoff, W. Münster: Unrast.

Deutsches Institut für Menschenrechte. 2010. Press release from 16 June 2010: Deutsches Institut für Menschenrechte unterstreicht Kritik des UN-Berichterstatters an zu engem Rassismusbegriff. Available at: http://www.institut-fuer-menschenrechte.de/de/aktuell/news/meldung/archive/2010/juni//article/pressemitteilung-deutsches-institut-fuer-menschenrechte-unterstreicht-kritik-des-un-berichterstatte.html?tx_ttnews[day]=16&cHash=2629629cf3 [accessed: 20 July 2010].

Dietze, G., Haschemi Yekani, E. and Michaelis, B. 2007. 'Checks and Balances'. Zum Verhältnis von Intersektionalität und Queer Theory, in *Gender als interdependente Kategorie: neue Perspektiven auf Intersektionalität, Diversität und Heterogenität*, edited by Walgenbach, K., Dietze, G., Hornscheidt, A. and Palm, K. Opladen: Barbara Budrich, 107–39.

Dorlin, E. 2009. *Sexe, race, classe. Pour une épistémologie de la domination*. Paris: Presses Univ. de France.

Eggers, M.M., Kilomba, G., Piesche, P. and Arndt, S. (eds) 2005. *Mythen, Masken, Subjekte. Kritische Weißseinsforschung in Deutschland*. Münster: Unrast.

Erel, U., Gutiérrez Rodríguez, E. and Klesse, C. 2008. Intersectionality or simultaneity?! Conceptualizing multiple oppressions, in *Out of Place: Silences in Queerness/Raciality*, edited by Miyake, E. and Kuntsman, A. York: Raw Nerve Books, 203–30.

European Commission 2007. Tackling Multiple Discrimination. Practices, policies and laws. European Commission Directorate-General for Employment, Social Affairs and Equal Opportunities Unit G.4. Luxembourg: Office for Official Publications of the European Communities.

Fassin, D. und Fassin, E. 2006. *De la question sociale à la question raciale?* Paris: La Découverte.

feministische studien 2009. Kritik üben – Übungen in Kritik, 27(1).

Frankenberg, R. 1993. *White Women, Race Matters: The social construction of whiteness*. Minneapolis: University of Minnesota Press.

Grabham, E., Cooper, D., Krishnadas, J. and Herman, D. (eds) 2008. *Intersectionality and Beyond: Law, Power and the Politics of Location*. London: Routledge.

Gümen, S. 1998. Das Soziale des Geschlechts. Frauenforschung und die Kategorie 'Ethnizität'. *Argument*, 40(224), 187–202.

Gummich, J. 2010. Migrationshintergrund und Beeinträchtigung. Vielschichtige Herausforderungen an einer diskriminierungsrelevanten Schnittstelle, in *Gendering Disability. Intersektionale Aspekte von Behinderung und Geschlecht*, edited by Jacob, J., Köbsell, S. and Wollrad, E. Bielefeld: transcript, 131–52.

Ha, K.N., Lauré al-Samarai, N. and Mysorekar, S. 2007. *Einleitung, in re/visionen. Postkoloniale Perspektiven von People of Color auf Rassismus, Kulturpolitik und Widerstand in Deutschland.* Münster: Unrast.

hooks, b. 1992. *Black Looks: Race and Representation.* Boston,: South End Press.

Hutson, C. 2010. Mehrdimensional verletzbar. Eine Schwarze Perspektive auf Verwobenheiten zwischen Ableism und Sexismus, in *Gendering Disability. Intersektionale Aspekte von Behinderung und Geschlecht*, edited by Jacob, J., Köbsell, S and Wollrad, E. Bielefeld: transcript, 61–72.

Ignatiev, N. 1995. *How the Irish became White.* New York: Routledge.

Jacobsen, M.F. 1999. *Whiteness of a Different Color: European Immigrants and the Alchemy of Race.* Cambridge, MA: Harvard University Press.

Johnston, J. 1973. *Lesbian Nation: The Feminist Solution.* New York: Simon and Schuster.

King, D.K. 1988. Multiple Jeopardy, Multiple Consciousness: The Context of Black Feminist Ideology. *Signs: Journal of Women in Culture and Society*, 14(1), 42–72.

Knapp, G.-A. 2009. Resonanzräume – Räsonierräume: Zur transatlantischen Reise von Race, Class und Gender, in *Gender Mobil? Geschlecht und Migration in transnationalen Räumen*, edited by Lutz, H. Münster: Westfälisches Dampfboot, 215–33.

Knudsen, S.V. 2006. Intersectionality – A theoretical inspiration in the analysis of minority cultures and identities in textbooks, in *Caught in the web or lost in the textbook?*, edited by Bruillard, E. et al. Caen: IAERTEM, 61–76.

Lutz, H. 2001. Differenz als Rechenaufgabe? in *Unterschiedlich Verschieden. Differenz in der Erziehungswissenschaft*, edited by Lutz, H. and Wenning, N. Opladen: Leske und Budrich, 11–24.

Lutz, H. and Gawarecki, K. (eds) 2005. *Kolonialismus und Erinnerungskultur. Die Kolonialvergangenheit im kollektiven Gedächtnis der deutschen und niederländischen Einwanderungsgesellschaft.* Münster: Waxmann.

Lutz, H., Phoenix, A. and Yuval-Davis, N. (eds) 1995. *Crossfires: Nationalism, racism and gender in Europe.* London: Pluto Press.

Lutz, H. and Wenning, N. (eds) 2001. Differenzen über Differenz – Einführung in die Debatten, in *Unterschiedlich verschieden: Differenz in der Erziehungswissenschaft.* Opladen: Leske und Budrich, 11–24.

Lykke, N. 2005. Intersectionality revisited: problems and potentials. *Kvinnovetenskapling tidskrift*, 26(2–3), 7–17.

Lykke, N. 2010. *Feminist Studies: A Guide to Intersectional Theory, Methodology and Writing.* New York, London: Routledge.

Margiotta, C. 2008. *Quando la "razza" conta? Fra pratiche discriminatorie e trattamenti eguaglianti.* Available at: http://www.nazioneindiana. com/2008/06/10/quando-la-razza-conta/ [accessed: 13 July 2010].

McCall, L. 2005. The Complexity of Intersectionality. *Signs: Journal of Women in Culture and Society*, 30(3), 1771–1800.

Meekosha, H. 1990. Is feminism able-bodied? Reflections from between the trenches. *Refractory Girl*, August, 34–42.

Meekosha, H. 2006. What the hell are you? An intercategorical analysis of race, ethnicity, gender and disability in the Australian body politic. *Scandinavian Journal of Disability Research*, 8(2–3), 161–76.

Mohanty, C.T. 2003. *Feminism Without Borders: Decolonizing Theory, Practicing Solidarity.* Durham: Duke University Press.

Moraga, C. and Anzaldúa, G. (eds) 1981. *This Bridge Called My Back: Writings by Radical Women of Color.* New York: Kitchen Table, Women of Color Press.

Morris, J. 1989. *Able Lives: Women's experience of paralysis.* London: The Women's Press.

Morrison, T. 1992. *Playing in the Dark: Whiteness and the Literary Imagination.* New York: Vintage Books.

N'Diaye, P. 2009. *La condition noire. Essai sur une minorité française.* Paris: Gallimard.

Ogbar, J.O.G. 2004. *Black Power: Radical Politics and African American Identity.* Baltimore: Johns Hopkins UP.

Oguntoye, K., Opitz, M. and Schultz, D. (eds) 1985. *Farbe bekennen. Afro-Deutsche Frauen auf den Spuren ihrer Geschichte.* Berlin: Orlanda.

Platero, R. 2007. Intersecting gender and sexual orientation: An analysis of sexuality and citizenship in gender equality policies in Spain. 'Contesting Citizenship Comparative Analyses'. *Critical Review of International Social and Political Philosophy*, 10(4): 575–97.

Prins, B. 2006. Narrative accounts of origins: A blind spot in the intersectionality approach. *European Journal of Women's Studies*, 15(3), 277–90.

Raab, H. 2007. Intersektionalität in den Disability Studies. Zur Interdependenz von Behinderung, Heteronormativität und Geschlecht, in *Disability Studies, Kultursoziologie und Soziologie der Behinderung. Erkundungen in einem neuen Forschungsfeld*, edited by Waldschmidt, A. and Schneider, W. Bielefeld: transcript, 127–48.

Raab, H. 2010. Shifting the Paradigm: 'Behinderung, Heteronormativität und Queerness', in *Gendering Disability. Intersektionale Aspekte von Behinderung und Geschlecht*, edited by Jacob, J., Köbsell, S. and Wollrad, E. Bielefeld: transcript, 73–94.

Radicalesbians 1970. *The Woman-Identified Woman.* Pittsburgh: Know Inc.

Rich, A. 1980. Compulsory Heterosexuality and Lesbian Existence. *Signs: Journal of Women in Culture and Society*, 5(4), 631–60.

Rodríguez Martínez, P. (ed.) 2006. *Feminismos periféricos. Discutiendo las categorías de sexo, clase y raza (y etnicidad) conFloya Anthias.* Granada: Editorial Alhuila.

Rommelspacher, B. 1999. Ethnizität und Geschlecht, in *Ethnizität, Differenz und Geschlechterverhältnisse*, edited by Lutz, H., Amos, K. and Guitérrez-Rodriguez, E. Frankfurt/M.: Cornelia Goethe Centrum, 19–32.

Rose, N. 2006. Introduction to the Discussion of Race and Ethnicity in Nature Genetics. *Biosocieties*, 1(3), 307–311.

Roth, B. 2004. *Separate Roads to Feminism: Black, Chicana and White Feminist Movements in America's Second Wave*. Cambridge: Cambridge University Press.

Saharso, S. 2002. Een vrouw met twee missies. Reactie op Helma Lutz. *Tijdschrift voor Genderstudies*, 3, 18–23.

Schiek, D. and Chege, V. (eds) 2008. *European Union Non-Discrimination Law: Comparative Perspectives on Multidimensional Equality Law*. London: Routledge Cavendish.

Schiek, D. and Lawson, A. (eds) 2010. *EU Non-Discrimination Law and Intersectionality: investigating the triangle of racial, gender and disability discrimination*. Aldershot: Ashgate.

Soiland, T. 2008. Die Verhältnisse gingen und die Kategorien kamen. Intersectionality oder Vom Unbehagen an der amerikanischen Theorie. *Querelles-Net* 26. Available at: http://www.querelles-net.de/index.php/qn/issue/view/09-3 [accessed: 30 July 2010].

Solanke, I. 2009. *Making Anti-Racial Discrimination Law*. London: Routledge.

Søndergaard, D.M. 2005. Academic Desire Trajectories: Retooling the concepts of subject. *European Journal of Women's Studies*, 12(3), 297–314.

Spivak, G.C. 1988. Can the Subaltern Speak?, in *Marxism and the Interpretation of Culture*, edited by Grossberg, L. and Nelson, G. Houndmills: Macmillan Education, 271–353.

Staunæs, D. 2003. Where have all the subjects gone? Bringing together the concepts of intersectionality and subjectification. *Nora*, 11(2), 101–10.

Supik, L. 2005. *Dezentrierte Positionierung. Stuart Halls Konzept der Identitätspolitiken*. Bielefeld: transcript.

Taylor, Y., Hines, S. and Casey, M.E. (eds) 2010. *Theorizing Intersectionality and Sexuality*. London, Houndmills: Palgrave Macmillan.

Tißberger, M., Dietze, G., Hrzán, D. and Husmann-Kastein, J. (eds) 2006. *Weiß – Weißsein – Whiteness. Kritische Studien zu Gender und Rassismus*. Critical Studies on Gender and Racism. Frankfurt/M.: Lang.

UN Human Rights Council. 2010. Report of the Special Rapporteur on contemporary forms of racism, racial discrimination, xenophobia and related intolerance, Githu Mugai, addendum Mission to Germany. United Nations. Available at: http://www.institut-fuer-menschenrechte.de/fileadmin/user_upload/PDF-Dateien/UN-Dokumente/Sonderberichterstatter/report_Muigai_mission__Germany__2009.pdf [accessed: 30 July 2010].

Verloo, M. 2006. Multiple inequalities, intersectionality and the European Union. *European Journal of Women's Studies*, 15(3), 211–228.

Vingelli, G. 2009. Intersectionality in Italy: State of the Art, in *Teaching Intersectionality. Putting Gender at the Centre*, edited by Franken, M., Woodward, A., Cabó, A. and Bagilhole, B.M. Utrecht: Athena Book Series,

133–40. Available at: http://www.athena3.org/images/documents/teaching_intersectionality.pdf [accessed: 30 July 2010].

Walgenbach, K. 2007. Gender als interdependente Kategorie, in *Gender als interdependente Kategorie: neue Perspektiven auf Intersektionalität, Diversität und Heterogenität*, edited by Walgenbach, K., Dietze, G., Hornscheidt, A. and Palm, K. Opladen: Barbara Budrich, 23–64.

Ware, V. 1992. *Beyond the pale: White women, racism and history*. London: Verso.

Ware, V. and Back, L. 2002. *Out of Whiteness: Color, politics, and culture*. Chicago: University of Chicago Press.

Wekker, G. 2004. Still Crazy after All Those Years. Feminism for the New Millennium. *European Journal of Women's Studies*, 11(4), 487–500.

Winker, G. and Degele, N. 2009. *Intersektionalität. Zur Analyse sozialer Ungleichheiten*. Bielefeld: transcript.

Yuval-Davis, N. 2006. Intersectionality and Feminist Politics. *European Journal of Women's Studies*, 13(3), 193–209.

PART I
Intersectionality's Transatlantic Travels: Geographies of the Debate

Chapter 1

Demarginalising the Intersection of Race and Sex: A Black Feminist Critique of Anti-discrimination Doctrine, Feminist Theory, and Anti-racist Politics[1]

Kimberlé W. Crenshaw

One of the very few black women's studies books is entitled *All the Women Are White, All the Blacks Are Men, But Some of Us are Brave!* (Hull et al. 1982). I have chosen this title as a point of departure in my efforts to develop a black feminist criticism[2] because it sets forth a problematic consequence of the tendency to treat race and gender as mutually exclusive categories of experience and analysis.[3] In this chapter, I want to examine how this tendency is perpetuated by a single-axis framework that is dominant in anti-discrimination law and that is also reflected in feminist theory and anti-racist politics.

I will centre black women in this analysis in order to contrast the multi-dimensionality of black women's experience with the single-axis analysis that distorts these experiences. Not only will this juxtaposition reveal how black women are theoretically erased, it will also illustrate how this framework imports its own theoretical limitations that undermine efforts to broaden feminist and anti-racist analyses. With black women as the starting point, it becomes more apparent how

---

1   This is a shortened version of the original text, reprinted by permission from *The University of Chicago Legal Forum*, 139 (1989). Shortenings are marked through square brackets.

2   For other work setting forth a black feminist perspective on law, see Judy Scales Trent (1989) or Regina Austin (1989).

3   The most common linguistic manifestation of this analytical dilemma is represented in the conventional usage of the term 'blacks and women'. Although it may be true that some people mean to include black women in either 'blacks' or 'women', the context in which the term is used actually suggests that often black women are not considered. See, for example, Elizabeth Spelman (1988: 114–15), discussing an article on blacks and women in the military where 'the racial identity of those identified as "women" does not become explicit until reference is made to Black women, at which point it also becomes clear that the category of women excludes Black women'. It seems that if black women were explicitly included, the preferred term would be either 'blacks and white women' or 'black men and all women'.

dominant conceptions of discrimination condition us to think about subordination as disadvantage occurring along a single categorical axis. I want to suggest further that this single-axis framework erases black women in the conceptualisation, identification and remediation of race and sex discrimination by limiting inquiry to the experiences of otherwise-privileged members of the group. In other words, in race discrimination cases, discrimination tends to be viewed in terms of sex- or class-privileged blacks; in sex discrimination cases, the focus is on race- and class-privileged women.

This focus on the most privileged group members marginalises those who are multiply burdened and obscures claims that cannot be understood as resulting from discrete sources of discrimination. I suggest further that this focus on otherwise-privileged group members creates a distorted analysis of racism and sexism because the operative conceptions of race and sex become grounded in experiences that actually represent only a subset of a much more complex phenomenon.

After examining the doctrinal manifestations of this single-axis framework, I will discuss how it contributes to the marginalisation of black women in feminist theory and in anti-racist politics. I argue that black women are sometimes excluded from feminist theory and anti-racist policy discourse because both are predicated on a discrete set of experiences that often does not accurately reflect the interaction of race and gender. These problems of exclusion cannot be solved simply by including black women within an already established analytical structure. Because the intersectional experience is greater than the sum of racism and sexism, any analysis that does not take intersectionality into account cannot sufficiently address the particular manner in which black women are subordinated. Thus, for feminist theory and anti-racist policy discourse to embrace the experiences and concerns of black women, the entire framework that has been used as a basis for translating 'women's experience' or 'the black experience' into concrete policy demands must be rethought and recast.

As examples of theoretical and political developments that miss the mark with respect to black women because of their failure to consider intersectionality, I will briefly discuss the feminist critique of rape and separate spheres ideology, and the public policy debates concerning female-headed households within the black community.

The Anti-discrimination Framework

A. The Experience of Intersectionality and the Doctrinal Response

One way to approach the problem of intersectionality is to examine how courts frame and interpret the stories of black women plaintiffs. While I cannot claim to know the circumstances underlying the cases that I will discuss, I nevertheless believe that the way courts interpret claims made by black women is itself part of black women's experience and, consequently, a cursory review of cases involving black female plaintiffs is quite revealing. To illustrate the difficulties inherent in judicial treatment of intersectionality, I will consider [one] Title VII[4] case: *DeGraffenreid v. General Motors:*[5]

DeGraffenreid v. General Motors   In *DeGraffenreid*, five black women brought suit against General Motors, alleging that the employer's seniority system perpetuated the effects of past discrimination against black women. Evidence adduced at trial revealed that General Motors simply did not hire black women prior to 1964 and that all of the black women hired after 1970 lost their jobs in a seniority-based layoff during a subsequent recession. The district court granted summary judgment for the defendant, rejecting the plaintiffs' attempt to bring a suit not on behalf of blacks or women, but specifically on behalf of black women. The court stated:

> [P]laintiffs have failed to cite any decisions which have stated that Black women are a special class to be protected from discrimination. The Court's own research has failed to dispose such a decision. The plaintiffs are clearly entitled to a remedy if they have been discriminated against. However, they should not be allowed to combine statutory remedies to create a new 'super-remedy' which would give them relief beyond what the drafters of the relevant statutes intended. Thus, this lawsuit must be examined to see if it states a cause of action for race discrimination, sex discrimination, or alternatively either, but not a combination of both.[6]

Although General Motors did not hire black women prior to 1964, the court noted that 'General Motors has hired ... female employees for a number of years prior to the enactment of the Civil Rights Act of 1964'.[7] Because General Motors did hire women – albeit *white* women – during the period that no black women were hired, there was, in the court's view, no sex discrimination that the seniority system could conceivably have perpetuated.

After refusing to consider the plaintiffs' sex discrimination claim, the court dismissed the race discrimination complaint and recommended its consolidation with another case alleging race discrimination against the same employer.[8] The plaintiffs responded that such consolidation would defeat the purpose of their suit since theirs was not purely a race claim, but an action brought specifically on

---

4   Civil Rights Act of 1964, 42 USC § 2000e, et seq. as amended (1982).
5   413 F Supp 142 (E D Mo 1976). 6. 708 F2d 475 (9th Cir 1983).
6   *DeGraffenreid*, 413 F Supp 143. 9; ibid., 144.
7   Ibid., 144.
8   Ibid., 145. In *Mosley v. General Motors*, 497 F Supp 583 (E D Mo 1980), plaintiffs, alleging broad-based racial discrimination at General Motors' St. Louis facility, prevailed in a portion of their Title VII claim. The seniority system challenged in *DeGraffenreid*, however, was not considered in *Mosley*.

behalf of black women alleging race *and* sex discrimination. The court, however, reasoned:

> The legislative history surrounding Title VII does not indicate that the goal of the statute was to create a new classification of 'black women' who would have greater standing than, for example, a black male. The prospect of the creation of new classes of protected minorities, governed only by the mathematical principles of permutation and combination, clearly raises the prospect of opening the hackneyed Pandora's box.[9]

Thus, the court apparently concluded that Congress either did not contemplate that black women could be discriminated against as 'black women' or did not intend to protect them when such discrimination occurred.[10] The court's refusal in *DeGraffenreid* to acknowledge that black women encounter combined race and sex discrimination implies that the boundaries of sex and race discrimination doctrine are defined respectively by white women's and black men's experiences. Under this view, black women are protected only to the extent that their experiences coincide with those of either of the two groups.[11] Where their experiences are distinct, black women can expect little protection as long as approaches, such as that in *DeGraffenreid*, which completely obscure problems of intersectionality prevail. [...]

---

9   Ibid., 145.

10   Interestingly, no case has been discovered in which a court denied a white male's attempt to bring a reverse discrimination claim on similar grounds, that is, that sex and race claims cannot be combined because Congress did not intend to protect compound classes. White males in a typical reverse discrimination case are in no better position than the frustrated plaintiffs in *DeGraffenreid*: if they are required to make their claims separately, white males cannot prove race discrimination because white women are not discriminated against, and they cannot prove sex discrimination because black males are not discriminated against. Yet it seems that courts do not acknowledge the compound nature of most reverse discrimination cases. That black women's claims automatically raise the question of compound discrimination and white males' 'reverse discrimination' cases do not suggest that the notion of compoundedness is somehow contingent upon an implicit norm that is not neutral but is white male. Thus, black women are perceived as a compound class because they are two steps removed from a white male norm, while white males are apparently not perceived to be a compound class because they somehow represent the norm.

11   I do not mean to imply that all courts that have grappled with this problem have adopted the *DeGaffenreid* approach. Indeed, other courts have concluded that black women are protected by Title VII. See, for example, *Jefferies v Harris Community Action Ass'n.*, 615 F2d 1025 (5th Cir 1980). I do mean to suggest that the very fact that the black women's claims are seen as aberrant suggests that sex discrimination doctrine is centred in the experiences of white women. Even those courts that have held that black women are protected seem to accept that black women's claims raise issues that the 'standard' sex discrimination claims do not. See Elaine W. Shoben (1980) criticising the *Jefferies* use of a sex-plus analysis to create a sub-class of black women.

Perhaps it appears to some that I have offered inconsistent criticisms of how black women are treated in anti-discrimination law: I seem to be saying that in one case, black women's claims were rejected and their experiences obscured because the court refused to acknowledge that the employment experience of black women can be distinct from that of white women, while in other cases the interests of black women were harmed because black women's claims were viewed as so distinct from the claims of either white women or black men that the court denied to black females representation of the larger class. It seems that I have to say that black women are the same and harmed by being treated differently, or that they are different and harmed by being treated the same. But I cannot say both.

This apparent contradiction is but another manifestation of the conceptual limitations of the single-issue analyses that intersectionality challenges. The point is that black women can experience discrimination in any number of ways and that the contradiction arises from our assumptions that their claims of exclusion must be unidirectional. Consider an analogy to traffic in an intersection, coming and going in all four directions. Discrimination, like traffic through an intersection, may flow in one direction, and it may flow in another. If an accident happens in an intersection, it can be caused by cars travelling from any number of directions and, sometimes, from all of them. Similarly, if a black woman is harmed because she is in the intersection, her injury could result from sex discrimination or race discrimination.

Judicial decisions which premise intersectional relief on a showing that black women are specifically recognised as a class are analogous to a doctor's decision at the scene of an accident to treat an accident victim only if the injury is recognised by medical insurance. Similarly, providing legal relief only when black women show that their claims are based on race or on sex is analogous to calling an ambulance for the victim only after the driver responsible for the injuries is identified. But it is not always easy to reconstruct an accident. Sometimes the skid marks and the injuries simply indicate that they occurred simultaneously, frustrating efforts to determine which driver caused the harm. In these cases the tendency seems to be that no driver is held responsible, no treatment is administered, and the involved parties simply get back in their cars and zoom away.

To bring this back to a non-metaphorical level, I am suggesting that black women can experience discrimination in ways that are both similar to and different from those experienced by white women and black men. Black women sometimes experience discrimination in ways similar to white women's experiences; sometimes they share very similar experiences with black men. Yet often they experience double-discrimination – the combined effects of practices which discriminate on the basis of race, and on the basis of sex. And sometimes, they experience discrimination as black women – not the sum of race and sex discrimination, but as black women.

Black women's experiences are much broader than the general categories that discrimination discourse provides. Yet the continued insistence that black women's demands and needs be filtered through categorical analyses that completely obscure their experiences guarantees that their needs will seldom be addressed.

B. The Significance of Doctrinal Treatment of Intersectionality

DeGraffenreid [...] is a doctrinal manifestation of a common political and theoretical approach to discrimination which operates to marginalise black women. Unable to grasp the importance of black women's intersectional experiences, not only courts, but feminist and civil rights thinkers as well have treated black women in ways that deny both the unique compoundedness of their situation and the centrality of their experiences to the larger classes of women and blacks. Black women are regarded either as too much like women or blacks and the compounded nature of their experience is absorbed into the collective experiences of either group, or as too different, in which case black women's blackness or femaleness sometimes has placed their needs and perspectives at the margin of the feminist and black liberationist agendas.

While it could be argued that this failure represents an absence of political will to include black women, I believe that it reflects an uncritical and disturbing acceptance of dominant ways of thinking about discrimination. Consider first the definition of discrimination that seems to be operative in anti-discrimination law. Discrimination which is wrongful proceeds from the identification of a specific class or category; either a discriminator intentionally identifies this category, or a process is adopted which somehow disadvantages all members of this category.[12] According to the dominant view, a discriminator treats all people within a race or sex category similarly. Any significant experiential or statistical variation within this group suggests either that the group is not being discriminated against or that conflicting interests exist which defeat any attempts to bring a common claim.[13] Consequently, one generally cannot combine these categories. Race and sex, moreover, become significant only when they operate to explicitly *disadvantage* the victims; because the *privileging* of whiteness or maleness is implicit, it is generally not perceived at all.

---

12   In much of anti-discrimination doctrine, the presence of intent to discriminate distinguishes unlawful from lawful discrimination. See *Washington v Davis*, 426 US 229, 239–45 (1976) (proof of discriminatory purpose required to substantiate Equal Protection violation). Under Title VII, however, the Court has held that statistical data showing a disproportionate impact can suffice to support a finding of discrimination. See *Griggs*, 401 US at 432. Whether the distinction between the two analyses will survive is an open question. See *Wards Cove Packing Co., Inc. v Antonio*, 109 S Ct 2115, 2122–23 (1989) (plaintiffs must show more than mere disparity to support a prima facie case of disparate impact). For a discussion of the competing normative visions that underlie the intent and effects analyses, see Alan David Freeman (1978).

13   See, for example, *Moore*, 708 F2d: 479.

Underlying this conception of discrimination is a view that the wrong which anti-discrimination law addresses is the use of race or gender factors to interfere with decisions that would otherwise be fair or neutral. This process-based definition is not grounded in a bottom-up commitment to improve the substantive conditions for those who are victimised by the interplay of numerous factors. Instead, the dominant message of anti-discrimination law is that it will regulate only the limited extent to which race or sex interferes with the process of determining outcomes. This narrow objective is facilitated by the top–down strategy of using a singular 'but for' analysis to ascertain the effects of race or sex. Because the scope of anti-discrimination law is so limited, sex and race discrimination have come to be defined in terms of the experiences of those who are privileged *but for* their racial or sexual characteristics. Put differently, the paradigm of sex discrimination tends to be based on the experiences of white women; the model of race discrimination tends to be based on the experiences of the most privileged blacks. Notions of what constitutes race and sex discrimination are, as a result, narrowly tailored to embrace only a small set of circumstances, none of which include discrimination against black women. [...]

The problem is that they can receive protection only to the extent that their experiences are recognisably similar to those whose experiences tend to be reflected in anti-discrimination doctrine. If black women cannot conclusively say that 'but for' their race or 'but for' their gender they would be treated differently, they are not invited to climb through the hatch but told to wait in the unprotected margin until they can be absorbed into the broader, protected categories of race and sex.

Despite the narrow scope of this dominant conception of discrimination and its tendency to marginalise those whose experiences cannot be described within its tightly drawn parameters, this approach has been regarded as the appropriate framework for addressing a range of problems. In much of feminist theory and, to some extent, in anti-racist politics, this framework is reflected in the belief that sexism or racism can be meaningfully discussed without paying attention to the lives of those other than the race-, gender- or class-privileged. As a result, both feminist theory and anti-racist politics have been organised, in part, around the equation of racism with what happens to the black middle-class or to black men, and the equation of sexism with what happens to white women.

Looking at historical and contemporary issues in both the feminist and the civil rights communities, one can find ample evidence of how both communities' acceptance of the dominant framework of discrimination has hindered the development of an adequate theory and praxis to address problems of intersectionality. This adoption of a single-issue framework for discrimination not only marginalises black women within the very movements that claim them as part of their constituency, but it also makes the elusive goal of ending racism and patriarchy even more difficult to attain.

Feminism and Black Women: 'Ain't We Women?'

Oddly, despite the relative inability of feminist politics and theory to address black women substantively, feminist theory and tradition borrow considerably from black women's history. For example, 'Ain't I a Woman?' has come to represent a standard refrain in feminist discourse.[14] Yet the lesson of this powerful oratory is not fully appreciated because the context of the delivery is seldom examined. I would like to tell part of the story because it establishes some themes that have characterised feminist treatment of race and illustrates the importance of including black women's experiences as a rich source for the critique of patriarchy.

In 1851, Sojourner Truth declared 'Ain't I a Woman?' and challenged the sexist imagery used by male critics to justify the disenfranchisement of women.[15] The scene was a Women's Rights Conference in Akron, Ohio; white male hecklers, invoking stereotypical images of 'womenhood', argued that women were too frail and delicate to take on the responsibilities of political activity. When Sojourner Truth rose to speak, many white women urged that she be silenced, fearing that she would divert attention from women's suffrage to emancipation. Truth, once permitted to speak, recounted the horrors of slavery, and its particular impact on black women:

> Look at my arm! I have ploughed and planted and gathered into barns, and no man could head me – and ain't I a woman? I could work as much and eat as much as a man when I could get it and bear the lash as well! And ain't I a woman? I have borne thirteen children, and seen most of 'em sold into slavery, and when I cried out with my mother's grief, none but Jesus heard me – and ain't I a woman? (Flexner 1975: 91)[16]

By using her own life to reveal the contradiction between the ideological myths of womanhood and the reality of black women's experience, Truth's oratory provided a powerful rebuttal to the claim that women were categorically weaker than men. Yet Truth's personal challenge to the coherence of the cult of true womanhood was useful only to the extent that white women were willing to reject the racist attempts to rationalise the contradiction that because black women were something less than real women, their experiences had no bearing on true womanhood. Thus, this nineteenth-century black feminist challenged not only patriarchy, but she

---

14   See Phyllis Palmer (1983) posing the question of why 'white women in the women's movement had not created more effective and continuous alliances with Black women' when 'simultaneously… Black women [have] become heroines for the women's movement, a position symbolised by the consistent use of Sojourner Truth and her famous words, "Ain't I a Woman?"'

15   See Paula Giddings (1984).

16   See also bell hooks (1981: 159–60).

also challenged white feminists wishing to embrace black women's history to relinquish their vestedness in whiteness.

Contemporary white feminists inherit not the legacy of Truth's challenge to patriarchy but, instead, Truth's challenge to their forbears. Even today, the difficulty that white women have traditionally experienced in sacrificing racial privilege to strengthen feminism renders them susceptible to Truth's critical question. When feminist theory and politics that claim to reflect *women's* experience and *women's* aspirations do not include or speak to black women, black women must ask: 'Ain't *We* Women?' If this is so, how can the claims that 'women are', 'women believe' and 'women need' be made when such claims are inapplicable or unresponsive to the needs, interests and experiences of black women?

The value of feminist theory to black women is diminished because it evolves from a white racial context that is seldom acknowledged. Not only are women of colour in fact overlooked, but their exclusion is reinforced when *white women* speak for and as *women*. The authoritative universal voice – usually white male subjectivity masquerading as non-racial, non-gendered objectivity[17] – is merely transferred to those who, but for gender, share many of the same cultural, economic, and social characteristics. When feminist theory attempts to describe women's experiences through analysing patriarchy, sexuality, or separate-spheres ideology, it often overlooks the role of race. Feminists thus ignore how their own race functions to mitigate some aspects of sexism and, moreover, how it often privileges them over and contributes to the domination of other women.[18] Consequently, feminist theory remains *white*, and its potential to broaden and deepen its analysis by addressing non-privileged women remains unrealised. […]

Because ideological and descriptive definitions of patriarchy are usually premised upon white female experiences, feminists and others informed by feminist literature may make the mistake of assuming that since the role of black women in the family and in other black institutions does not always resemble the familiar manifestations of patriarchy in the white community, black women are somehow exempt from patriarchal norms. For example, black women have traditionally worked outside the home in numbers far exceeding the labour participation rate of white women (see generally Jones 1985, Davis 1981).

An analysis of patriarchy that highlights the history of white women's exclusion from the workplace might permit the inference that black women have not been burdened by this particular gender-based expectation. Yet the very fact that black women must work conflicts with norms that women should not, often creating personal, emotional, and relationship problems in black women's lives. Thus, black

---

17 'Objectivity' is itself an example of the reification of white male thought (Hull et al. 1982: xxv).

18 For example, many white females were able to gain entry into previously all white male enclaves not through bringing about a fundamental reordering of male versus female work, but in large part by shifting their 'female' responsibilities to poor and minority women.

women are burdened not only because they often have to take on responsibilities that are not traditionally feminine but, moreover, their assumption of these roles is sometimes interpreted within the black community as either black women's failure to live up to such norms or as another manifestation of racism's scourge upon the black community.[19] This is one of the many aspects of intersectionality that cannot be understood through an analysis of patriarchy rooted in white experience.

Another example of how theory emanating from a white context obscures the multi-dimensionality of black women's lives is found in feminist discourse on rape. A central political issue on the feminist agenda has been the pervasive problem of rape. Part of the intellectual and political effort to mobilise around this issue has involved the development of a historical critique of the role that law has played in establishing the bounds of normative sexuality and in regulating female sexual behaviour (see generally Brownmiller 1975, Estrich 1987). Early carnal knowledge statutes and rape laws are understood within this discourse to illustrate that the objective of rape statutes traditionally has not been to protect women from coercive intimacy but to protect and maintain a property-like interest in female chastity (see Brownmiller 1975:17, generally Estrich 1987). Although feminists quite rightly criticise these objectives, to characterise rape law as reflecting male control over female sexuality is for black women an oversimplified account and an ultimately inadequate account.

Rape statutes generally do not reflect *male* control over *female* sexuality, but *white* male regulation of *white* female sexuality.[20] Historically, there has been absolutely no institutional effort to regulate black female chastity.[21] [...] Also, while it was true that the attempt to regulate the sexuality of white women

---

19   As Elizabeth Higginbotham (1982: 95) in her article 'Two Representative Issues in Contemporary Sociological Work on Black Women' noted, 'women, who often fail to conform to "appropriate" sex roles, have been pictured as, and made to feel, inadequate even though as women, they possess traits recognised as positive when held by men in the wider society. Such women are stigmatised because their lack of adherence to expected gender roles is seen as a threat to the value system.'

20   One of the central theoretical dilemmas of feminism that is largely obscured by universalising the white female experience is that experiences that are described as a manifestation of male control over females can be instead a manifestation of dominant group control over all subordinates. The significance is that other non-dominant men may not share in, participate in, or connect with the behaviour, beliefs, or actions at issue, and may be victimised themselves by 'male' power. In other contexts, however, 'male authority' might include non-white men, particularly in private sphere contexts. Efforts to think more clearly about when black women are dominated as *women* and when they are dominated as *black women* are directly related to the question of when power is *male* and when it is *white male*.

21   See Wriggins (1983: 117-123) discussing the historical contemporary evidence suggesting that black women are generally not thought to be chaste. See also hooks (1981: 54) stating that stereotypical images of black womanhood during slavery where based on the myth that 'all black women were immoral and sexually loose', Smith (1982: 110)

placed unchaste women outside the law's protection, racism restored a fallen white woman's chastity where the alleged assailant was a black man.[22] No such restoration was available to black women.

The singular focus on rape as a manifestation of male power over female sexuality tends to eclipse the use of rape as a weapon of racial terror.[23] When black women were raped by white males, they were being raped not as women generally, but as black women specifically: Their femaleness made them sexually vulnerable to racist domination, while their blackness effectively denied them any protection (Lerner 1972: 173). This white male power was reinforced by a judicial system in which the successful conviction of a white man for raping a black woman was virtually unthinkable (see generally Wriggins 1983: 103).

In sum, sexist expectations of chastity and racist assumptions of sexual promiscuity combined to create a distinct set of issues confronting black women.[24] These issues have seldom been explored in feminist literature nor are they prominent in anti-racist politics. The lynching of black males, the institutional practice that was legitimised by the regulation of white women's sexuality, has historically and contemporaneously occupied the black agenda on sexuality and violence. [...] The suspicion is compounded by the historical fact that the protection of white female sexuality was often the pretext for terrorising the black community. Even today some fear that anti-rape agendas may undermine anti-racist objectives. This is the paradigmatic political and theoretical dilemma created by the intersection of race

---

noting that '...white men for centuries have justified their sexual abuse of Black women by claiming that we are licentious, always "ready" for any sexual encounter'.

22 Because of the way the legal system viewed chastity, black women could not be victims of forcible rape. One commentator has noted that '[a]ccording to governing stereotypes *[sic]*, chastity could not be possessed by Black women. Thus, Black women's rape charges were automatically discounted, and the issue of chastity was contested only in cases where the rape complainant was a white woman' (Wriggins 1983: 126). Black women's claims of rape were not taken seriously regardless of the offender's race. A judge in 1912 said: 'This court will never take the word of a nigger against the word of a white man [concerning rape]' (ibid.: 120). On the other hand, lynching was considered an effective remedy for a black man's rape of a white woman. Since rape of a white woman by a black man was 'a crime more horrible than death' (ibid.: 125), the only way to assuage society's rage and to make the woman whole again was to brutally murder the black man.

23 See 'The Rape of Black Women as a Weapon of Terror', in Gerda Lerner (1972: 172–193). See also Brownmiller (1975). Even where Brownmiller acknowledges the use of rape as racial terrorism, she resists making a 'special case' for black women by offering evidence that white women were raped by the Klan as well (1975: 139). Whether or not one considers the racist rape of black women a 'special case', such experiences are probably different. In any case, Brownmiller's treatment of the issue raises serious questions about the ability to sustain an analysis of patriarchy without understanding its multiple intersections with racism.

24 Paula Giddings (1984: 82) notes the combined effect of sexual and racial stereotypes: 'Black women were seen having all of the inferior qualities of white women without any of their virtues.'

and gender: black women are caught between ideological and political currents that combine first to create and then to bury black women's experiences.

When and Where I Enter: Integration – an Analysis of Sexism into Black Liberation Politics

Anna Julia Cooper, a nineteenth-century black feminist, coined a phrase that has been useful in evaluating the need to incorporate an explicit analysis of patriarchy in any effort to address racial domination (Cooper 1969). Cooper often criticised black leaders and spokespersons for claiming to speak for the race, but failing to speak for black women. Referring to one of Martin Delaney's public claims that where he was allowed to enter, the race entered with him, Cooper countered: 'Only the Black Woman can say, when and where I enter ... then and there the whole Negro race enters with me' (ibid.: 31). [...]

While there are a number of reasons – including anti-feminist ones – why gender has not figured directly in analyses of the subordination of black Americans, a central reason is that race is still seen by many as the primary oppositional force in black lives.[25] If one accepts that the social experience of race creates both a primary group identity as well as a shared sense of being under collective assault, some of the reasons that black feminist theory and politics have not figured prominently in the black political agenda may be better understood.[26]

The point is not that African Americans are simply involved in a more important struggle. Although some efforts to oppose black feminism are based on this assumption, a fuller appreciation of the problems of the black community will reveal that gender subordination does contribute significantly to the destitute conditions of so many African Americans and that it must therefore be addressed. Moreover, the foregoing critique of the single-issue framework renders problematic the claim that the struggle against racism is distinguishable from,

---

25   An anecdote illustrates this point. A group of female law professors gathered to discuss 'Isms in the Classroom'. One exercise led by Patricia Cain involved each participant listing the three primary factors that described herself. Almost without exception, white women in the room listed their gender either primarily or secondarily; none listed their race. All of the women of colour listed their race first, and then their gender. This seems to suggest that identity descriptions seem to begin with the primary source of opposition with whatever the dominant norm is. Explaining the exercise and noting that 'no white woman ever mentions race, whereas every woman of color does', and that, similarly, 'straight women do not include "heterosexual" ... whereas lesbians who are open always include "lesbian"' (Cain 1989: 210–11).

26   For a comparative discussion of Third World feminism paralleling this observation, see Kumari Jayawardena (1986: 1–24). Jayawardena states that feminism in the Third World has been 'accepted' only within the central struggle against international domination. Women's social and political status has improved most when advancement is necessary to the broader struggle against imperialism.

much less prioritised over, the struggle against sexism. Yet it is also true that the politics of racial otherness that black women experience along with black men prevent black feminist consciousness from patterning the development of white feminism. For white women, the creation of a consciousness that was distinct from and in opposition to that of white men figured prominently in the development of white feminist politics. Black women, like black men, live in a community that has been defined and subordinated by colour and culture.[27] Although patriarchy clearly operates within the black community, presenting yet another source of domination to which black women are vulnerable, the racial context in which black women find themselves makes the creation of a political consciousness that is oppositional to black men difficult.

Yet while it is true that the distinct experience of racial otherness militates against the development of an oppositional feminist consciousness, the assertion of racial community sometimes supports defensive priorities that marginalise black women. Black women's particular interests are thus relegated to the periphery in public-policy discussions about the presumed needs of the black community. The controversy over the movie *The Color Purple* is illustrative. The animating fear behind much of the publicised protest was that by portraying domestic abuse in a black family, the movie confirmed the negative stereotypes of black men (Matthews 1985, 1986; but cf. Siskel 1986, Page 1986). The debate over the propriety of presenting such an image on the screen overshadowed the issue of sexism and patriarchy in the black community. Even though it was sometimes acknowledged that the black community was not immune from domestic violence and other manifestations of gender subordination, some nevertheless felt that in the absence of positive black male images in the media, portraying such images merely reinforced racial stereotypes.[28] The struggle against racism seemed to compel the subordination of certain aspects of the black female experience in order to ensure the security of the larger black community.

The nature of this debate should sound familiar to anyone who recalls Daniel Moynihan's (1965) diagnosis of the ills of black America. Moynihan's report depicted a deteriorating black family, foretold the destruction of the black male householder and lamented the creation of the black matriarch. His conclusions prompted a massive critique from liberal sociologists[29] and from civil rights

---

27 For a discussion of how racial ideology creates a polarising dynamic which subordinates blacks and privileges whites, see Kimberlé Crenshaw (1988: 1331, 1371–76).

28 A consistent problem with any negative portrayal of African Americans is that they are seldom balanced by positive images. On the other hand, most critics overlooked the positive transformation of the primary male character in *The Color Purple*.

29 See Lee Rainwater and William I. Yancey (1967: 427–29) containing criticisms of the Moynihan Report by, among others, Charles E. Silberman, Christopher Jencks, William Ryan, Laura Carper, Frank Riessman and Herbert Gans.

leaders.[30] Surprisingly, while many critics characterised the report as racist for its blind use of white cultural norms as the standard for evaluating black families, few pointed out the sexism apparent in Moynihan's labelling black women as pathological for their 'failure' to live up to a white female standard of motherhood.[31]

The latest versions of a Moynihan-esque analysis can be found in the Moyers televised special, *The Vanishing Black Family*, and, to a lesser extent, in William Julius Wilson's *The Truly Disadvantaged*. In *The Vanishing Black Family*, Moyers presented the problem of female-headed households as a problem of irresponsible sexuality, induced in part by government policies that encouraged family breakdown.[32] The theme of the report was that the welfare state reinforced the deterioration of the black family by rendering the black male's role obsolete. As the argument goes, because black men know that someone will take care of their families, they are free to make babies and leave them. A corollary to the Moyers view is that welfare is also dysfunctional because it allows poor women to leave men upon whom they would otherwise be dependent.

Most commentators criticising the programme failed to pose challenges that might have revealed the patriarchal assumptions underlying much of the Moyers report. They instead focused on the dimension of the problem that was clearly recognisable as racist.[33] White feminists were equally culpable. There was little, if any, published response to the Moyers report from the white feminist community. Perhaps feminists were under the mistaken assumption that since the

---

30   Ibid.: 395–97: critics included Martin Luther King, Jr., Benjamin Payton, James Farmer, Whitney Young, Jr., and Bayard Rustin.

31   One of the notable exceptions is Jacquelyne Johnson Jackson (1973: 185–86).

32   Columnist Mary McGrory (1986), applauding the show, reported that Moyers found that sex was as common in the black ghetto as a cup of coffee. George Will (1986) argued that over-sexed black men were more of a menace than Bull Conner, the Birmingham Police Chief who in 1968 achieved international notoriety by turning fire hoses on protesting school children.

My guess is that the programme has influenced the debate about the so-called underclass by providing graphic support to pre-existing tendencies to attribute poverty to individual immorality. During a recent and memorable discussion on the public-policy implications of poverty in the black community, one student remarked that nothing can be done about black poverty until black men stop acting like 'roving penises', black women stop having babies 'at the drop of a hat', and they all learn middle-class morality. The student cited the Moyers report as her source.

33   Although the nearly exclusive focus on the racist aspects of the programme poses both theoretical and political problems, it was entirely understandable given the racial nature of the subsequent comments that were sympathetic to the Moyers view. As is typical in discussions involving race, the dialogue regarding the Moyers programme covered more than just the issue of black families; some commentators took the opportunity to indict not only the black underclass, but the black civil-rights leadership, the war on poverty, affirmative action, and other race-based remedies. See for example Will (1986).

report focused on the black community, the problems highlighted were racial, not gender-based. Whatever the reason, the result was that the ensuing debates over the future direction of welfare and family policy proceeded without significant feminist input.

The absence of a strong feminist critique of the Moynihan/Moyers model not only impeded the interests of black women, but it also compromised the interests of growing numbers of white women heads of household who find it difficult to make ends meet.[34]

William Julius Wilson's *The Truly Disadvantaged* modified much of the moralistic tone of this debate by reframing the issue in terms of a lack of marriageable black men (Wilson 1987: 96). According to Wilson, the decline in black marriages is not attributable to poor motivation, bad work habits, or irresponsibility but instead is caused by structural economics which have forced black unskilled labour out of the workforce. Wilson's approach represents a significant move away from that of Moynihan/Moyers in that he rejects their attempt to centre the analysis on the morals of the black community. Yet, he too considers the proliferation of female-headed households as dysfunctional *per se*, and fails to explain fully why such households are so much in peril. Because he incorporates no analysis of the way the structure of the economy and the workforce subordinates the interests of women, especially child-bearing black women, Wilson's suggested reform begins with finding ways to put black men back in the family.[35] In Wilson's view, we must change the economic structure with an eye towards providing more black jobs for black men. Because he offers no critique of sexism, Wilson fails to consider economic or social reorganisation that directly empowers and supports these single black mothers.[36]

My criticism is not that providing black men with jobs is undesirable; indeed, this is necessary not only for the black men themselves, but for an entire community, depressed and subject to a host of sociological and economic ills that accompany massive rates of unemployment. But as long as we assume that the massive social

---

34   Their difficulties can also be linked to the prevalence of an economic system and family policy that treat the nuclear family as the norm and other family units are aberrant and unworthy of societal accommodation.

35   Wilson's (1987: 154) suggestions include macroeconomic policies which promote balanced economic growth, a nationally oriented labour-market strategy, a child support assurance programme, a child-care strategy, and a family allowances programme which would be both means-tested and race-specific.

36   Nor does Wilson include an analysis of the impact of gender on changes in family patterns. Consequently, little attention is paid to the conflict that may result when gender-based expectations are frustrated by economic and demographic factors. This focus on demographic and structural explanations represents an effort to regain the high ground from the Moyers/Moynihan approach, which is more psychosocial. Perhaps because psychosocial explanations have come dangerously close to victim-blaming, their prevalence is thought to threaten efforts to win policy directives that might effectively address deteriorating conditions within the working-class and poor black communities.

reorganisation Wilson calls for is possible, why not think about it in ways that maximise the choices of black women?[37] A more complete theoretical and political agenda for the black underclass must take into account the specific and particular concerns of black women; their families occupy the bottom rung of the economic ladder, and it is only through placing them at the centre of the analysis that their needs and the needs of their families will be directly addressed.[38]

Expanding Feminist Theory and Anti-racist Politics by Embracing the Intersection

If any real efforts are to be made to free black people of the constraints and conditions that characterise racial subordination, then theories and strategies purporting to reflect the black community's needs must include an analysis of sexism and patriarchy. Similarly, feminism must include an analysis of race if it hopes to express the aspirations of non-white women. Neither black liberationist politics nor feminist theory can ignore the intersectional experiences of those whom the movements claim as their respective constituents. In order to include black women, both movements must distance themselves from earlier approaches in which experiences are relevant only when they are related to certain clearly identifiable causes (for example, the oppression of blacks is significant when based on race, of women when based on gender). The praxis of both should be centred on the life chances and life situations of people who should be cared about without regard to the source of their difficulties.

I have stated earlier that the failure to embrace the complexities of compoundedness is not simply a matter of political will, but is also due to the influence of a way of thinking about discrimination which structures politics so that struggles are categorised as singular issues. Moreover, this structure imports a descriptive and normative view of society that reinforces that status quo.

It is somewhat ironic that those concerned with alleviating the ills of racism and sexism should adopt such a top-down approach to discrimination. If their efforts instead began with addressing the needs and problems of those who are most disadvantaged and with restructuring and remaking the world where necessary, then others who are singularly disadvantaged would also benefit. In addition, it seems that placing those who currently are marginalised in the centre is the most effective way to resist efforts to compartmentalise experiences and undermine potential collective action.

---

37   For instance, Wilson (1987: 153) only mentions in passing the need for daycare and job training for single mothers. No mention at all is made of other practices and policies that are racist and sexist, and that contribute to the poor conditions under which nearly half of all black women must live.

38   Pauli Murray (1975: 351–61) observes that the operation of sexism is at least the partial cause of social problems affecting black women.

It is not necessary to believe that a political consensus to focus on the lives of the most disadvantaged will happen tomorrow in order to re-centre discrimination discourse at the intersection. It is enough, for now, that such an effort would encourage us to look beneath the prevailing conceptions of discrimination and to challenge the complacency that accompanies belief in the effectiveness of this framework. By so doing, we may develop language which is critical of the dominant view and which provides some basis for unifying activity. The goal of this activity should be to facilitate the inclusion of marginalised groups for whom it can be said: 'When they enter, we can enter.'

Bibliography

Austin, R. 1989. Sapphire–Bound!*Wise Women's L J.*

Brownmiller, S. 1975. *Against Our Will. Men, Women and Rape*. New York: Simon and Schuster.

Cain, P.A. 1989. Feminist Jurisprudence: Grounding the Theories. *Berkeley Women's Law Journal*, 4(2), 199–214.

Cooper, A.J. 1969. *A Voice from the South*. New York: Negro Universities Press. (reprint of the Aldine Printing House, Ohio, 1892).

Crenshaw, K. 1988. Race, Reform and Retrenchment: Transformation and Legitimation in Antidiscrimination Law. *Harvard Law Review*, 101(7), 1331–87.

Davis, A. 1981. *Women, Race and Class. An Activist Perspective*. New York: Random House.

Estrich, S. 1987. *Real Rape. How the Legal System Victimizes Women Who Say No*. Cambridge, MA: Harvard University Press.

Flexner, E. 1975. *Century of Struggle: The Women's Rights Movement in the United States*. Cambridge, MA: Belknap Press of Harvard University Press.

Freeman, A.D. 1978. Legitimizing Racial Discrimination through Antidiscrimination Law. A Critical Review of Supreme Court Doctrine. *Minnesota Law Review*, 62, 1049–1119.

Giddings, P. 1984. When and Where I Enter: The Impact of Black Women on Race and Sex in America. New York: William Morrow and Co.

Higginbotham, E. 1982. Two Representative Issues in Contemporary Sociological Work on Black Women, in *All the Women Are White, All the Blacks Are Men, but Some of Us Are Brave*, edited by Hull, G.; Bell Scott, P. and B. Smith. New York: The Feminist Press, 93–97.

hooks, B. 1981. *Ain't I a Woman. Black Women and Feminism*. Boston: South End Press.

Hull, G., Bell Scott, P. and Smith, B. (eds) 1982. *All the Women Are White, All the Blacks Are Men, But Some of Us Are Brave*. New York: The Feminist Press.

Jackson, J.J. 1973. Black Women in a Racist Society, in *Racism and Mental Health*, edited by Willie, C.V., Kramer, B.M. and Brown, B.S. Pittsburgh: University of Pittsburgh Press, 185–268.

Jayawardena, K. 1986. Feminism and Nationalism in the Third World. London: Zed Books.

Jones, J. 1985. *Labor of Love, Labor of Sorrow; Black Women, Work, and the Family from Slavery to the Present.* New York: Basic Books.

Lerner, G. (ed.) 1972. The Rape of Black Women as a Weapon of Terror, in *Black Women in White America.* New York: Pantheon Books, 172–93.

Matthews, J. 1985. Some Blacks Critical of Spielberg's Purple. *Los Angeles Times*, 20 December, 1.

Matthews, J. 1986. Three Color Purple Actresses Talk About Its Impact. *Los Angeles Times*, 31 January, 1.

McGrory, M. 1986. Moynihan was Right 21 Years Ago. *The Washington Post*, 26 January.

Moynihan, D.P. 1965. *The Negro Family: The Case for National Action.* Office of Policy Planning and Research, United States Department of Labour.

Murray, P. 1975. The Liberation of Black Women, in *Women: A Feminist Perspective*, edited by Freeman, J. Mountain View, CA: Mayfield, 351–62.

Page, C. 1986. Toward a New Black Cinema. *Chicago Tribune*, 12 January, 3.

Palmer, P. 1983. The Racial Feminization of Poverty. Women of Color as Portents of the Future for All Women. *Women's Studies Quarterly*, 11(3), 4–6.

Rainwater, L. and Yancey, W.I. 1967. *The Moynihan Report and the Politics of Controversy.* Cambridge, Mass.: MIT Press.

Scales Trent, J. 1989. Black Women and the Constitution: Finding Our Place, Asserting Our Rights (Voices of Experience: New Responses to Gender Discourse). *Harvard Civil Rights – Civil Liberties Law Review*, 24(9), 23–27.

Shoben, E.W. 1980. Compound Discrimination: The Interaction of Race and Sex in Employment Discrimination. *New York University Law Review*, 55, 793–803.

Siskel, G. 1986. Does Purple Hate Men? *Chicago Tribune*, 05 January, 16.

Smith, B. 1982. Black Women's Health: Notes for a Course, in *All the Women Are White, All the Blacks Are Men, but Some of Us Are Brave*, edited by Hull, G., Bell Scott, P. and Smith, B. New York: The Feminist Press, 103–14.

Spelman, E. 1988. *The Inessential Woman. Problems of exclusion in feminist thought.* Boston: Beacon Press.

The Vanishing Black Family. 1986. PBS Television Broadcast, January.

Will, G. 1986. Voting Rights Won't Fix It. *The Washington Post*, 23 January.

Wilson, W.J. 1987. *The Truly Disadvantaged: The Inner City, The Underclass and Public Policy.* Chicago: University of Chicago Press.

Wriggins, J. 1983. Rape, Racism, and the Law. *Harvard Women's Law Journal*, 6, 103–41.

Chapter 2

Intersectionality as Buzzword: A Sociology of Science Perspective on What Makes a Feminist Theory Successful[1]

Kathy Davis

Intersectionality is heralded as the 'most important contribution that women's studies has made so far' (McCall 2005: 1771). Feminist scholars from different disciplines (philosophy, social sciences, humanities, economics and law), theoretical perspectives (phenomenology, structuralist sociology, psychoanalysis, and deconstructionism) and political persuasions (feminism, anti-racism, multiculturalism, queer studies, disability studies) all seem to be convinced that intersectionality is exactly what is needed.

While most feminist scholars today would agree that intersectionality is essential to feminist theory, it has also generated heated theoretical debates throughout the US and Europe. Some suggest that intersectionality is a theory, others regard it as a concept[2] or heuristic device, and still others see it as a reading strategy for doing feminist analysis. Controversies have emerged about whether intersectionality should be conceptualised as a crossroad (Crenshaw 1991), as 'axes' of difference (Yuval-Davis 2006) or as a dynamic process (Staunæs 2003). It is not at all clear whether intersectionality should be limited to understanding individual experiences, to theorising identity, or whether it should be taken as a property of social structures and cultural discourses.

This raises the question how a theory which is so vague could come to be regarded by so many as the cutting edge of contemporary feminist theory. And does it need – as some have argued – a more coherent conceptual framework and methodology in order for it to live up to its potential and to grasp the complex realities it was initially intended to address (McCall 2005)?

---

1   Shortened reprint of Kathy Davis, *Feminist Theory* 9(1), 67–85, © 2008 by SAGE, Reprinted by Permission of SAGE.

2   For an understanding of intersectionality as a 'conceptual nodal point' see Lykke in this volume.

In this chapter, I look at the phenomenon of intersectionality's spectacular success as well as the uncertainties it generates.[3] I shall not be providing suggestions about how to clarify the ambiguities surrounding the concept, nor how to alleviate uncertainties about how it should be used. Quite the contrary, I shall be arguing that, paradoxically, precisely the vagueness and open-endedness of 'intersectionality' may be the very secret to its success. To this end, I draw upon insights from the sociology of science.[4] This branch of sociology is concerned with processes of scientific activity, the relationship between theories and their audience, and, more generally, how a specific theory or theoretical perspective can persuade an (academic) audience to view some aspect of the world in a certain way.

In particular, I shall be turning to the work of Murray S. Davis, who, several decades ago, produced two – in my view – sadly underrated articles called, respectively, 'That's Interesting!' (1971) and 'That's Classic!' (1986).[5] In these articles, Davis explored what enables a specific social theory to capture the imagination of a broad audience of academics. Borrowing from phenomenology and the rhetoric of science, he analyses how theories that are widely circulated or are 'in the air' (Davis 1971: 312) come to be viewed as interesting by their audiences and, in some cases, even go on to achieve the venerable status of 'classic'. He draws his examples from the grand theories of sociology (Marx, Durkheim, Weber), but his arguments can be applied to any theory – including, as I shall show, feminist theory. Davis is not concerned with whether a specific theory is good (as in valid or able to adequately explain certain aspects of the social world) or coherent (in terms of the logic of its propositions or consistency of its arguments). Indeed, he argues that no theory ever became famous because it was 'true' or coherent. Quite the contrary, in fact. Davis claims that successful theories thrive on ambiguity and incompleteness. Successful theories appeal to a concern regarded as fundamental by a broad audience of scholars, but they do so in a way which is not only unexpected, but inherently hazy and mystifyingly open-ended.

At first glance, intersectionality would appear to have all the makings of a successful feminist theory.[6] Leaving aside the issue of whether intersectionality can be treated as a full-fledged 'theory', I shall take a closer look at what it is about intersectionality that has allowed it to 'move' the minds of a broad audience of feminist scholars, not only whetting their interest, but compelling them to enter into theoretical debates and look for ways to use the concept in their own inquiries. Drawing upon Davis's explanation for what makes a theory successful, I explore the features of intersectionality that account for its success: its focus on a pervasive

---

3   For a discussion of the blackboxing effect on the intersectionality concept, that is, its turning to a rhetorical device, see Lykke's contribution in this volume.

4   For a seminal formulation, see Merton (1973).

5   Since I always get this question, I should note that Murray Davis and I are not related, although we have the same last name.

6   Even – as Knapp (2005) has argued – one of feminism's most well-known 'travelling theories'.

and fundamental concern in feminist theory, its provision of novelty, its appeal to the generalists as well as the specialists of the discipline, and its inherent ambiguity and open-endedness that beg for further critique and elaboration. After addressing the secret of intersectionality's success within contemporary feminist theory, I raise the question of whether embracing such a chimerical and – some would argue – scientifically unsound[7] concept should be only a reason for celebration or also a reason for some alarm.

Fundamental Concern

According to Davis (1986), the first characteristic of a successful social theory is that it speaks to a primary audience concern. It needs to be recognisable as 'imperative', 'crucial', or 'key' to understanding something that a particular audience holds near and dear. This concern must, in fact, be so pervasive that in order to be successful at all, a theory will simply have to address it (Davis 1986: 287).[8] But Davis warns that in order to be fundamental, a concern must not simply be shared by a broad and disparate audience of scholars. It also needs to address a problem which collides with something that the audience holds dear, something which – as he puts it – 'is about to destroy their ideally immovable valued object' (Davis 1986: 290). This provides the context of desperation necessary to compel an audience to invest time and energy into trying to get the problem under control, thereby eliminating the source of their anxiety.

'Intersectionality' addresses the most central theoretical and normative concern within feminist scholarship: namely, the acknowledgement of differences among women. This is because it touches on the most pressing problem facing contemporary feminism – the long and painful legacy of its exclusions (Zack 2007: 197). Intersectionality addresses precisely the issue of differences among women by providing a 'handy catchall phrase that aims to make visible the multiple positioning that constitutes everyday life and the power relations that are central to it' (Phoenix 2006: 187). At the same time, it promises to address (and redress) the exclusions

---

7   For the record, I do not subscribe to the notion that a theory needs to meet certain scientific criteria in order to be useful. However, as any student in the social sciences will know, considerable attention has been given to what is required for a 'good' theory. Thus, by 'soundness' I am referring to the scientific conventions for good theory.

8   For sociology, the fundamental concern was the relationship between individual and society – a concern which was recycled in endless debates about social order and social role, structure and agency, and cultural discourses and processes of subjectification. That concern kept sociological debates flourishing well into the twenty-first century, when it was ousted by a new 'fundamental concern', namely globalisation.

which have played such a distressing role in feminist scholarship through the (deceptively) easy procedure of 'asking the other question':[9]

> The way I try to understand the interconnection of all forms of subordination is through a method I call 'ask the other question'. When I see something that looks racist, I ask, 'Where is the patriarchy in this?' When I see something that looks sexist, I ask, 'Where is the heterosexism in this?' When I see something that looks homophobic, I ask, 'Where are the class interests in this?' (Matsuda 1991: 1189)

While the issues of difference and diversity were important both to the political project of exploring the interactions of race, class and gender and to the deconstructive project of postmodern feminist theory, which can be defined as two of the most important strands of contemporary feminist thought, they also evoked some uncertainty among feminist scholars about the viability of the feminist enterprise in general. If the 'old' ideal of an inclusive feminism – the 'common world of women' scenario, as Chandra T. Mohanty put it – is abandoned as theoretically and politically ethnocentric and imperialistic (Lugones and Spelman 1983, Mohanty 1988), where were feminist scholars to find a platform unified enough to warrant labelling their theoretical enterprise 'feminist'?

Intersectionality coincides with the need to problematise the theoretical hegemony of gender and the exclusions of white Western feminism, and yet it provides a platform for feminist theory as a shared enterprise. It promises an almost universal applicability, useful for understanding and analysing any social practice, any individual or group experience, any structural arrangement, and any cultural configuration. Moreover, it can – by definition – be employed by any (feminist) scholar willing to use her own social location, whatever it may be, as an analytic resource rather than just an identity marker. Intersectionality offers a new *raison d'être* for doing feminist theory and analysis. The success of intersectionality is therefore, at least in part, attributable to the implicit reassurance it provides that the focus on difference will not make feminist theory obsolete or superfluous.[10] In other words, intersectionality promises feminist scholars of all identities, theoretical perspectives, and political persuasions that they can 'have their cake and eat it, too'.

---

9   I say 'deceptively' because, as anyone knows who has tried to employ this procedure, it merely marks the beginning of the analysis. The hard work of making sense of the connections between categories of difference and interpreting them in terms of power has yet to be done.

10   Or, as Pfeil (1994) notes, a 'disabling fetish' which ignores the effort of differently located feminists to discover affinities and possibilities for alliance 'on the ground'.

Novel Twist

The second characteristic of successful social theories is that they provide a novel twist to an old problem. According to Davis, social theories flourish precisely because they manage to 'deny ...the assumed while affirming the unanticipated' (Davis 1971: 343). Successful theories capture the attention of an audience by disputing or unsettling something that it had previously believed. They make unexpected connections between unlikely events in ways that the audience could not have imagined before (Davis 1971: 310–11).

At first glance, intersectionality might not seem to fit the bill. After all, it was hardly a new idea. Kimberlé Crenshaw may have introduced the term,[10] but she was by no means the first to address the issue of how black women's experiences have been marginalised or distorted within feminist discourse. Nor was she making a particularly new argument when she claimed that their experiences had to be understood as multiply shaped by race and gender. Black feminists on both sides of the Atlantic and Third World feminist scholars had already produced numerous critiques of how the experiences of women of colour had been neglected in feminist discourse, and had already underscored the importance of theorising multiple identities and sources of oppression.[11] As a result, race/class/gender became the new mantra within women's studies and it became *bon ton* to speak in the plural – of genders instead of gender, feminisms instead of feminism (Zack 2007). If all these ideas were already 'in the air', then, what was so special about intersectionality?

Although intersectionality addressed an old problem within feminist scholarship, it did so with a new twist. It offered a novel link between critical feminist theory on the effects of sexism, class, and racism and a critical methodology inspired by postmodern feminist theory, bringing them together in ways that could not have been envisioned before. While feminist theories of race, class and gender and poststructuralist feminist theory shared many of the same concerns, there were also some theoretical and methodological incompatibilities, such as the search for ways to abandon categorical thinking altogether (McCall 2005).[12] On the other hand, the emphasis on identity politics in specific historical contexts has been a

---

11　It is impossible to do justice to this writing, but here are some of the most well-known and frequently cited works: Combahee River Collective in Hull et al. 1982, Davis 1981, hooks 1981, Carby 1982, Smith 1983, Moraga and Anzaldúa 1983, Ware 1992, Zinn and Dill 1994, and Collins 1990.

12　A case in point is Judith Butler's well-known critique of the 'embarrassed "etc."' which ends the list of predicates (gender, race, ethnicity, class, sexuality, able-bodiedness) that 'strive to encompass a situated subject, but invariably fail to be complete' (Butler 1989: 143).

critical, and even more effective, strategy of resistance than the deconstruction of categories for combatting the effects of racism and sexism (Crenshaw 1991).[13]

Intersectionality takes up the political project of making the social and material consequences of the categories of gender/race/class visible, but does so by employing methodologies compatible with the poststructuralist project of deconstructing categories, unmasking universalism, and exploring the dynamic and contradictory workings of power (Brah and Phoenix 2004: 82).[14] It offers the race/class/gender feminists a theoretically sophisticated methodology that can help them avoid some of the pitfalls of additive approaches to multiple identities. It gives poststructuralist feminist theory political credibility, enabling it to counter some of the criticisms of multicultural feminism that it has become distanced from the material realities of women's lives and too relativistic to be of use for women's concrete political struggles. In short, intersectionality provides the basis for a mutually beneficial collaboration between theoretical projects which had previously found themselves on somewhat uneasy footing. Thus, while the idea of intersectionality may not have been new, it provided a new platform – 'a joint nodal point' – for disparate theoretical approaches within feminist scholarship (Lykke 2005).[15]

Generalists and Specialists

The third characteristic of successful social theories is that they must appeal to a broad academic audience, bridging the gap between theory generalists and specialists. They must 'contain enough seemingly easily grasped famous concepts to attract generalists, and enough difficult (but not impossible) to grasp complexity within and between these concepts to attract the specialists' (Davis 1986: 295). For generalists, the theory is often experienced as a few 'famous concepts' or easily remembered 'clichés' (Davis 1986: 294). In contrast, theory specialists devote their entire career towards understanding a particular theory.

Intersectionality has proved particularly adept in appealing to both generalists and specialists in feminist academic audiences. On the one hand, it has all the makings of a buzzword, which can easily capture the interest of the generalists. It appears frequently in the titles of articles in feminist journals on any number

---

13   Similar arguments were made by hooks (1992, 1994), Spivak (1993), Moya (2001) and Mohanty (2003).

14   It is not surprising that many of the debates about intersectionality have concerned precisely the problem of categories and the necessity to rely upon them in intersectional analysis. See, for example, Yuval-Davis's (2006) critique of the 'crossroad' metaphor which implies that once a road is taken, all other roads become irrelevant, at least for the time being. Knapp (2005) has also expressed concern about the lack of attention in intersectional theory to the specific ontologies and histories of categories of social inequality.

15   See also Lykke's contribution in this volume.

of subjects,[16] providing a catchy and convenient way of expressing the author's normative commitments. It allows her to express her familiarity with the latest developments in feminist theory, without necessarily exploring all the ramifications of the theoretical debates. In sum, it is no wonder that intersectionality has been taken up by many generalists as a welcome helpmeet for engaging in feminist inquiry.

On the other hand, intersectionality has many attractions for the theory specialists among feminist academics. Since its introduction as a theoretical concept, it has been the subject of numerous theoretical debates on both sides of the Atlantic. Theorists have found plenty to lock horns about. For example, heated debates have emerged about which categories (and how many) should be included in intersectional analysis (Lutz 2002)[17] and whether the seemingly endless proliferation of difference might not, after all, be the 'Achilles heel of intersectionality' (Ludwig 2006: 247), leaving the 'most salient' differences (race, class, and gender) undertheorised (Knapp 1999, Skeggs 1997).[18] Still other theorists have debated at length the problem of using categories at all, suggesting that what is needed is a more transversal approach – a thinking *across* categories (Yuval-Davis 2006) or focusing on 'sites' where multiple identities are performed rather than on the categories themselves (Staunæs 2003).[19] Discussions have emerged about the scope of intersectional analysis (Staunæs 2003, Buitelaar 2006, Prins 2006) and about the uses to which intersectional theory should be put. Should it be deployed primarily for uncovering vulnerabilities or exclusions or

---

16   An Internet search yielded 2,450 hits under 'intersectionality' and encompassed fields ranging from law, international relations, human rights, psychotherapy, identity politics, literature, popular culture and many more.

17   Lutz (2002) has provided a list of no less than 14 lines of difference (gender, sexuality, race or skin colour, ethnicity, national belonging, class, culture, religion, able-bodiedness, age, sedentariness, property ownership, geographical location, and status in terms of tradition and development). The list is, however, potentially much longer. See also Lutz and Wenning (2001).

18   Leiprecht and Lutz (2006) offer an interesting compromise, whereby race, class and gender are taken as a 'minimum standard' for intersectional analysis to which other categories can be added, depending upon the context and the specifics of the research problem.

19   As McCall (2005: 1779) points out, much of the literature on intersectionality has been critical of broad and sweeping generalisations of categorisation rather than critical of categorisation *per se*. Crenshaw (1991) deliberately takes issue with what she calls 'vulgar constructionist' attempts to dismantle categories altogether in the name of anti-essentialism. Given the significance of categories such as race and gender for the experiences and struggles of women of colour, it makes more sense to challenge the social and material consequences of categories rather than the process of categorisation *per se*. Identity politics do not need to be abandoned because of their reliance on categories, but rather need to recognise the multiplicity of identities and the ways categories intersect at specific sites (Crenshaw 1991: 1297–9).

should we be examining it as a resource, a source of empowerment (Saharso 2002, Burman 2003, Lutz and Davis 2005)? In short, as Ann Phoenix has aptly noted, there seems to be enough in the concept of intersectionality to attract and repel feminist theorists and to keep them going for a long time to come (Phoenix 2006: 187). Intersectionality is successful not only because it is both catchy and complex enough to stimulate theoretical debate but because it provides a much needed bridge between feminist researchers (generalists) and feminist theoreticians. In a well-known (and hotly debated) article for *Feminist Theory*, Liz Stanley and Sue Wise criticised recent developments in feminist theory, arguing that theory has become 'the distinct activity and special preserve of a priestly caste determinedly maintaining an elite position' (Stanley and Wise 2000: 276). In their view, feminist theory has become limited to the esoteric theoretical ruminations of a handful of 'theory stars' rather than an activity in which all feminist researchers are engaged. They make a passionate plea for a return to the conception of theory as the 'commonly owned and shared production of feminist ideas' (Stanley and Wise 2000: 276). This is precisely what intersectionality seems to do. It mends the division between the generalists (feminist researchers) and specialists ('theory'), compelling the specialists to ground their meta-concerns in the concrete social and political contexts of women's lives and the generalists to reclaim theory as an integral part of feminist inquiry.

Ambiguity and Incompleteness

The fourth characteristic of successful theory is that it is, paradoxically, inherently ambiguous and obviously incomplete. Davis (1986) takes issue with one of the shibboleths within the sociology of science to the effect that disputes about theoretical articulations mark the end of a theoretical paradigm. Davis regards inconsistencies and missing pieces as part of what makes a theory famous in the first place. Theories thrive on ambiguity and incompleteness. Given the myriad and often hostile divisions in any academic audience, a successful theory has to be fuzzy and indeterminate enough that disparate groups will be able to interpret it in 'congenial, if mutually incompatible, ways' (Davis 1986: 296). The more incoherent a theory is, the more it will require synthesis and elaboration. Pointing out the incongruities in a theory is the first step towards looking for ways to improve upon the original – an activity which is the bread and butter of theorising. If ambiguity stimulates synthesis, then incompleteness can motivate an academic audience to elaborate or 'test' the theory by applying it to new areas of social life that were not addressed in the original theory (Davis 1986: 297).

In short, successful theories are successful precisely because they do not settle matters once and for all; they open them up for further discussion and inquiry.

It is precisely because intersectionality is so imperfect – ambiguous and open-ended – that it has been so productive for contemporary feminist scholarship. Its lack of clear-cut definition or even specific parameters has enabled it to be drawn upon in nearly any context of inquiry. The infinite regress built into the concept – which categories to use and when to stop – makes it vague, yet also allows endless constellations of intersecting lines of difference to be explored. With each new intersection, new connections emerge and previously hidden exclusions come to light. Intersectionality offers endless opportunities for interrogating one's own blind spots and transforming them into analytic resources for further critical analysis. In short, intersectionality, by virtue of its vagueness and inherent open-endedness, initiates a process of discovery which not only is potentially interminable, but promises to yield new and more comprehensive and reflexively critical insights. What more could one desire from feminist inquiry?

Assessing Intersectionality's Success

In this chapter, I have raised the question of how the vague and open-ended concept of intersectionality could become such a success within contemporary feminist theory. I have shown that the success of intersectionality can be explained by the paradox that its so-called weaknesses are what allowed it to become so successful in the first place. The concept's very lack of precision and its myriad missing pieces are what have made it such a useful heuristic device for critical feminist theory.

Obviously, successful theories are not necessarily 'good' theories – and, indeed, as Davis has shown, the most successful theories are often not the best ones in the sense of being coherent or capable of providing encompassing or irrefutable explanations of social life. Some feminist scholars – much in line with this sociological common sense concerning 'good theory' – have argued that while intersectionality is clearly important, the ambiguity and open-endedness of the concept stand in the way of its usefulness for feminist theory. In order to achieve its full potential, intersectionality is in need of a definition, a set of clearly demarcated parameters, and a methodology which would eliminate any confusion among researchers concerning how, where and when it should be applied.

Of course, the notion of 'good theory' is itself highly contested. It might be argued that feminist theory is – or should be – less concerned with considerations of clarity and comprehensiveness than with how a theory can be deployed for specific normative or political purposes. As Judith Butler and Joan Scott note, feminist theory needs to 'generate analyses, critiques, and political interventions, and open up a political imaginary for feminism that points the way beyond some of the impasses by which it has been constrained' (Butler and Scott 1992: xiii). In their view, a 'good' feminist theory would not end the confusion once and for all, but would allow us to attend to and critically analyse the multiplicity of divisions and inequalities. It would open up space for critique and intervention, while enabling us to be reflexive about the range and limitations of our own theoretical enterprise.

While intersectionality may not fit the sociological common sense concerning 'good theory' as coherent, comprehensive and sound, it does provide an instance of *good* feminist theory in the sense that Judith Butler and Joan W. Scott describe. Intersectionality initiates a process of discovery, alerting us to the fact that the world around us is always more complicated and contradictory than we ever could have anticipated. It compels us to grapple with this complexity in our scholarship. It does not provide written-in-stone guidelines for doing feminist inquiry, a kind of feminist methodology to fit all kinds of feminist research. Rather, it stimulates our creativity in looking for new and often unorthodox ways of doing feminist analysis. Intersectionality does not produce a normative straitjacket for monitoring feminist inquiry in search of the 'correct line'. Instead, it encourages each feminist scholar to engage critically with her own assumptions in the interests of reflexive, critical and accountable feminist inquiry.

In this sense, intersectionality has precisely the ingredients which are required of a good feminist theory. It encourages complexity and avoids premature closure, tantalising feminist scholars to raise new questions and explore uncharted territory. Of course, at some point we may discover that intersectionality is not addressing the issues that seem most important to us. Or it may not be addressing them in a sufficiently novel and unexpected way. We may discover that theoretical debates about intersectionality have become too detailed and convoluted for our liking, or that the research has become so predictable that we cannot suppress a yawn at the thought of having to read even one more article on intersectionality. When that day comes, I would hope that a new theory enters the scene – a theory which speaks to an even more fundamental concern in a delightfully novel but irritatingly ambiguous way, thereby irresistibly compelling us, specialists and generalists alike, to roll up our sleeves and get to work.

Bibliography

Brah, A. and Phoenix, A. 2004. Ain't I a Woman? Revisiting Intersectionality. *Journal of International Women's Studies*, 5(3), 75–86.

Buitelaar, M. 2006. 'I Am the Ultimate Challenge': Accounts of Intersectionality in the Life-Story of a Well-Known Daughter of Moroccan Migrant Workers in the Netherlands. *European Journal of Women's Studies*, 13(3), 259–76.

Burman, E. 2003. From Difference to Intersectionality: Challenges and Resources. *European Journal of Psychotherapy, Counselling and Health*, 6(4), 293–308.

Butler, J. 1989. *Gender Trouble: Feminism and the Subversion of Identity.* New York: Routledge.

Butler, J. and Scott, J.W. 1992. Introduction, in *Feminists Theorize the Political*, edited by Butler, J. and Scott, J.W. New York: Routledge, xiii–xvii.

Carby, H. 1982. White Woman Listen! Black Feminism and the Boundaries of Sisterhood, in *The Empire Strikes Back: Race and Realism in 70s Britain*, edited by The Centre for Contemporary Studies. London: Hutchinson, 212–35.

Collins, P.H. 1990. *Black Feminist Thought: Knowledge, Power and the Politics of Empowerment*. Boston: Unwin Hyman.

Crenshaw, K. 1991. Mapping the Margins: Intersectionality, Identity Politics, and Violence against Women of Color. *Stanford Law Review*, 43(6), 1241–99.

Davis, A.Y. 1981. *Women, Race, and Class*. New York: Random House.

Davis, M.S. 1971. 'That's Interesting!' Towards a Phenomenology of Sociology and a Sociology of Phenomenology. *Philosophy of the Social Sciences*, 1, 309–44.

Davis, M.S. 1986. 'That's Classic!' The Phenomenology and Rhetoric of Successful Social Theories. *Philosophy of the Social Sciences*, 16, 285–301.

hooks, b. 1981. *Ain't I a Woman?: Black Women and Feminism*. Boston, MA: South End Press.

hooks, b. 1992. *Black Looks: Race and Representation*. Boston, MA: South End Press.

hooks, b. 1994. *Outlaw Culture: Resisting Representations*. New York: Routledge.

Hull, G.T., Scott, P.B. and Smith, B. (eds) 1982. *All the Women Are White, All the Blacks Are Men, But Some of Us Are Brave: Black Women's Studies*. Old Westbury: Feminist Press.

Knapp, G.-A. 1999. Fragile Foundations, Strong Traditions, Situated Questioning: Critical Theory in German-Speaking Feminism, in *Adorno, Culture and Feminism*, edited by O'Neill, M. London: Sage, 119–41.

Knapp, G.-A. 2005. Race, Class, Gender: Reclaiming Baggage in Fast Travelling Theories. *European Journal of Women's Studies*, 12(3), 249–66.

Leiprecht, R. and Lutz, H. 2006. Intersektionalität im Klassenzimmer: Ethnizität, Klasse, Geschlecht, in *Schule in der Einwanderungsgesellschaft*, edited by Leiprecht, R. and Kerber, A. Schwalbach: Wochenschau Verlag, 218–34.

Ludwig, A. 2006. Differences between Women? Intersecting Voices in a Female Narrative. *European Journal of Women's Studies*, 13(3), 245–58.

Lugones, M. and Spelman, E.V. 1983. Have We Got a Theory for You! Feminist Theory, Cultural Imperialism, and the Demand for 'The Woman's Voice'. *Women's Studies International Forum*, 6(6), 573–81.

Lutz, H. 2002. Zonderblikken of blozen. Het standpunt van de (nieuw-) realisten. *Tijdschriftvoor Genderstudies*, 5(3), 7–17.

Lutz, H. and Davis, K. 2005. Geschlechterforschung und Biografieforschung: Intersektionalität als biographische Ressource am Beispiel einer außergewöhnlichen Frau, in *Biographieforschung im Diskurs*, edited by Völter, B., Dausien, B.; Lutz, H. and G. Rosenthal. Wiesbaden: VS, 228–47.

Lutz, H. and Wenning, N. 2001. Differenzen über Differenz – Einführung in die Debatten, in *Unterschiedlich verschieden. Differenz in der Erziehungswissenschaft*, edited by Lutz, H. and Wenning, N. Opladen: Leske & Budrich, 11–24.

Lykke, N. 2005. Intersectionality Revisited: Problems and Potentials. *Kvinnovetenskaplig tidskrift*, 2(3), 7–17.

Matsuda, M.J. 1991. Beside My Sister, Facing the Enemy: Legal Theory out of Coalition. *Stanford Law Review*, 43(6), 1183–92.

McCall, L. 2005. The Complexity of Intersectionality. *Signs*, 30(3), 1771–800.

Merton, R.K. 1973. *The Sociology of Science: Theoretical and Empirical Investigations.* Chicago, IL: University of Chicago Press.

Mohanty, C.T. 1988. Under Western Eyes: Feminist Scholarship and Colonial Discourses. *Feminist Review*, 30(6), 1–88.

Mohanty, C.T. 2003. *Feminism without Borders: Decolonizing Theory, Practicing Solidarity.* Durham, NC: Duke University Press.

Moraga, C. and Anzaldúa, G. (eds) 1983. *This Bridge Called My Back: Writing by Radical Women of Color.* New York: Kitchen Table Press.

Moya, P.M.L. 2001. Chicana Feminism and Postmodernist Theory. *Signs*, 26(2), 441–83.

Pfeil, F. 1994. No Basta Teorizar: In-Difference to Solidarity in Contemporary Fiction, Theory, and Practice, in *Scattered Hegemonies: Postmodernity and Transnational Feminist Practices*, edited by Grewal, I. and Kaplan, C. Minneapolis and London: University of Minnesota Press, 197–230.

Phoenix, A. 2006. Editorial: Intersectionality. *European Journal of Women's Studies*, 13(3), 187–92.

Prins, B. 2006. Narrative Accounts of Origins: A Blind Spot in the Intersectional Approach. *European Journal of Women's Studies*, 13(3), 277–90.

Saharso, S. 2002. Eenvrouw met twee missies. Reactie op Helma Lutz. *Tijdschriftvoor Genderstudies*, 5(3), 18–23.

Skeggs, B. 1997. *Formations of Class and Gender: Becoming Respectable.* London: Sage.

Smith, B. (ed.) 1983. *Home Girls: A Black Feminist Anthology.* New York: Kitchen Table/Women of Color Press.

Spelman, E. 1988. *Inessential Woman: Problems of Exclusion in Feminist Thought.* Boston: Beacon Press.

Spivak, G.C. 1993. *Outside in the Teaching Machine.* London: Routledge.

Stanley, L. and Wise, S. 2000. But the Empress has no Clothes! Some Awkward Questions about the 'Missing Revolution' in Feminist Theory. *Feminist Theory*, 1(3), 261–88.

Staunæs, D. 2003. Where have all the Subjects Gone? Bringing together the Concepts of Intersectionality and Subjectification. *Nora*, 11(2), 101–10.

Ware, V. 1992. *Beyond the Pale: White Women, Racism and History.* London: Verso.

Yuval-Davis, N. 2006. Intersectionality and Feminist Politics. *European Journal of Women's Studies*, 13(3), 193–210.

Zack, N. 2007. Can Third Wave Feminism Be Inclusive? Intersectionality, its Problems, and New Directions, in *Feminist Philosophy*, edited by Alcoff, L.M. and Kittay, E.F. Oxford: Blackwell Publishing, 193–207.

Zinn, M.B. and Dill, B.T. (eds) 1994. *Women of Color in US Society.* Philadelphia: Temple University Press.

Chapter 3

The Discursive Politics of Feminist Intersectionality

Myra Marx Ferree

As critical frame analysis has shown, even when concepts are expressed in the same words, they may have different meanings (Verloo 2007). Intersectionality is itself one of these contested terms within feminist thought. In this chapter, I take up the challenge of considering what feminists talk about when we talk of intersectionality.

Because intersectionality as a concept derives from the activist critiques that women of colour in the US and UK made in the 1970s and 1980s about an overly homogeneous political discourse in which 'all the women are white and all the blacks are men' (Hull, Scott and Smith 1982, Crenshaw 1989; this volume, Brah and Phoenix 2004), it is important to consider how its meaning changes when it is stretched to cover other inequalities and exclusions. I begin by adopting the dynamic and institutional understanding of intersectionality suggested by Leslie McCall (2005) and Ange-Marie Hancock (2007). Rather than identifying *points* of intersection, this approach sees the dimensions of inequality themselves as dynamic, located in changing, mutually constituted *relationships* with each other from which they cannot be disentangled (Glenn 2002, Walby 2007). Categories (such as women and black) and the dimensions along which they are ordered (such as gender and race) are not therefore deemed 'false' or 'insignificant' even though they are imperfect, variable and contested.

I then develop this argument to suggest how historically realised social relations in any place or time have an irreducible complexity in themselves, from which the abstraction of any dimension of comparison is an imperfect but potentially useful conceptual achievement of simplification, not an inherent property of the world. I offer a model of political discourse that is equally dynamic, and use it to illustrate how structurally anchored discursive opportunities in continental Europe differ from the frameworks for political discourse on which US and UK women of colour originally drew. I argue that across different political contexts, various actors engage in trying to 'shrink' the meaning of intersectionality and limit the areas in which it can be applied, to 'bend' it to better fit with other issues on their agenda, and to 'stretch' it to meet emergent needs (Lombardo, Meier and Verloo 2009).

Intersections, Systems and Discourses

The dynamic version of intersectionality insists that it cannot be located at any one level of analysis, whether individual or institutional. The 'intersection of gender and race' is not any number of specific *locations* occupied by individuals or groups (such as black women) but a *process* through which 'race' takes on multiple 'gendered' meanings for particular women and men (and for those not neatly located in either of those categories) depending on whether, how and by whom race-gender is seen as relevant for their sexuality, reproduction, political authority, employment or housing. These domains (and others) are to be understood as *organisational fields* in which multidimensional forms of inequality are experienced, contested and reproduced in historically changing forms.

This is what Baukje Prins (2006) defines as a constructionist rather than structural understanding of intersectionality, but I prefer to call it 'interactive intersectionality' to emphasise its structuration as an ongoing historical process from which neither structure nor agency can be erased (Giddens 1990). Sylvia Walby (2007) introduces complexity theory to develop further this idea of intersectionality as an active system with both positive and negative feedback effects, non-linearity of relations, and non-nested, non-hierarchical overlaps among institutions. In such a complex system, gender is not a dimension limited to the organisation of reproduction or family, class is not a dimension equated with the economy, and race is not a category reduced to the primacy of ethnicities, nations and borders, but all of the processes that systematically organise families, economies and nations are co-constructed along with the meanings of gender, race and class that are presented in and reinforced by these institutions separately and together. In other words, each institutional system serves as each other's environment to which it is adapting.

To McCall's dynamically interactive view of intersectionality and Walby's notion of co-constructed systems, I add an emphasis on *discourse* as a political process by which this co-creation occurs. My approach rests on understanding the co-formation of knowledge and power, stresses the historical development of institutions that shape consciousness and practice, and identifies discourse as a crucial arena of political activity (Foucault 1977).[1] Two of the central processes of discursive politics are categorising and ordering. These human actions have political consequences in themselves because of the inherent reflexivity of the social world; that is, we use categories and ranks not only to understand but to control the world. Feedback from the environment to the system comes in terms of information about success and failure (Espeland and Sauder 2007). As lists, ranks, metaphors and distinctions proliferate, they guide our understanding of who we are and with whom we are more or less related. Thus, for example, when the dimension of 'race' is constructed and 'fixed' in national censuses, it generates

---

1   For another anti-categorical and discourse-based approach to intersectionality, compare Paula-Irene Villas' contribution to this volume (171f).

meaningful and contestable categories (such as 'Asian') which can always be further decomposed, but which serve to distribute real resources and recognition in response to which identities and activities become oriented.

The understandings of all forms of inequality are mutually stretched and bent as they encounter each other. Like other forms of social reflexivity, the relatively new framing of intersectionality in Europe is being done in a social world that already incorporates intersectional relations in historically specific and yet contestable and changing ways (Knapp 2005, Verloo 2006). By bringing attention to discourse as a central political concept for understanding both intersectionality and social change, and arguing that rights are better understood as a discourse than as a single 'master frame', I suggest that there are concrete struggles involved in making intersectionality a useful concept. I then apply this web of meaning approach to illustrate some ways in which intersectionality is differently controversial and radical in Europe than in the US, and conclude by suggesting that the agency involved in choosing one's struggles will shape the future meaning of intersectionality in each context.

Frameworks and Framing Work

Framing means connecting beliefs about social actors and beliefs about social relations into more or less coherent packages that define what kinds of actions are necessary, possible and effective for particular actors. The point of frames is that they draw connections, identify relationships and create perceptions of social order out of the variety of possible mental representations of reality swirling around social actors. By actively making links among people, concepts, practices and resources, frames allow for a coordination of activity for oneself that also is open to interpretation by others (Goffman 1974). Drawing a relationship or connection, not the individual element, is the key unit for *framing work*. Framing creates the known world: it actively gives concepts meaning by embedding them in networks of other more or less widely shared and practically relevant meanings (Benford and Snow 2000, Snow 2004). Although Robert Benford and David A. Snow both emphasise framing as a process of attaching ideas to given meaning structures, I stress mutual transformations of the structures and ideas promoted by movements. The institutionalised networks of meaning are what I call *frameworks*.

Frameworks in politics can be understood in part by analogy to how systems of meaning work in other areas. For example, scientific disciplines have histories that privilege certain ways of knowing and direct those who would be productive within them to follow certain practices rather than others. Rather than by a disciplinary canon, the framework for political debate is given by *authoritative texts* such as constitutions, laws, judicial decisions, treaties and administrative regulations. Such texts never 'speak for themselves' but need to be interpreted, implemented and enforced. But they offer a discursive structure – an institutionalised framework of connections made among people, concepts, events – that shapes the opportunities of political actors by making some sorts of connections appear inevitable and making others conspicuously uncertain and so especially inviting for debate.

Such frameworks will be variably useful or constraining to speakers, thus it makes sense to speak of them as discursive *opportunity* structures (Ferree 2003). As critical frame analysis emphasises, the authoritative texts in any particular context have themselves been created by fixing their meaning in a network of strong connections with other concepts, a process that always takes political work to accomplish and, once achieved, shapes future political work (Stone 1988, Bacchi 1999). A discursive opportunity structure is thus open, dynamic and imbued with power, not just something that exists passively as texts 'on paper'.

Looking at a discursive opportunity structure as a set of authoritative texts (e.g. laws), in other words, should not obscure how their authority fits in a wider system. A given law is a part of a wider legal culture, and each such text also provides a resource over which politically mobilised actors struggle by offering interpretations and drawing out implications for actions. By its very nature, law is a system of dispute; if there were no opposing interests, there would be no need for treaties, regulations or decisions. Laws, constitutions, treaties and directives thus form policy frameworks that are historically constructed, path-dependent, opportunity structures for the discursive struggles of the present time.

Framing work is the term describing the ever-present struggle over political meaning by diverse social actors. All social movements challenge the prevailing frameworks for politics: they try to de-institutionalise some texts and bring other laws or principles of governance into force. Some social movements are discursively radical; these are the ones that name new rights (freedom from sexual harassment) and recognise new social actors (naming them citizens). Other so-called reform efforts extend the enforceability of nominally existing rights. The framing work in which movements engage is an essential means to claim legitimacy for their ways of defining right and wrong, justice and injustice.

Frame analysis gains an important dimension of agency when it attends to the historical political processes by which contemporary authoritative texts were created, interpreted and used as resources for mobilisation. Studies of policy development, such as Nicholas Pedriana (2006) offers with regard to equal employment law in the US and Kathrin Zippel (2006) provides for sexual harassment law in Germany, the US and the EU, provide an important window into these processes. These studies indicate the reflexive impact of securing, institutionalising and applying new ways of thinking about rights, making them real in their consequences.

Pedriana (2006) shows, for example, that the framework of 'equal rights' provided in US law had to be actively connected to a specific practical meaning in its interpretation, application and enforcement. Inclusion of 'sex' as a category to be protected from discrimination by law, although a political accomplishment, did not itself mean that courts would understand this as disallowing protective legislation or even the 'customary' segregation of jobs by sex. Only after contests in and out of court around the scope of meaning that the literal words of the law should carry, did the equal rights frame become the 'self-evident' understanding of this language in the US. Paradoxically, this stretching of meaning to protect women, 'like blacks', from discrimination created a discursive connection to 'desegregation'. This allowed the opposition to frame the proposed Equal Rights Amendment to the US Constitution as threatening to abolish women's restrooms and women's colleges (Mathews and DeHart 1990) and blocked the continued expansion of women's legal rights that had seemed 'self-evident' only a decade before (Mansbridge 1986).

The relationality and fluidity of meaning carried in and to frames even in institutionalised texts challenges the more familiar idea of a 'master frame' (Snow 2004). Although there is a strong consensus among many scholars that 'rights' is an exceptionally powerful idea in the United States, what 'rights' means is contested on an ongoing basis in the courts, legislature and executive branch and shifts over time in its application. For example, 'equal rights' claims made in the Civil Rights movement were 'shrunk' over time to no longer imply any but the most formal legal rights, separated from the concept of 'social justice' and tied instead to the idea of 'diversity', which was in turn carefully restricted to imply that no 'special rights' could be considered (Edelman, Fuller and Mara-Drita 2001). Because frames are not isolated concepts, but *connections* to other concepts that provide the meanings of words-in-use, framing spins a web of meaning in which self-references and cross-references are inherently multiple.

Thus, rather than thinking of US political discourse as providing 'rights' as a singular master frame that exists outside of or above the web of meaning in which more particular frames are being constructed, it is useful to consider rights as one of the more centrally located and densely linked ideas in a network of political meanings. Rights discourses draw on one or more of the particular connections available to the concept of rights and thus 'stretch' it in some particular direction or another (for example to include gay marriage or not, Hull 1997). The density and stability of the cross-referencing system of meaning at the core of American thinking about 'rights' offers a rich and diverse periphery of potential interpretations to actors in a variety of positions along its 'edges' (Skrentny 2006). Seeing rights discourse as a framework in which rights is centrally located highlights both how all the elements in it are shaped by the ways they are linked to each other, but also emphasises how the concept of 'rights' itself is defined by its links to other ideas.

This network of meaning is a *rights discourse*. Specific rights discourses vary in different contexts, which is why intersectionality enters into these frameworks in different ways. By contrast, 'rights' as a singular master frame would be the one most important element and carry one fixed definition. It would then connect hierarchically to a range of abstract and interchangeable elements such as 'equality', 'difference' or 'protection'. These subordinate concepts would be thought to have stable definitions regardless of the local framework in which they are found, and vary only in how likely they are to be embraced, rather than taking their meaning from the discourse in which they are used. The 'women' who have these understood rights would also constitute a category of known membership, rather than 'woman' itself being a contested object of political debate in which women of different ethnicities, sexualities, ages and occupations are more or less included. Intersectionality as a concept is often used to stretch the concept of women to include marginalised groups, however they might be understood in a specific socio-historical context. Attempts to list all such possible exclusions are therefore bound to fail, defeated by the fluidity of power relations in practice.

Intersectional Framing and Institutionalised Rights Discourses

Thinking of rights discourses as multiple, historically produced frameworks for feminist struggles over power highlights the challenges that travelling concepts such as intersectionality face when they arrive in new contexts of meaning. Using the interactional definition of intersectionality, 'race' and 'gender' take operational meaning in any given situation in part from the multiple institutions in play (such as family or nation) and in part from the other dimensions of inequality that are also engaged in giving meaning to each other and to the institutional context. This is what Walby (2007) means by avoiding the 'segregationary reductionism' that places class, race and gender each into just one key institutional 'system' (economy, state or family). She instead looks for the interpenetration of meaning and action in systems that are not 'saturated' by one concept alone. Similarly, in the dynamic definition of discourse, there is an equally complex (that is, non-nested and non-saturated) system of meanings being referenced when political actors speak of 'rights' in the US or the 'rule of law' (*Rechtsstaat*) in Germany. Rights discourse is both a discursive environment for systems structuring national, economic, familial and other social relations of power and a system of meaning embedded in an environment of material inequality. These terms reach across a variety of institutional contexts.

Each of these dynamic models specifically rejects the emphasis on generating long lists of diverse 'frames' and of 'axes of inequality' that has been part of the study of both intersectionality and framing (and critiqued by McCall 2005 and Benford 1997, respectively). Instead, both discourse and intersectionality can be more productively approached through the study of *configurations*, a term McCall (2005) uses to describe attention to patterns, interactions among elements that have paradoxical and conflicting meanings depending on the specific context as a whole. Such configurations – both of discourses and of intersectionality in both discursive and material aspects of the social order – have stability but also change. It is an empirical matter in any given context to see what concepts are important to the configuration of inequalities in discourse and in practice.

This means 'rights' (or 'women') is not a master frame that has a 'real' meaning that could ever be fully known or 'correctly' used, but is a more or less meaningful and discursively powerful way of speaking depending on the panoply of meanings attached to it. Unlike the way that Benford and Snow (2000) talk about 'frame amplification' or 'frame extension' as if it were an operation performed on a single conceptual claim, I contend that actors who make political claims that 'stretch' the meaning of a concept are not 'extending' their single ideas to apply to new groups or new elements that were simply missing before, but rather 'stretching' their whole web of meaning to encompass people or practices that were connected in different patterns. They thereby change the shape and structure of the web as a whole. What 'women' are and want and need is meaningfully different depending on who is included in that concept.

To argue, as contemporary transnational feminist organisations do, that 'women's rights are human rights' is to stretch the concepts of *both* 'human' and 'rights' to mean something different than they did before, not just to extend their stably existing meanings to a new group, 'women'. Because gender equality is framed in the discursive structure of a political system through its relationships to other ideas, actors and actions, some actors' frames for gender will embrace many of these existing connections (Ferree 2003), while other (radical) efforts will aim to transform the very framework in which the idea of gender equality is embedded.

The differently institutionalised relationships among gender, race and class in the frameworks of the US and Europe offer both opportunities for pragmatic gains and prospects for radical transformation in different discursive dimensions. The European social model constructs social equality in terms of economic relations, institutionalises processes of class representation (parties and unions), and views the redistributive role of the state as legitimate. Class mobilisations were successful in constructing this framework, and women's mobilisation for their rights drew on the ideas of citizenship and justice that were institutionalised through this class struggle. By contrast, US women's struggle for democratic citizenship was intertwined with the claims of racialised minorities, especially enslaved blacks, to be recognised as fully human individuals. Thus the framing of 'rights' formed by class-centred meanings of social citizenship dominated in Europe, but race-centred attributions of personal inferiority to legitimate exclusions from 'rights' were historically central to the US (Ferree 2008).

As a consequence, placing race and gender together as forms of social inequality appropriately recognises that these struggles are fundamental to American understandings of rights as political recognition, but to place gender with 'race' (ethnic heritage, language, skin colour or religion) rather than with class in Europe is to wrench gender out of its existing framework of meaning. Because feminists are suspicious that defining gender as a form of 'diversity' will place it in a lower tier of rights, the alliance of white feminists with persons of colour in Europe is problematic for them. Unlike US feminists, who could benefit by the gender-race analogy, many feminists in Europe see little to gain for themselves in terms of rights by alliance with immigrant groups. At the same time, the active framing work of European politicians to define gender equality as (already) characteristic of this region undermines European feminist critiques of their own countries and aligns the supposed interests of (white) women against 'immigrants' (Brown and Ferree

2005, Rottmann and Ferree 2008).[2] In a quite different but no less significant way, if gender is defined intersectionally as 'like class' in the US, it becomes a matter of competitive achievement in which trying to be part of the elite is a moral duty.

The rights discourses that frame feminism are therefore stretched in quite different directions in different frameworks. Which particular feminist claims are going to radically challenge this configuration thus will be different too. In both regions, full citizenship for all women remains a goal rather than an achievement, but the available discursive tools for the necessary activist framing work that movements in both contexts pursue differ. By beginning from an analysis of social inequality that is already understood to be intersectional in a dynamic sense, the frameworks that connect race, class and gender with rights and citizenship can be examined for *how* they empower and disempower people in different structural locations.

Conclusion

The meaning of gender inequality is not simply different across countries or contexts but is anchored in a history in which the boundaries and entitlements of racialised nationhood, the power of organised class interests to use the state, and the intersection of both of these with the definition of women as reproducers of the nation have always been part of politics (Yuval-Davis 1990). Recognising gender as part of a system of intersectional inequality that cuts across institutions, reflects historical struggles, and depends on the meanings that categories carry in context makes clear that intersectional analysis will never be able to be simplified into just a list of oppressions.

Instead, the institutionalised frameworks for understanding even the most fundamental political terms such as rights, security, power, freedom and democracy should be addressed as the products of historical struggles. Feminist efforts have always been part of that long process of state-making, and feminist framing work is integrally part of contemporary struggles to shift boundaries of inclusion and exclusion within the category called 'women' as well as between women and men. This applies not only to rights discourses specific to particular nation states, but also to the choices feminists make about their relationship to EU and global discourses (Hellgren and Hobson 2008). For example, the framing of 'national security' today, no less than that of 'human rights', is in need of feminist stretching and bending, particularly in the US. The weak connection of social class and economic inequality with American understandings of gender and race as individual traits constitutes the central challenge of communicating a feminist discourse of intersectionality within the US framework.

---

2   From a different angle, Gudrun-Axeli Knapp, in this volume (187f), arrives at another explanation for the problematic connection of race and gender in the German discourse. Also see the discussion of race in Europe in this volume's introduction.

People make categories to understand the world, and do so from the standpoints that we occupy, but the point of our understanding this world of inequality and injustice is to change it. Descriptions of inequalities feed back in both positive and negative ways into the continued existence of these configurations of inequality. Positive feedback reinforces the status quo in the classic vicious circle expressed as path-dependencies in systems. However, the institutionalisation of certain patterns with their inherent contradictions also allows for negative feedback, in which small changes multiply and drive a system further and further from its previous, precarious equilibrium. This potential instability – whether noted as Marx's 'dialectic' of class, Myrdal's 'dilemma' of racial exclusions, or Wollstonecraft and Scott's 'paradox' of gender difference and equality – affects all forms of inequality and gives mobilisations to transform frameworks of inequality their hope for success.

But transformatory politics will not be identifiable by some list of their particular characteristics or target groups, any more than politically significant frames or social inequalities can be captured in a list, however long. A system-based view of intersectionality recognises the inherent potential of reforms, however modest, to be the 'butterfly wings' that begin a longer process of radical change that is difficult for even its advocates to foresee. Politics is the action of taking risks in a future that is unknowable because it is being co-determined by all the other actors with whom one must necessarily struggle (Zerilli 2005). Feminist 'identity politics' actively construct the meaning of 'feminism' by the choices of with and against whom feminists engage politically.

Feminists today, as in the past, have no special claim on insight or ability to find the one correct analysis. Feminist actors can never predict how their actions will ultimately be understood or how the process of struggle will unfold, since they are not the only actors engaged in contests over meanings, resources and power. Yet, uncertain as the ends of a framing process must be, framing cannot be avoided if action is to be taken at all. A modest claim to limited, fallible but strategically useful framing might open the door to dialogue with others, who have developed their own frames from their own circumstances, allowing a reflexive approach to finding alliances with which feminists can more broadly challenge the frameworks of inequality that enmesh us all.

Bibliography

Bacchi, C. 1999. *Women, Politics and Policies: The Construction of Policy Problems*. Thousand Oaks CA: Sage.

Benford, R. 1997. An Insider's Critique of the Social Movement Framing Perspective. *Sociological Inquiry*, 67(4), 409–30.

Benford, R. and Snow, D.A. 2000. Framing Processes and Social Movements: An Overview and Assessment. *Annual Review of Sociology*, 26, 611–39.

Brah, A. and Phoenix, A. 2004. Ain't I A Woman? Revisiting Intersectionality. *Journal of International Women's Studies*, 5(3), 75–87.

Brown, J.A. and Ferree, M.M. 2005. Close Your Eyes and Think of England: Pronatalism in the British Print Media. *Gender & Society*, 19(1), 5–24.

Crenshaw, K.W. 1989. Demarginalizing the Intersection of Race and Sex: A Black Feminist Critique of Antidiscrimination Doctrine, Feminist Theory and Antiracist Politics. *University of Chicago Legal Forum*, 139–67.

Edelman, L.B., Fuller, S.R. and Mara-Drita, I. 2001. Diversity Rhetoric and the Managerialization of Law. *American Journal of Sociology*, 106(6), 1589–1641.

Espeland, W.N. and Sauder, M. 2007. Rankings and Reactivity: How Public Measures Recreate Social Worlds. *American Journal of Sociology*, 113(1), 1–40.

Ferree, M.M. 2003. Resonance and Radicalism: Feminist Abortion Discourses in Germany and the United States. *American Journal of Sociology*, 109(2), 304–44.

Ferree, M.M. 2008. Framing Equality: The Politics of Race, Class, Gender in the US, Germany, and the Expanding European Union, in *The Gender Politics of the European Union*, edited by Roth, S. New York: Berghahn Publishers, 237–55.

Foucault, M. 1977. *Discipline and Punish: The Birth of the Prison.* (Translated from the French by A. Sheridan) New York: Pantheon Books.

Giddens, A. 1990. *The Consequences of Modernity.* Stanford: Stanford University Press.

Glenn, E.N. 2002. *Unequal Labor: How Race and Gender shaped American Citizenship and Labor.* Cambridge, MA: Harvard University Press.

Goffman, E. 1974. *Frame Analysis: An Essay on the Organization of Experience.* New York: Harper and Row.

Hancock, A.-M. 2007. When Multiplication Doesn't Equal Quick Addition: Examining Intersectionality as a Research Paradigm. *Perspectives on Politics*, 5(1), 63–79.

Hellgren, Z. and Hobson, B. 2008. Gender and Ethnic Minority Claims in Swedish and EU Frames: Sites of Multi-level Political Opportunities and Boundary Making, in *Gender Politics and Women's Movements in the Expanding European Union*, edited by Roth, S. New York: Berghahn Books, 211–33.

Hull, K.E. 1997. The Political Limits of the Rights Frame: The Case of Same-Sex Marriage in Hawaii. *Sociological Perspectives*, 44(2), 207–32.

Hull, G., Scott, P.B. and Smith, B. 1982. *All the Women are White, All the Blacks are Men, but Some of Us are Brave: Black Women's Studies.* Old Westbury NY: Feminist Press.

Knapp, G.-A. 2005. Race, Class, Gender: Reclaiming Baggage in Fast-Travelling Theories. *European Journal of Women's Studies*, 12(3), 249–65.

Lombardo, E., Meier, P. and Verloo, M. (eds) 2009. *The Discursive Politics of Gender Equality: Stretching, Bending and Policy-making*. London: Routledge.

Mansbridge, J. 1986. *Why we Lost the ERA*. Chicago: University of Chicago Press.

Mathews, D. and DeHart, J.S. 1990. *Sex, Gender and the Politics of the ERA: A State and the Nation*. New York: Oxford University Press.

McCall, L. 2005. The Complexity of Intersectionality. *Signs: Journal of Women in Culture and Society*, 30(3), 1771–1880.

Pedriana, N. 2006. From Protective to Equal Treatment: Legal Framing Processes and Transformation of the Women's Movement in the 1960s. *American Journal of Sociology*, 111(6), 1718–61.

Prins, B. 2006. Narrative Accounts of Origins: A Blind Spot in the Intersectional Approach? *European Journal of Women's Studies*, 13(3), 277–90.

Rottmann, S.B. and Ferree, M.M. 2008. Citizenship and Intersectionality: German Feminist Debates about Headscarf and Anti-discrimination Laws. *Social Politics*, 15(4), 481–513.

Skrentny, J. 2006. Policy-Elite Perceptions and Social Movement Success: Understanding Variations in Group Inclusion in Affirmative Action. *American Journal of Sociology*, 111(6), 1762–1815.

Snow, D.A. 2004. Framing Processes, Ideology, and Discursive Fields, in *The Blackwell Companion to Social Movements*, edited by Snow, D.A., Soule, S.A. and Kriesi, H. Malden, MA: Blackwell, 380–412.

Stone, D.A. 1988. *Policy Paradox and Political Reason*. Glenview, IL: Scott, Foresman.

Verloo, M. 2006. Multiple Inequalities, Intersectionality and the European Union. *European Journal of Women's Studies*, 13(3), 211–28.

Verloo, M. (ed.) 2007. *Multiple Meanings of Gender Equality: A Critical Frame Analysis of Gender Policies in Europe*. Budapest: CPS Books.

Walby, S. 2007. Complexity Theory, Systems Theory, and Multiple Intersecting Social Inequalities. *Philosophy of the Social Sciences*, 37(4), 449–70.

Yuval-Davis, N. 1990. *Gender and Nation*. Thousand Oaks CA: Sage Publications.

Zerilli, L. 2005. *Feminism and the Abyss of Freedom*. Chicago: University of Chicago Press.

Zippel, K. 2006. *The Politics of Sexual Harassment: A Comparative Study of the United States, the European Union, and Germany*. New York: Cambridge University Press.

PART II
Emerging Fields in Intersectionality: Masculinities, Heteronormativity and Transnationality

Chapter 4

Marginalised Masculinity, Precarisation and the Gender Order

Mechthild Bereswill and Anke Neuber
[translated by Gerard Holden]

The arguments put forward in this chapter are connected with a conference that took place in January 2009. The title of the conference took the form of a question, 'Celebrating Intersectionality?', thus inviting the participants to debate a concept that is becoming increasingly popular. On the cover of the flyer announcing the conference programme was a striking illustration that also appears on the cover of this volume. We would like to start by looking at this image again, and using it to clarify some of the central considerations and open questions which, in our view, are significant for theoretical debates about, and empirical investigations of, the constellations of difference and hierarchy that have traditionally been the focus of feminist approaches.

If we look at the flyer, we see that the subject of the conference is reflected in the image of a bundle of thrown Mikado sticks, with the implication that there is a connection between a game of skill and concentration such as Mikado and the complexity associated with the intersection and overlapping of various axes of difference and of associated constellations of inequality.[1] This is how the game is played: one player throws all the sticks onto a table, with the highest-value stick placed in the middle of the bundle. The result is a random arrangement of intersecting sticks; these sticks have different values, and the highest-value stick has a special master status and is the most prized trophy. The other players have to try to pick up as many sticks as possible, and of course the most valuable ones, out of the arrangement without disturbing the arrangement as a whole. If the first player causes the whole thing to move, it is the next player's turn.

The associations to which this gives rise suggest interesting connections with some fundamental questions. In addition to the provocative idea of society as a randomly thrown conglomerate which starts to wobble if the necessary steady hand is lacking, the image corresponds to some open questions about different axes of social inequality. With reference to the category of gender, one question is how we can grasp theoretically, and explore empirically, the points of overlap and intersection between various constellations of difference without employing gender

---

1   This game is also sometimes known as spellicans, pick-up sticks or jackstraws.

as a privileged master category, but also without losing sight of the structuration of gender relations – as if gender hierarchies were the result of a random throw of sticks with different values and profit margins.[2]

If we put the question of the contingency of societal relations to one side and concentrate on the image of the falling sticks, we can ask some further questions. Do the sticks fall differently every time, or are there repeated patterns? What is the meaning of the colours, red and blue? What do the different values of the sticks represent? And finally: what is it that begins to move when someone moves one stick, or, to put it another way, which constellations begin to wobble and how far can this disruption go before it begins to shake the arrangement as a whole?

The image gives rise to questions that are initially playful, but these lead us to fundamental theoretical issues in women's and gender research and to the question of how best to theoretically refine the concept of intersectionality. What value or weight should be attached to gender in the interplay between various determinants of inequality? Is gender a central pillar in the structuration of social inequality? What is the current status of the central paradigm of women's and gender research, the idea that gender is a structural category and that we are universally confronted with a hierarchical gender relationship?

Questions such as these, and the associated critical objections to the primacy of the category of gender over other axes of difference, had been formulated long before the recent rise of intersectionality in the context of German-language women's and gender research. Approaches from research on racism and migration were important here, together with postcolonial theories, all of which were sharply critical of a one-dimensional and homogeneous version of gender which ignored both the life situations and gender arrangements of black and immigrant women and men and the significance of whiteness and dominance for the position of white people (Mohanty 1988, Spelman 1988, Schultz 1990, Lutz 1992, Ware 1992, Frankenberg 1993, Gümen 1998, Bereswill and Ehlert 1996).[3]

These criticisms were designed to decentre gender as part of an attempt to find an appropriate way of approaching the overlapping and intersection of, and connections between, different social positions and relations of oppression. Kimberlé Crenshaw, in an article published in 1989, discussed the need to overcome a one-dimensional perspective on gender and looked for strategies that would make it possible to grasp the complex interrelations between race, class and gender rather than just adding them together to produce a multiple category of oppression. Crenshaw's image of an intersection, which has been taken up by many other authors, must also be seen in the context of a concrete empirical finding and the search for improved ways of intervening legally on behalf of African American

---

2   The controversial question of the primacy of gender over other categories of inequality is tackled as well by Dubravka Zarkov in this volume.

3   However, this was never only a question of 'women', but rather of gender relations and the social construction of difference and hierarchy in the historically constituted relation of tension between majorities and minorities.

women. At the beginning of the 1990s, black underclass women were appearing in court to face criminal charges much more frequently than white women. In 1991 Crenshaw published a text with the programmatic title 'Mapping the Margins', which drew attention to the connection between marginalisation and gender. This is very important, not only in the context of societal constructions of criminality. This perspective also raises the question of how the interplay between different axes of social inequality changes a category such as gender and the insights and assumptions related to gender theory that are associated with the category. This means that we can only grasp 'what is social about the category of gender' adequately if we assume that gender is a structuring factor in societal relations, but also that gender relations are simultaneously structured by other axes of inequality (Gümen 1998). Against this background, we are able to incorporate constellations in which there are intersections between social revaluations and devaluations following different logics, and we can see that these may also take the form of simultaneous dynamics running contrary to social privilege and disadvantage. Configurations such as a version of femininity that is subordinate to masculinity, or the privileged position of whites, thus give rise to further questions about the structuring effects of gender. One can also pursue these questions in relation to constellations where hegemonic masculinity breaks down as a result of downgrading, heteronormativity or ethnicisation. The next question, which we have already posed (see above), is: Are women as a social group in a fundamentally disadvantaged position in relation to men as a social group? This question can be posed in the context of a possible bringing together of different theoretical perspectives on the relationship between inequality and gender, and also with regard to the issue of axes of inequality which may overlap with, intersect or contradict one another. The constellations we find particularly interesting are those in which tension arises between hegemonic and subordinate positions in gender relations within a single constellation.

Against this background, our argument in this chapter takes as its starting point a constellation in which deviancy, marginalisation and gender move closer together and a constellation of social inequality that is full of tension becomes visible. Our theoretical reflections have been developed in connection with long-term empirical studies of the biographies of young men who received prison sentences in the late 1990s in East and West Germany.[4] The life situations and life plans of this group

---

4   These long-term biographical studies were carried out by the authors, together with Almut Koesling, at the Criminological Research Institute of Lower Saxony. The first investigation was entitled 'The Consequences of Incarceration' (1997–2004, funded by the Volkswagen Foundation) and focused on ways of dealing with imprisonment in the context of biographies shaped by gender. In the second investigation, 'Fragile Transitions' (2005–2007, funded by the Stiftung Deutsche Jugendmarke), we reconstructed the educational and working biographies of the young men and illuminated the connection between education, work and social integration. In the framework of these projects, we had a unique opportunity to investigate the biographical processes of 30 young adults over a period of up to nine years, with the help of regular interviews.

of male adolescents reveal a specific constellation of social marginality which, in the context of gender-theoretical considerations and with reference to the findings of studies of masculinity, can be characterised as representations of 'marginalised masculinity' (Connell 1987, 1995, 1999, 2002, Messerschmidt 1993, Findeisen and Kersten 1999, Bereswill 2007, Neuber 2009, Hearn this volume). At the same time, the risks of social exclusion and recognition conflicts experienced by this group are connected with deep-rooted transformation processes in industrialised societies. Questions arise here about changes in gender relations and changes in masculine domination. Could it be that new connections between social inequality and gender are emerging? What interactions might be at work between these developments and new axes of inequality such as ethnicity, the significance and weight of which are also shifting as social change occurs? Against the background of these changes, a view 'from the margins' is able to open up a perspective on central dynamics of societal subordination and superiority which are also relevant to debates about intersectionality.

In this chapter, we provide a brief outline of the empirical constellation we have mentioned, and in doing this show how the dynamics of marginalised masculinity work (section 1). This constellation gives rise to theoretical questions about social change and change in gender relations (section 2). These questions bring together debates from social theory as reflected in contemporary women's and gender research with issues from masculinity research (section 3). One issue that arises here is a possible disruption of male dominance. In conclusion, we discuss the question of the differences and commonalities between these different approaches in relation to intersectionality (section 4).

Marginalised Masculinity – A Contradictory Constellation

In this section, we provide more detail on the findings of our qualitative studies (see footnote 4) on the deep-rooted and ongoing conflicts related to integration and masculinity experienced by young men from East and West Germany. The biographies of a group classified in education and transition research as 'suffering from multiple disadvantages' are characterised by family experiences of difficult situations, poverty, and educational disadvantage, as well as a range of experiences with institutions providing help and supervision (Bereswill, Koesling and Neuber 2008). For example, it is not unusual to find that at the age of no more than 20, a young man may have experienced more than 10 moves from one place of residence to another and from one caregiver or (psychological) parent to another. As in the primary socialisation contexts, one finds a development in the educational biographies of these young men that is shaped by constant change, ups and downs, official reprimands, breaks and interventions by social-pedagogic institutions. More than half of those who participated in our investigations had not finished school at the time they were first sent to prison, and the majority had experienced what can be described as 'careers in support programmes'

('*Maßnahmenkarrieren*') involving the administrative procedures of agencies responsible for helping young people choose careers or find work (Walther 2000, 2002). There has been no fundamental change in this constellation since the 1970s, but things have got considerably worse in relation to the lack of opportunities for training and employment available to young men (and young women) who are socially especially vulnerable, both in the education system and after that when they are looking for their first job (Kersten 1986, Solga 2006). This serves to illustrate the most important characteristic of the biographical processes we have investigated: these biographies are extremely discontinuous.[5] Biographical discontinuity directs our attention to ways in which the biographical regimes of the welfare state are struggling to meet demands they are structurally unable to cope with, and to cumulative dynamics of social exclusion. In concrete terms, this means that institutions such as the family, school, training and profession do not simply succeed each other in a biography or exist alongside one another in a coherent manner. The biographies of these young men are characterised instead by continual collisions between different interventions and measures and by alternating institutional inclusions and exclusions.

The obstacles to integration we have sketched and the associated biographical conflicts of the subject are connected, in the case of the group we have investigated, with an institutional dynamic in which expectations of masculinity are greatly overemphasised. In prison, or to be more accurate in institutions for young offenders, the dominant cultural interaction patterns are those of hypermasculinity, combined with ideals of masculine domination of a violent kind.[6] In the subculture, the inmates project an image that suggests they are prepared to resist and to use violence, while the representatives of the institution expect them to conform to a normal male biography shaped by integration into training and work. We are therefore confronted at present by a very paradoxical constellation: the idea of the disciplined, gainfully employed male, which continues to be upheld as a model within the prison, has for some time now been crumbling as a societal ideal even though it has not completely lost its socially integrating potential (Kronauer 2006, Scholz 2008).

We can summarise the situation as follows: the already established social marginality of a disadvantaged group of men is worsening as a general process of social precarisation advances. This process of downgrading needs to be analysed against the background of the loss of a fundamental social construct of masculinity, the idea of 'industrial worker masculinity' (Meuser 2004), and also in the context of broader societal processes of precarisation. Against this background, we need to

---

5   We use the term biographical discontinuity in order to emphasise the subjective dimension of a biography, the character of which is shaped by constant changes in the factors and influences which give it structure.

6   Over the long term and in individual cases, this collective display of exaggerated masculinity can turn out to be extremely fragile (Bereswill 2003a, 2003b, 2006, Neuber 2008, 2009).

reformulate the question of how social inequalities and existing gender hierarchies currently interlock with each other. How is the constitution and construction of masculinity imposing itself, given the contradictory coexistence between hegemonic positions and socially marginalised ones? In our view, questions such as this about the persistence of and changes in inequalities in gender relations should immediately direct attention to the open question of the contribution conceptions of intersectionality can make to the analysis of inequality. With this in mind, we will now move on to discuss a range of theoretical perspectives on social change which are also connected with debates about critiques of power, and which focus particularly on masculine domination.

Exhaustion or Persistence of Masculine Domination? Social Change and Change in Gender Relations

Within feminist scholarship, there is currently a lively debate going on about what considerations from social theory concerning precarisation and social inequality imply for changes in the meaning of the category of gender. This controversy also relates to questions about changes in masculine domination, or in the capacity of masculine domination to persist. In broad terms, there are two competing positions: a praxeological perspective (Völker 2006, 2007, Dölling and Völker 2008) and a structural-theoretical perspective on profound changes in the industrial society and society based on work (Becker-Schmidt 2008). The praxeologically based argument put forward by Dölling and Völker, who work on gender arrangements under precarious conditions, is that at present not only the institutions of the welfare state but also individual identities and the lifestyle forms being practised are becoming precarious (Dölling and Völker 2008: 58). They argue that there is a need to 'pay attention to the specific logic of the cultural dimension of the social, or rather the (ambivalent and paradoxical) connections between economic, political, and cultural processes' and not to focus for analytic and conceptual purposes on economic factors, because this produces what Pierre Bourdieu calls 'misjudgement effects' (Dölling and Völker 2008: 58).[7] Irene Dölling and Susanne Völker argue that women's and gender research should understand current transformations as processes of social destructuring and disintegration, in which forces of social cohesion and stratification that have existed up to now, such as the gender arrangements associated with 'normal male working relations', are becoming exhausted (Dölling and Völker 2008: 58). This means that the ascriptions and classifications of the gender order, which up until now had been thought stable, are becoming questionable. Dölling and Völker argue that in methodological

---

7   'Misjudgement effects' means that connections and (implicit) hierarchies, which are unconscious or unreflected, become invisible and so cannot be objects of scholarly investigation (Dölling and Völker 2007).

terms, this means that researchers have to look very closely at the everyday action figurations of the actors themselves:

> An exclusively macrosociological approach or an examination of structures and institutions is insufficient if we want to be able to bring such uncertainties, including uncertainties related to categories, into the analysis. The exhaustion of normative and practical arrangements and uncertainties which had been considered 'self-evident' are experienced for the first time practically, as friction between (gendered) habitus and conditions and figurations of changing or dissolving everyday action, as disturbances of everyday arrangements that have been practised up until now. (Dölling and Völker 2008: 59)

If we translate these premises into the thought experiment with the Mikado sticks we proposed at the start of this chapter, and use them to reconsider the question of the relationship between various axes of difference, these authors are saying that we should look at the everyday patterns of action and interpretation and should consider the ensemble of different sticks from the perspective of the actors involved. It may turn out, Dölling and Völker are arguing, that the master status gender enjoys in the structuring of social relations has been 'exhausted' or used up, has lost its value, and has been shaken. For our empirical example, this leads to the question of whether we might now be dealing with a constellation of marginalised masculinity in which there is no longer any 'patriarchal dividend' (Connell) in prospect and (young) men who are socially extremely vulnerable must work out for themselves gender arrangements which cannot be satisfactorily grasped with the usual categories of masculine domination. To put this point differently, we would have to investigate whether socially marginal young men are still privileged in relation to young women in comparable life situations, because they participate in masculine domination and therefore enjoy advantages over women. One could also ask what criteria we use to determine whether a social group is privileged or disadvantaged by comparison with another group. If we take, for example, the idea of equality in education, which is currently being widely discussed in both academic and popular debates, the evidence relating to qualifications obtained at school suggests that it is young women who are privileged. If, on the other hand, we look at the transition from school to various forms of training in the dual education system, young men are privileged even though their school-leaving qualifications are not as good as those of young women (Dombrowski and Solga 2009: 20).

Against the background of this complex situation, Regina Becker-Schmidt insists that there has been no break in gender hierarchies (and so no weakening of masculine domination), and questions whether we can speak of 'exhausted forces of stratification'. She argues that 'class' and 'gender' should be retained as structural categories, even though changes in society mean modifications are necessary (Becker-Schmidt 2008: 40). Becker-Schmidt bases this argument on the observation that current societal changes are having effects that are still and increasingly to the disadvantage of women, and she supports this thesis with reference to a number of studies of the new financial market capitalism: 'The opportunities provided by the ruling market economy are becoming less and less compatible with the tasks that have to be carried out in privately-organised reproduction processes, which are predominantly the responsibility of women' (Becker-Schmidt 2008: 40). She argues further that the devaluation of work in the private sphere performed largely by women suggests that both economic calculation and the hegemonic aspirations of male organisations continue to exert their influence (Becker-Schmidt 2008: 40).

If we apply this argument to the image of the Mikado sticks, it is not the case that the sticks always fall in a different arrangement, and they are not subject to the actions of the actors alone. It would be more accurate to say that the practice of the actors is less important than the logic of the capitalist economy and masculine domination. Gender and class relations may be transformed, but masculine domination is by no means exhausted. This means that marginalised masculinity is a dimension of masculine domination. The group of young men we have presented as an example are disadvantaged by comparison with other men. From the perspective of structural theory, though, young women in a comparably marginal life situation would be more disadvantaged than young men in the same position. According to Becker-Schmidt this structural inequality is, despite any societal change that may take place, embedded in the gendered division of labour and in the difference in the social value attached to the public and private spheres.

The question of how, and for whom, male hegemony continues to have an effect today, and the related question of change and the force of persistence in gender relations, directs us towards approaches from research on masculinity. We take up these approaches in the following section, and refer to two influential approaches from social theory – Bourdieu's analysis of masculine domination and Robert W./Raewyn Connell's concept of hegemonic masculinity.[8] The theoretical perspectives involved here treat temporality in different ways: Bourdieu concentrates on the reproduction of masculine domination and its persistence, while Connell makes it possible to examine changes in the configurations of hegemonic masculinity. Both approaches are valuable for the debate about intersectionality.

The Serious Games in the Competition? The Reproduction of Masculine Domination with the Help of Hegemonic Masculinity

In his work on masculine domination, Bourdieu develops theoretical arguments concerning a gendered and gendering habitus. With reference to symbolic dominance, he asks how relations of dominance – in this case, gender relations

---

8   For a discussion of Bourdieu's theory of masculine domination, see also Nira Yuval-Davis's contribution in this volume.

– are (re)produced. In a nutshell, the argument is that gender-specific socialisation produces a gender-specific habitus, and this in turn ensures a continuation of the relations (of dominance) between the genders.

Bourdieu argues that in this process, masculinity is produced and stabilised not only in relation to femininity but above all in a homosocial space: 'Male habitus is constructed and completed only in connection with the space reserved for men, the space in which the serious games of the competition are played among men' (Bourdieu 1997: 203). With this frequently cited image of the exclusive and 'serious games of the competition', Bourdieu emphasises the competitive structure of masculinity and the significance of the homosocial character of the social fields in which this competition takes place (Meuser and Scholz 2005). Femininity, or to be more accurate women, are no more than objects in this game, either as a stake or as 'flattering mirrors' which show the best side of masculinity.

If we once again apply these considerations to the Mikado game, masculinity would be the most sought-after stick that falls out of the middle of the bundle, and which everyone wants to get hold of without disturbing the arrangement. Masculinity is thus the master category that structures the game and subordinates the other sticks. From this perspective, what at first glance appeared to be Mikado's principle of pure chance turns out to have a single, permanent scale of reference – this exclusive stick. More importantly, though, Bourdieu's theory of masculine domination is a very inflexible concept which raises further questions. If we adopt Bourdieu's perspective, how can we account for other dimensions of inequality? For example, which men are allowed to take part in which games? What are the stakes with regard to class, ethnicity, age, sexuality? Do men belonging to different classes play different games, or do the same basic patterns always apply? Are women still not allowed to play, even in the twenty-first century? These questions indicate that Bourdieu's concept of masculine domination is applied at a stage *before* the intersectionality perspective is opened up. If we want to reflect on intersectionality, though, we need to find a way of grasping masculine domination.

A summary of Bourdieu's view of this question reveals that two different things are expressed in the gender habitus: a strategy of difference and a position in the gender order. This means that a conception of male gender habitus brings into focus both how being a man comes into existence as a process of demarcation from being a woman (the difference dimension), and how masculine domination emerges through the production of difference (the inequality dimension). Difference and dominance thus mutually constitute one another: difference is produced in dominance, and difference is produced through dominance. At this point Michael Meuser (2005) connects Bourdieu's theory with Connell's concept of hegemonic masculinity, arguing that hegemonic masculinity needs to be grasped as 'the generative principle of masculine domination' (Meuser and Scholz 2005).

Connell develops his/her concept of hegemonic masculinity with the help of Gramsci's concept of hegemony. He/she argues that masculinity, or to be more precise the cultural dominance of the male, is a relational phenomenon in two respects: dominance and relations of superiority and subordination exist, and come into existence, not only between the genders but also within the group of men (Connell 1999). Connell describes the differentiations between various non-hegemonic masculinities, which take hierarchical forms, as marginalised, subordinated and complicit masculinities. However, these positions are not fixed; they are related dynamically to one another and can change. Connell and James W. Messerschmidt (2005) have re-examined the concept of hegemonic masculinity and developed it further, emphasising what they see as a decisive dimension of the concept from the perspective of social theory. They argue that it is not just a 'simple model of cultural control', but also captures 'the dynamics of structural change involving the mobilisation and demobilisation of whole classes' (Connell and Messerschmidt 2005: 831). Categories such as race and class structure these configurations from the start, and lead to different forms of masculinity (or femininity[9]). In their jointly authored article, Connell and Messerschmidt present these considerations in a more concrete form with the help of some examples. They argue, for example, that masculinity and ethnicity drift apart when young immigrants cannot attain the ideal of hegemonic masculinity and fall back instead on constructions of hypermasculinity. On the other hand, there are cases in which femininity and hegemonic masculinity come together when middle-class, well-educated women occupy professional positions that are usually occupied by men. Connell's concept of hegemonic masculinity thus directs our attention to the wide range of configurations of superiority and subordination, and provides us with ways of posing the question of intersections between different kinds of social inequality. Hegemonic masculinity remains, though, a central point of reference for the structuring of inequality.

Let us now return once again to the game of Mikado. Connell's concept of hegemonic masculinity, which treats gender as 'configurations of practice', suggests initially that the sticks fall in a new, accidental pattern every time they are thrown. The master stick, the Mikado, would be hegemonic masculinity, the sought-after ideal. When we look more closely, though, we see that the master stick is not (as it is in Bourdieu's treatment) the central point of reference for the game as a whole, but at most a desirable trophy which both men and women want to get hold of. It is quite possible for the master stick to be located after a throw at the edge of the bundle, rather than in the centre, and for another stick, that is to say a different dimension of inequality, to be at the centre. This dynamic may initially seem to be accidental, but it is more easily explained if we consider the implications of the concept of hegemonic masculinity as a contribution to social theory. We can then see that the sticks may indeed fall differently every time, but this is not accidental.

---

9   Even though all approaches to research on masculinity which use Connell's concepts repeatedly stress the relationality between masculinity and femininity, there is no doubt that much of this research not only focuses explicitly on men but also loses sight of this relationality. For critical observations on this point, see Connell and Messerschmidt 2005: 837.

Despite the fact that, for example, black men in top-level sport and successful women in professional life can lay claim to hegemonic masculinity, this does not change the cultural ideal of hegemonic white masculinity in any fundamental way, and this ideal subordinates both femininity and marginalised masculinity.

Future Prospects

What are the differences and commonalities between the various approaches we have discussed, and how can these considerations be related to intersectionality? One general shared element is that the situations of inequality and experiences of women and men are examined, and all the approaches pose the question of changes in and the persistence of hierarchies in gender relations, and so the significance of masculine domination. On the other hand, the theoretical approaches have very different lines of vision and focus on different dimensions of inequality.

Becker-Schmidt's structural-theoretical perspective shares one feature with Bourdieu's concept of masculine domination (though not with his praxeological perspective): they both emphasise the persistence of masculine domination in gender relations. Applied to the question of marginalised masculinity we have raised, this leads to the conclusion that processes of societal precarisation, especially the loosening of the connection between masculinity and gainful employment, which has for a long time now been an increasingly important factor for socially marginalised men, do not lead to the 'exhaustion' of hierarchies in gender constellations. Instead, the disadvantaged situations of women in comparable precarisation processes are also worsening, and women as a social group are still disadvantaged by comparison with men as a social group. This means that gender is and remains a master category in the analysis of social inequality. It follows that marginalised masculinity is a dimension of masculine domination. What this means for the theoretical conceptualisation of intersectionality is that gender remains one of the main axes of inequality.

Dölling and Völker question this with reference to the theory of practice, another of Bourdieu's main theoretical concerns. They argue that in the current process of societal change certain forces generating social ties and stratification are becoming exhausted, and that this also applies to gender. Connell, too, is interested in configurations of practice, though his/her concept of practice has a different theoretical derivation.[10] The concept of hegemonic masculinity and the praxeological perspective share a conception of gender relations that does not see them as a firmly fixed structural relationship. They both leave open the question of the mediation between the practical appropriation of social relations and the

---

10   Dölling and Völker refer to Bourdieu's concept of practice, while Connell uses Sartre's (see Wolde 2007: 34).

conditions of constitution of these relations themselves.[11] However, there is also one major difference between these two approaches. Dölling and Völker, looking at the question from the perspective of the actors, observe the exhaustion of the structural category of gender. Connell, although his/her concept assumes that women can practise or represent hegemonic masculinity and that black sportsmen, whose position relates to marginalised masculinity, can be collectively admired, does not consider that these flexible cultural positions change structurally rooted relations of inequality in their dual relationality – between men and women, and within the group of men. If we apply this to the case of marginalised men, the question to be asked from the praxeological perspective is whether marginalised men can discard 'exhausted' formats of the gender order and work out new sketches of masculinity for themselves. From Connell's perspective, they have a place in the relations of superiority and subordination between men and want to participate in hegemonic masculinity. Following this argument, and with reference to Dölling and Völker, the central question would be whether this is still possible in present circumstances – whether, in the course of social change, hegemonic masculinity still pays out a 'patriarchal dividend' for all positions. Becker-Schmidt thinks it does, and Connell would agree – as can be seen from his/her recent work on new forms of neoliberal, globalised hegemonic masculinity (Connell 2005).

Where, though, can the concept of intersectionality be fitted into the different theoretical frameworks? What are we looking at here? At first glance it is the commonalities between Connell's concept of hegemonic masculinity and the concept of intersectionality that catch the eye, and this is worth a closer look. Both of these concepts have experienced a scholarly boom in the last 10 years and have become buzzwords, as Kathy Davis (2008; this volume) stresses for the concept of intersectionality. These concepts are 'travelling theories' (Knapp 2005), which have spread round the world in a very short space of time and have provided the starting points for numerous theoretical and empirical investigations. It is appropriate to ask why they have become so popular. As Davis stresses for the intersectionality approach (in this volume), we would argue that it is their vagueness and lack of clarity that make these concepts so popular and so easy to apply in investigations of the most varied theoretical and empirical questions. Connell emphasises that he/she is interested in the analysis of configurations of practice and positions[12] in gender relations; Helma Lutz and others speak of investigating positions and practices (Lutz and Davis 2005, Leiprecht and Lutz 2006). In these investigations, they fall back on categories such as gender, class, ethnicity and age.

---

11   Bourdieu's treatment of the incorporation of relations of dominance remains very abstract, and he does not explain how the processes themselves function (see Stövesand 2007: 66).

12   The 'positions' of men refers both to men's positions in society and to the male body.

Lutz and Davis say that such categories should be seen as phenomena which are 'not static, but fluid and shifting' (Lutz and Davis 2005: 231).[13] This makes it possible to look at numerous different configurations, but it simultaneously strengthens the impression that something rather vague is going on because it looks as though almost anything could be included (see Winker and Degele 2009: 18). How many categories of difference are there – three (race, class, gender), 13 (Lutz and Wenning 2001), or 15 (Leiprecht and Lutz 2006)? It seems this list could be extended indefinitely. Who decides which category is relevant? Are such categories of difference defined in advance of the analysis? Do the meaning and the effects of difference emerge from the field under investigation, or are they generated in the theoretical discourse? There is no end to the questions one can ask, and they all relate in one way or another to the fundamental question of the relationship between theory and empirical work.

These questions direct our attention to the need for further concretisation of axes of inequality and the need to embed them within social theory; there have been repeated calls for this to be done (Soiland 2008, Winker and Degele 2009: 16). This criticism also applies to Connell's conception of hegemonic masculinity, which – at least in German-language scholarship – has been increasingly used as a contribution to the theory of action and interaction rather than as an approach to social theory.

Some related questions arise here. In which dimension of social reality are hegemonic masculinity and intersectionality located? Do these concepts enable us to analyse cultural representations, day-to-day practices, or institutional structures? Do these approaches contribute to the analysis of relations of dominance and the interdependencies between them? Or are subject positions in discourse the main concern? Alternatively, do these concepts relate to identity constructions and identifications? How are the lines of difference seen?[14]

In Lutz's view the many categories of difference are an effect of interactions, a matter of doing gender or doing ethnicity (Lutz 2007: 223). This reveals a further commonality between the concept of hegemonic masculinity and that of intersectionality: both approaches have taken a strong turn towards the theory of action. To sum this up as simply as possible, gender and ethnicity are understood as things we produce or do. This formula runs the risk of seeing social inequality in excessively narrow terms as part of construction and interaction theory (Gottschall 2000). What does this mean in concrete terms? If we return at this point to our own investigations of the relationship between marginalisation, masculinity, and deviance, we see that interaction and action theories have been prioritised in this field too. Violent action on the part of young men, for example, is interpreted as 'doing masculinity' and as a class-specific and ethnicity-specific way of managing

---

13   See also Ferree in this volume.

14   These questions are posed by Hearn (2004) and Meuser and Scholz (2005: 211) in relation to the concept of hegemonic masculinity, and by Knapp (2008) in relation to the intersectionality approach.

gender (Messerschmidt 1993, Kersten 1997, Meuser 2002). If we look specifically at the social situation of the group we investigated, 'doing masculinity' and 'doing class' would be folded into one another as part of the struggle to attain a position recognised by society. This way of looking at the question through the lens of interaction theory is not wrong, but it requires us to ask the further question of the relationship between structures of inequality and inter-subjective action structures. This question cannot be answered from a 'doing gender' perspective alone, and multiplying the categories of difference does not help either.

This argument can be made clearer with the help of a further example. If social inequality between women is treated as 'doing ethnicity' (Lutz 2007: 224–27), the successful career woman who employs an immigrant woman to do the housework seems to be exploiting her employee directly (Soiland 2008). To put this in simpler terms, using action theory to provide a perspective on social inequality runs the risk of reducing the phenomenon of the transnational societal division of labour between the genders to the construction logic of actors. Once again, this criticism requires us to pose the question of the connection between practice and social relations.

If we apply these concluding considerations once again to the game of Mikado, the sticks do not represent different categories every time, and it is not the case that there are an unlimited number of categories which become meaningful when they fall in a certain pattern or when the players pick them up while causing as little disturbance as possible to the overall arrangement. If we want to find a theoretically satisfactory way of grasping complicated and contradictory societal developments in the production and reproduction process and the effects these have on gender relations, it is in our view important to use the tools provided by structural-theoretical approaches and to start from the assumption that the sticks do not fall in an accidental pattern. Or, as Cornelia Klinger puts it: 'It makes no sense to argue that aspects of class, race and gender overlap or intersect in individuals' worlds of experience unless you can also say how, and by what factors, class, race and gender are constituted as social categories' (Klinger 2003: 25).

Despite the great success of, and the important contributions that have been inspired by, the concepts of hegemonic masculinity and intersectionality (or perhaps precisely because they have become so popular), the limitations of these approaches have become apparent in their failure to provide a theoretically convincing and empirically well-founded way of grasping complex social relations. We are therefore confronted with a variety of challenges for the future. In addition to the further sounding out of the limitations and possibilities of each concept and of the gaps that need to be filled in, the debate about intersectionality brings us back to familiar and fundamental questions about gender research, and not only about that field. The first of these is the question of mediation between different principles of social structure and forms of power. This abstract thought can be pursued further with the help of our research findings on marginalised masculinity using the examples of relations of violence and employment relations. We also need to meet the challenge of reflecting on the different theoretical starting points of our work. Are we treating gender as a structural category, as an aspect of the social order, or as a social construction? Where are the points of connection between the different theoretical assumptions and implications, and where are they incompatible with one another? In our view, this is also connected with another very familiar sociological challenge – the need to deal with the dialectical unity of structure and agency, or of societal and subjective dynamics, not by privileging one or the other aspect but by exploring them in their contradictory interaction. The constitution and construction of masculinity is, we would argue, a contradictory interweaving of hegemonic and socially marginalised positionings which, from the point of view of societal actors, has started to shake quite dramatically. We need to debate this situation further in theoretical terms, and to explore it empirically with the help of appropriately creative methods, in order to work out what it means for the continuation of masculine domination and of inequalities in gender relations.

Bibliography

Becker-Schmidt, R. 2008. Gesellschaftliche Transformationsprozesse, soziale Ungleichheit und Geschlecht. *Zeitschrift für Frauenforschung und Geschlechterstudien*, 26(3+4), 38–56.

Bereswill, M. 1997. Migration und Rassismus: eine Herausforderung des westlichen Feminismus. *Ariadne*, 32, 65–71.

Bereswill, M. 2003a. Gewalt als männliche Ressource? Theoretische und empirische Differenzierungen am Beispiel junger Männer mit Hafterfahrungen, in *Geschlecht Gewalt Gesellschaft*, edited by Lamnek, S and Boatcă, M. Opladen: Leske und Budrich, 123–37.

Bereswill, M. 2003b. Gewalthandeln, Männlichkeitsentwürfe und biographische Subjektivität am Beispiel inhaftierter junger Männer, in *Gewalt und Geschlecht. Konstruktionen, Positionen, Praxen*, edited by Koher, F. and Pühl, K. Opladen: Leske und Budrich, 189–212.

Bereswill, M. 2006. Zur Beziehung zwischen Männlichkeit und Gewalt. Empirische Einsichten und theoretische Reflexionen am Beispiel von Gewalt zwischen Männern in der geschlossenen Institution Gefängnis. *Feministische Studien*, 2, 242–55.

Bereswill, M. 2007. Undurchsichtige Verhältnisse. Marginalisierung und Geschlecht im Kontext der Männlichkeitsforschung, in *Achsen der Ungleichheit – Achsen der Differenz. Verhältnisbestimmungen von Klasse, Geschlecht, Rasse/Ethnizität*, edited by Klinger, C., Knapp, G.-A. and Sauer, B. Frankfurt am Main & New York: Campus, 84–99.

Bereswill, M. and Ehlert, G. 1996. *Alleinreisende Frauen zwischen Selbst- und Welterfahrung*. Königstein/Taunus: Ulrike Helmer Verlag.

Bereswill, M., Koesling, A. and Neuber, A. 2008. *Umwege in Arbeit. Die Bedeutung von Tätigkeit in den Biographien junger Männer mit Hafterfahrung*.

Interdisziplinäre Beiträge zur kriminologischen Forschung, Band 34. Baden-Baden: Nomos.

Bourdieu, P. 1997. Die männliche Herrschaft, in *Ein alltägliches Spiel. Geschlechterkonstruktionen in der Praxis*, edited by Krais, B. and Dölling, I. Frankfurt am Main: Suhrkamp, 153–217.

Connell, R.W. 1987. *Gender and Power*. Cambridge: Polity Press.

Connell, R.W. 1994. Psychoanalysis on Masculinity, in *Theorizing Masculinities*, edited by Brod, H. and Kaufman, M. Thousand Oaks: Sage, 11–38.

Connell, R.W. 1995. *Masculinities*. Berkeley and Los Angeles: University of California Press.

Connell, R.W. 1999. *Der gemachte Mann. Konstruktion und Krise von Männlichkeiten*. Opladen: Leske und Budrich.

Connell, R.W. 2002. *Gender*. Cambridge: Polity Press.

Connell, R.W. 2005. Globalization, Imperialism, and Masculinities, in *Handbook of Studies on Men & Masculinities*, edited by Kimmel, M.S., Hearn, J. and Connell, R.W. London, New Delhi: Sage, 71–89.

Connell, R.W. and Messerschmidt, J.W. 2005. Hegemonic Masculinity: Rethinking the Concept. *Gender & Society*, 19(6), 829–59.

Crenshaw, K. 1989. Demarginalizing the Intersection of Race and Class. A black feminist critique of antidiscrimination doctrine. *University of Chicago Legal Forum*, 139–67.

Crenshaw, K. 1991. Mapping the Margins: Intersectionality, Identity Politics and Violence against Women of Color. *Stanford Law Review*, 6, 1241–99.

Davis, K. 2008. Intersectionality as buzzword: A sociology of science perspective on what makes a feminist theory successful. *Feminist Theory*, 9(1), 67–85.

Dölling, I. and Völker, S. 2007. Komplexe Zusammenhänge und die Praxis von Akteur/inn/en in den Blick nehmen! Anmerkungen zum Bericht 'Zur Lage in Ostdeutschland'. *Berliner Debatte INITIAL*, 18(4/5), 105–20.

Dölling, I. and Völker, S. 2008. Prekäre Verhältnisse, erschöpfte Geschlechterarrangements – eine praxeologische Perspektive auf Strategien sozialer Kohäsion. *Zeitschrift für Frauenforschung und Geschlechterstudien*, 26(3+4), 57–71.

Dombrowski, R. and Solga, H. 2009. *Soziale Ungleichheiten in schulischer und außerschulischer Bildung*. Stand der Forschung und Forschungsbedarf. Reihe: Arbeitspapier, Nr. 171. Düsseldorf (Hans-Böckler-Stiftung).

Findeisen, H.V. and Kersten, J. 1999. *Der Kick und die Ehre. Vom Sinn jugendlicher Gewalt*. München: Antje KunstmannVerlag.

Frankenberg, R. 1993. *The Social Construction of Whiteness: White Women, Race Matters*. Minneapolis: University of Minnesota Press.

Gottschall, K. 2000. *Soziale Ungleichheit und Geschlecht. Kontinuitäten und Brüche, Sackgassen und Erkenntnispotentiale im deutschen soziologischen Diskurs*. Opladen: Leske und Budrich.

Gümen, S. 1998. Das Soziale des Geschlechts. Frauenforschung und die Kategorie 'Ethnizität'. *Das Argument*, 224, 187–202.

Hearn, J. 2004. From hegemonic masculinity to the hegemony of men. *Feminist Theory*, 5(1), 49–72.

Kersten, J. 1986. Gut und (Ge)Schlecht: Zur institutionellen Verfestigung abweichenden Verhaltens bei Jungen und Mädchen. *Kriminologisches Journal*, 13(4), 241–57.

Kersten, J. 1997. Risiken und Nebenwirkungen: Gewaltorientierung und die Bewerkstelligung von 'Männlichkeit' und 'Weiblichkeit' bei Jugendlichen der underclass. *Kriminologisches Journal*, Beiheft 6, 103–14.

Klinger, C. 2003. Ungleichheit in den Verhältnissen von Klasse, Rasse und Geschlecht, in *Achsen der Differenz. Gesellschaftstheorie und feministische Kritik II*, edited by Knapp, G.-A. and Wetterer, A. Münster: Westfälisches Dampfboot, 14–48.

Knapp, G.-A. 2005. Traveling Theories: Anmerkungen zur neueren Diskussion über 'Race, Class, and Gender'. *Österreichische Zeitschrift für Geschichtswissenschaften*, 16(1), 88–110.

Knapp, G.-A. 2008. Verhältnisbestimmungen: Geschlecht, Klasse, Ethnizität in gesellschaftstheoretischer Perspektive, in *ÜberKreuzungen: Fremdheit, Ungleichheit, Differenz*, edited by Klinger, C. and Knapp G.-A. Münster: Westfälisches Dampfboot, 138–70.

Kronauer, M. 2006. 'Exklusion' als Kategorie einer kritischen Gesellschaftsanalyse. Vorschläge für eine anstehende Debatte, in *Das Problem der Exklusion. Ausgegrenzte, Entbehrliche, Überflüssige*, edited by Bude, H. and Willich, A. Hamburg: Hamburger Edition, 27–45.

Leiprecht, R. and Lutz, H. 2006. Intersektionalitat im Klassenzimmer: Ethnizitat, Klasse, Geschlecht, in *Schule in der Einwanderungsgesellschaft. Ein Handbuch*, edited by Leiprecht, R. and Kerber, A. Schwalbach/Ts., 218–34.

Lutz, H. 1992. Sind wir uns immer noch fremd? Konstruktionen von Fremdheit in der Frauenbewegung. *Widersprüche. Zeitschrift für sozialistische Politik im Bildungs-, Gesundheits- und Sozialbereich. Zur Produktion von Rassismus.* 45, 79–90.

Lutz, H. 2007. 'Die 24-Stunden-Polin'–Eine intersektionelle Analyse transnationaler Dienstleistungen, in *Achsen der Ungleichheit. Zum Verhältnis von Klasse, Geschlecht und Ethnizität*, edited by Klinger, C. and Knapp, G.-A. Frankfurt am Main: Campus, 210–34.

Lutz, H. and Davis, K. 2005. Geschlechterforschung und Biographieforschung: Intersektionalität als biographische Ressource am Beispiel einer außergewöhnlichen Frau, in *Biographieforschung im Diskurs*, edited by Völter, B., Dausien, B., Lutz, H. and Rosenthal, G. Wiesbaden: VS, 228–47.

Lutz, H. and Wenning, N. 2001. Differenzen über Differenz – Einführung in die Debatten, in *Unterschiedlich verschieden. Differenz in der Erziehungswissenschaft*, edited by Lutz, H. and Wenning, N. Opladen: Leske und Budrich, 11–24.

Messerschmidt, J.W. 1993. *Masculinities and Crime: Critique and Reconceptualization of Theory*. Boston: Rowman & Littlefield.

Meuser, M. 1998. *Geschlecht und Männlichkeit. Soziologische Theorie und kulturelle Deutungsmuster*. Opladen: Leske und Budrich.

Meuser, M. 2002. 'Doing Masculinity'. Zur Geschlechtslogik männlichen Gewalthandelns, in *Gewalt-Verhältnisse. Feministische Perspektiven auf Geschlecht und Gewalt*, edited by Dackweiler, R.-M. and Schäfer, R. Frankfurt am Main: Campus, 53–78.

Meuser, M. 2004. Nicht als alter Wein in neuen Schläuchen? Männlichkeitskonstruktionen im Informationszeitalter, in *Arbeit und Vernetzung im Informationszeitalter. Wie neue Technologien die Geschlechterverhältnisse verändern*, edited by Kahlert, H. and Kajatin, C. Frankfurt am Main: Campus, 73–93.

Meuser, M. 2005. Strukturübungen. Peergroups, Risikohandeln und die Aneignung des männlichen Geschlechtshabitus, in *Männliche Adoleszenz. Sozialisation und Bildungsprozesse zwischen Kindheit und Erwachsensein*, edited by King, V. and Flaake, K. Frankfurt am Main: Campus, 309–24.

Meuser, M. and Scholz, S. 2005. Hegemoniale Männlichkeit. Versuch einer Begriffsklärung aus soziologischer Perspektive, in *Handbuch Frauen- und Geschlechterforschung. Theorie, Methoden, Empirie*, edited by Dinges, M. Wiesbaden: VS, 112–21.

Mohanty, C.T. 1988. Aus westlicher Sicht: feministische Theorie und koloniale Diskurse. *beiträge zur feministischen theorie und praxis*, 23, 149–61.

Neuber, A. 2008. Gewalt und Männlichkeit bei inhaftierten Jugendlichen, in *Die soziale Konstruktion von Männlichkeit. Hegemoniale und marginalisierte Männlichkeiten in Deutschland*, edited by Luedtke, J. and Baur, N. Opladen: Budrich, 201–21.

Neuber, A. 2009. *Die Demonstration kein Opfer zu sein. Biographische Fallstudien zu Gewalt und Männlichkeitskonflikten*. Interdisziplinäre Beiträge zur kriminologischen Forschung, Band 35. Baden-Baden: Nomos.

Scholz, S. 2008. Männlichkeit und Erwerbsarbeit. Eine unendliche Geschichte? in *Geschlecht Macht Arbeit*, edited by Marburger Gender Kolleg. Münster: Westfälisches Dampfboot, 107–20.

Schultz, D. 1990. Der Unterschied zwischen Frauen –ein kritischer Blick auf den Umgang mit 'den Anderen' in der feministischen Forschung weißer Frauen. *Beiträge zur feministischen Theorie und Praxis*, 42, 45–57.

Soiland, T. 2008. Die Verhältnisse gingen und die Kategorien kamen. Intersectionality oder Vom Unbehagen an der amerikanischen Theorie., *querelles-net. Rezensionszeitschrift für Frauen- und Geschlechterforschung*, 26. Available at: http://www.querelles-net.de/index.php/qn/article/view/694/702 [accessed: 20 June 2010].

Solga, H. 2006. Ausbildungslose und die Radikalisierung ihrer sozialen Ausgrenzung, in *Das Problem der Exklusion. Ausgegrenzte, Entbehrliche, Überflüssige*, edited by Bude, H. and Willich, A. Hamburg: Hamburger Edition, 21–146.

Spelman, E. 1988. *Inessential Woman: Problems of Exclusion in Feminist Thought*. Boston: Beacon Press.

Stövesand, S. 2007. *Mit Sicherheit Sozialarbeit! Gemeinwesenarbeit als innovatives Konzept zum Abbau von Gewalt im Geschlechterverhältnis unter den Bedingungen neoliberaler Gouvernementalität*. Gender Studies in den Angewandten Wissenschaften. Gender Studies & Applied Sciences Vol. 5. Münster: LIT.

Völker, S. 2006. Praktiken der Instabilität. Eine empirische Untersuchung zu Prekarisierungsprozessen, in *FrauenMännerGeschlechterforschung, State of the Art*, edited by Aulenbacher, B., Bereswill, M., Löw, M., Meuser, M., Mordt, G., Schäfer, R. and Scholz, S. Forum Frauen- und Geschlechterforschung, Vol. 19. Münster: Westfälisches Dampfboot, 140–54.

Völker, S. 2007. Prekäre Transformationen – herausgeforderte Lebensführungen, in *Prekäre Transformationen: Pierre Bourdieus Soziologie der Praxis und ihre Herausforderungen für die Frauen- und Geschlechterforschung*. Querelles-Jahrbuch für Frauen- und Geschlechterforschung, edited by Bock, U., Dölling, I. and Krais, B. Göttingen: Wallenstein, 176–94.

Walther, A. 2000. *Spielräume im Übergang in die Arbeit. Junge Erwachsene im Wandel der Arbeitsgesellschaft in Deutschland, Italien und Großbritannien*. Weinheim und München: Juventa.

Walther, A. 2002. 'Benachteiligte Jugendliche': Widersprüche eines sozialpolitischen Deutungsmusters. Anmerkungen aus einer europäisch-vergleichenden Perspektive. *Soziale Welt*, 53(1), 87–106.

Ware, V. 1992. *Beyond the Pale: White Women, Racism and History*. London, New York: Verso.

Winker, G. and Degele, N. 2009. *Intersektionalität. Zur Analyse sozialer Ungleichheiten*. Bielefeld: transcript.

Wolde, A. 2007. *Väter im Aufbruch? Deutungsmuster von Väterlichkeit und Männlichkeit im Kontext von Väterinitiativen*. Wiesbaden: VS.

Chapter 5

Neglected Intersectionalities in Studying Men: Age(ing), Virtuality, Transnationality[1]

Jeff Hearn

Introduction

The notion of intersectionality, and the complex social phenomena to which it refers, go under many names and labels, including multiple oppressions, multiple social divisions, multiculturalism(s), multiple differences, 'diversity', postcolonialisms, hybridities. The concept of intersectionality has a rich feminist history (see, for example, Crenshaw 1989, 1991, McCall 2005). It has been used in many different ways – between relatively fixed social categories, in the making of such categories, in their mutual constitution, in transcending categories. Intersectionality can be understood, albeit very differently, within the full range of epistemologies, feminist or otherwise. Of special interest is in what times, places and situations do intersectionalities *appear* most evident.

Equally, the notion of intersectionality is not new. It was spoken in black feminism and the anti-slavery movement of the nineteenth century, and probably long before then too. More recently, in the elaborations that followed so-called Second Wave feminism of the 1960s, it was reaffirmed, though often under different names, especially in calling attention to the 'big three' intersections of class-gender-'race'. In 1981 Angela Davis published *Women, Race & Class*; in 1984 bell hooks wrote on black women and black men as potential allies in *Feminist Theory: From Margin to Center*; and in the same year Mary O'Brien drew attention to the dangers of commatisation (O'Brien 1984). And in 1989 Fiona Williams brought such ideas to the centre of critical debate on UK social policy, adding age, disability and sexuality to make the 'big six'. My own inspiration for considering intersectionality in relation to men (Hearn 1992) came partly from these debates, partly from feminist disability studies, notably the work of Helen Meekosha (1990, 2006), and partly from studying gender, sexuality and other intersections in work organisations (Hearn and Parkin 1993).

Much of the intersectionalities debate(s) has been directed towards the recognition of differences, yet commonalities, between women – and the complex intersections

---

1 This chapter is a revised version of the paper presented at the Celebrating Intersectionality? Debates on a Multi-faceted Concept in Gender Studies International Conference, Goethe-University Frankfurt, January 2009.

between such differences and divisions. These questions of difference, division and intersection apply equally to men (Kimmel and Messner [1989] 2009, Hearn and Collinson 2006), even if this has not been the primary concern of much feminist work.[2] Thus in this chapter I relate debates on intersectionality to men, and recent studies on men. My second task is to consider some neglected intersectionalities, or at least some social arenas where intersectionality theory might be developed more fully. In particular, three such neglects in studying men are discussed: ageing, disability and lived embodiment; virtuality; transnationality.[3] This chapter has a third, more specific aim: namely, that in addressing these neglected intersectionalities, and so challenging the gender hegemony of men, I point to how this questioning of a taken-for-granted social category of men can be an avenue to a possible abolition of men as a significant social category of power.

Studying Men and Intersectionality

Men can now be named as men: there is increasing recognition and analysis of men as gendered, not genderless, humans (Hanmer 1990, Collinson and Hearn 1994). Contemporary gendering of men has arisen from wide-ranging gendered socio-economic changes, including the impacts of feminism, gay movements, queer politics, and some men's responses to feminism, including pro-feminist approaches. Further critical, more or less gendered perspectives have problematised men and masculinities, including postcolonialism, critical race theory, poststructuralism, globalisation and transnational studies, pointing to, in different ways, intersectionalities amongst and between men.

Men involved and interested in feminism, women's studies and gender studies need to critique men: to deconstruct the dominant (Hearn 1996a). In this endeavour 'masculinities theory', particularly as propounded by Raewyn Connell and associates, has had a strong, perhaps surprising, popularity over the last 25 years. Within this, the concept of hegemonic masculinity has been especially influential. This approach can be understood as deriving partly from critique of sex role theory, and partly from qualified critique of patriarchy theory, especially deterministic theory. In another sense, such masculinities theory can be seen as a response to the intersectionalities debate – as applied to men. The most frequently cited definition of hegemonic masculinity is probably as 'the configuration of gender practice which embodies the currently accepted answer to the problem of legitimacy of patriarchy, which guarantees (or is taken to guarantee) the dominant position of men and the subordination of women' (Connell 1995: 77).

---

2   While the number of refereed journal articles on 'diversity and gender' and 'women and diversity' indexed by ISI Web of Science in January 2010 was 1,563 and 1,582 respectively, the number on 'diversity and men' was 660 (Jeanes et al. 2010).

3   The issue of embodiment is also addressed by Paula-Irene Villa in this volume.

Masculinities theory developed from the late 1970s at the same time as feminist auto-critiques of the concept of patriarchy. Both these debates around patriarchy and masculinities were very much about intersectionalities. The rethinking and problematisation of patriarchy and the identification of differential patriarchal arenas both fed into masculinities theory, and can be seen as part of debate on intersectionalities. Indeed, Jørgen Elm Larsen and Ann-Dorte Christensen (2008: 56) suggest that '*[t]he concept of intersectionality* complements the concept of hegemonic masculinities, in that it stresses the interaction between gender, class and other differentiating categories, and at the same time articulates different power structures and their reciprocating construction.'

Distinctions on historical periodising of patriarchy, other versions of gender systems, multiple arenas and structures, and pluralising of patriarchy to patriarchies can also be understood as debates on intersectionalities: that is, discussions on intersectionalities given social, historical or spatial form. The move from private to public patriarchy can be viewed as also one from the intersections of family, age, generation, sexuality, and work, with gender, to intersections of work, class, employment, occupation, and organisation with gender. Both entail intersections of gender with relations to law and the state, in terms of citizenship, nationality, ethnicity/'race', and often religion. The rethinking of patriarchy as multiple patriarchal structures in the 1980s (Walby 1986, 1990, Hearn 1987, 1992) can be reconceived as attempts to address intersectionalities (Hearn 2009).

Similarly, different masculinities can be seen as intersections of gender and other social divisions, especially class, ethnicity, racialisation and sexuality. Such social processes include hegemony, marginalisation, dominance/subordination and complicity. Hegemonic masculinity can be understood as formed in intersections of gender, class, ethnicity and sexuality, in legitimating patriarchy; subordinated masculinity in intersections of gender and sexuality, for example, gay masculinities; marginalised masculinity in intersections of class, ethnicity and racialisation, for example, black masculinities. Such thinking leads on to the notion of plural or multiple masculinities, such as black straight masculinity or white gay masculinities, which can be seen as further intersectionalities (Hearn and Collinson 1994, Aboim 2010). Having said that, there is lively debate on the limitations of not only hegemonic masculinities (Donaldson 1993, Whitehead 2002, Collinson and Hearn 2005), but also about the very concept of 'masculinity/ masculinities' for its historical specificity, ethnocentrism, false causality, possible psychologism, vagueness and confusions in some usages (Hearn 1996b, 2004a). Analysing multiple masculinities brings dangers of relativism, and infinite regress of multiple permutations. It may be more precise to talk of men's individual and collective practices, or men's identities or discourses on men, than the gloss 'masculinities'.

Hegemonic Masculinity and the Hegemony of Men

In studies on men and masculinities the concept of hegemony has figured strongly, especially as in hegemonic masculinity; however, one might argue that what is more hegemonic than this is the hegemony of men. Hegemony addresses relations of power and ideology, including domination of the 'taken-for-granted' and 'commonsense'. It highlights the importance of consent, even if that is provisional, contingent and backed by force. The notion of hegemonic masculinity developed from applying such ideas to gender relations within patriarchy (Connell 1995). Significantly, on some occasions Connell refers to hegemóny as *social process*; on others, hegemonic masculinity is described as a '*configuration of gender practice*', and a *form* of masculinity. Whilst the first two approaches are not easily compatible with seeing hegemonic masculinity as a *form* or *set of attributes* of masculinity, others have often used the term in this last way (see Jefferson 2002: 70–71). In linking hegemony to masculinity, the process usage of hegemony has been by no means as popular or influential as the other uses noted above: 'hegemony' as a key social process easily mutates to 'hegemonic' as a descriptor of certain forms of masculinity. Interestingly, in their 1985 paper discussing hegemonic masculinity, Tim Carrigan and colleagues noted that hegemony:

> ... always refers to an historical situation, a set of circumstances in which power is won and held. The construction of hegemony is not a matter of pushing and pulling of ready-formed groupings but is partly a matter of the *formation of these groupings*. To understand the different kinds of masculinity demands an examination of the practices in which hegemony is constituted and contested – in short, the political techniques of the patriarchal social order. (Carrigan et al. 1985: 594) [my emphasis]

Thus hegemony encompasses the formation of social groupings, not just their operation and collective action. Yet Carrigan et al. did not fully follow this insight through, in terms of specifying the gender hegemony of men (Hearn 2004a). One might argue that there is a quick slippage from the formation of these groupings to different forms of masculinity. Such slippages are one reason why the notions of hegemonic masculinity and multiple masculinities have been subject to various critiques since the early 1990s. In particular, a range of questions have yet to be clearly answered around hegemonic masculinity. These include: is hegemonic masculinity a cultural ideal, representations, everyday practices or institutional structures? Should one talk of hegemonic masculinities in the plural? How does hegemonic masculinity relate to postcolonial or queer critiques?

The focus on hegemonic masculinity is too narrow and restricted; rather the *hegemony of men* addresses the double complexity that men are both a *social category formed by intersectional gender systems* and *collective/individual, often dominant, agents*. As noted, 'the construction of hegemony is not a matter of pushing and pulling of ready-formed groupings but is partly a matter of *the formation of these groupings'*, but this has largely been translated to mean the formation of masculinities rather than of gender 'groupings' themselves, including men. The social category of 'men' is far more hegemonic than a particular form of masculinity, hegemonic or not. This is closer to the Gramscian notion of hegemony (Howson 2005), a concern oddly absent from most considerations of hegemonic masculinity. To understand, analyse, critique the category, men need to be thoroughly de-naturalised and deconstructed, just as postcolonial theory deconstructs and de-naturalises the white subject. There can be a danger in focusing primarily or solely on masculinities and in de-naturalising masculinities, that men are re-naturalised.[4]

The Hegemony of Men and Neglected Intersectionalities

The hegemony of men is a dialectical formulation, highlighting a strategic essentialism (Spivak 1988) in the gender class of men, yet critiquing how the taken-for-granted category of men obscures intersectionalities: *naming men as men and deconstructing men.* Naming men as men does not construct masculinities as simply variable within reformist or resistance (pro)feminism (Lorber 2005), but seeks the abolition of gender as power, including 'men' as a social category of power. As Nina Lykke (2010: 64) puts it, 'How is the category "men" created and recreated in concrete everyday life and institutional practices, and in interplay with categories such as class, ethnicity, sexuality...?' Crucially, intersectionalities are crucial not just in constructing masculinities but in the formation of the very category of men and relations to men's practices. Gender(ed) power, dominance and hegemony with respect to the social category of men, are defined through and in relation to other social divisions. Social divisions operate as sources of both gender power or lack of power for men. Gender hegemony of men is maintained by intersectional relations, as well studied in terms of class, sexuality, ethnicity and racialisation. Problematising hegemony entails attention to neglected intersectionalities.

---

4   The hegemony of men perspective raises key social processes: the hegemonic acceptance of the category of men; distinctions and categorisations between different forms of men and men's practices to women, children and other men ('masculinities'); which men and men's practices – in the media, the state, religion, and so on – are most powerful in setting those agendas of those systems of differentiations; the most widespread, repeated forms of men's practices; men's various, variable everyday, 'natural(ised)', 'ordinary', 'normal', most taken-for-granted practices to women, children and other men, and their contradictory, even paradoxical, meanings; how women may differentially support certain practices of men, and subordinate other practices of men or ways of being men; interrelations between 'men's' formation within hegemonic gender orders, which also form women, other genders and boys, and men's activity in different ways in (re-)forming hegemonic differentiations among men (Hearn 2004a).

Most analyses of men are restricted by class, ethnicity, racialisation, sexuality. Much less examined as part of the hegemony of men are: relations to age/disability/ bodies and lived embodiment (*'hierarchy of the social'*); bodily absence/virtuality (*'form and transformation of the social'*); and moves away from a focus on 'society' and nation to transnationalisations and transnationality (*'extension of the social'*). In the first, certain kinds of social division are prioritised over others. The second, virtuality, is of interest in several ways; intersectionalities occur within the virtual, but virtuality is also both a means and a form of sociality. The third, the transnational, can be thought of as an example of trans-sociality, that is, not simply about relations between two or more given nationalities or national identities, but trans-sectionalities (relations between relations) that are more than the sum of those parts.[5] By the term 'trans-section' I refer to the dynamic 'transformulation' of social, gender and sexual categories, rather than just their given mutual constitution and interrelation (Hearn 2008). In different ways these present challenges to 'men' as a significant social category of power.

Neglect 1: Age/ing, Disabilities, Older Men, Embodiment

Age and disability are the most neglected of the 'big six' social divisions. Age is an unusual social division, in its apparent universality yet constant change. It appears most readily in relation to the 'younger' and the 'older', away from age norms (Hearn 1999). Ageism is faced by all, though its severity varies (Calasanti 2005). Feminist theories have brought gender relations centre stage in studying age and ageing (Hockey and James 2003, Arber et al. 2004); gendering ageing means gendering both women's ageing and older women, and men's ageing and older men, and their relationality.

Age, ageing, men, maleness and masculinities intersect in many complex ways. Age is frequently highlighted in relation to young men, even simply 'youth'. Dominant constructions and images of men and masculinities are dominated by younger men and men 'of middle years', as if men/masculinities 'end' pre-old age. There is a frequent exclusion of older men, men with certain disabilities and dying men from analyses of and the category of 'men'.

Population ageing is likely to bring considerable changes in the social meanings of ageing. The numbers of older old men of 80+ are likely to increase proportionately more than those of younger older men in their 50s or 60s. In this situation, categories of 'old' and 'older' are subject to greater relative change, the older the age cohort concerned. There may be greater separation of older men as an age-set, through longer life, geographical mobility, and changes in work

---

5   These three concerns have been the focus of concern in the work of Theme 2, 'Deconstructing the Hegemony of Men and Masculinities: Contradictions of Absence', at the GEXcel Centre of Gender Excellence, Linköping and Örebro Universities. Available at: http://www.genderexcel.org/node/101 [accessed: 21 June 2010].

and family. Recognition of an age-set of the older old may be complicated by composite intersectionalities among older men. At the same time, blurring age categories of men – young(er), middle years, old(er) – may increase, alongside change in older men's activities, consumerism and representation. Dominant ways of being men may become less closely linked to youth, and how younger and middle years men are assumed to be.

(Older) Age is a contradictory source of power and disempowerment for men; the social category of older men is contradictory (Hearn 1995). In many societies age and ageing has been a 'traditional' source of patriarchal power, and of (some) men's power in relation to women, older women, younger men. Contemporary contradictions of men's ageing stem partly from intersections of sexism and ageism: older men benefit from sexism, while disadvantaged by ageism. Older men and older masculinities can be understood as an 'absent presence' (Hearn 1998); indeed (some) older men may become a contradictory Other to younger men, even younger women. However, age and ageing do not necessarily reduce men's power. Age and ageing are a source of financial power for some men, with ageing bringing greater economic divergence. Contemporary relations of men's age and gender power have thus become more complex. Though ageing can be a source of some men's lack of power, in relation to the body and loss of work, there can also be significant techno-extensions of the 'age of weakness'. Yet disruption of the associations of age power and gender power is certainly not new, for some people and some men. For example, in historical periods of war, disaster or refugee migration older men have become stateless, homeless or in other ways vulnerable by age.

In reviewing some of the critiques of hegemonic masculinity, Raewyn W. Connell and James Messerschmidt (2005) argue that too simple a model of global gender dominance should be rejected, and suggest reformulations of hegemonic masculinity towards: social *embodiment*; *geography* of masculinities; dynamics of masculinities; more holistic understanding of gender hierarchy. These are all useful points, though they do not fully engage with some critiques, such as phenomenology, sexual difference, queer theory and postcolonialism.[6] Hegemonic masculinity has limits as a framework for taking on board all the complexities of ageing (men). The complex picture, with men being both given status through ageing and old age but at the same time marginalised, is difficult to encompass or conceptualise within the frame of hegemonic masculinity (Hearn and Sandberg 2009). In various social contexts (older) age is a contradictory source of power and disempowerment for men, with intersections between ageism and sexism. Two areas of limitation for rethinking men and ageing, relating to the first two of the

---

6   Stephen Whitehead suggests that 'the concept of hegemonic masculinity goes little way towards revealing the complex patterns of inculcation and resistance which constitute everyday social interaction. … it is unable to explain the variant meanings attached to the concept of masculinity at this particular moment in the social history of Euro/American/ Australasian countries' (Whitehead 1999: 58).

auto-critiques noted above, are: first, the implications of a focus on *embodiment*, and, second, the implications of a focus on the contradictions of men's ageing seen in a context of *geography* and transnationalisation. These are especially important regarding men's relations to ageing, older men, and the interrelations of men, ageing and power. While to some extent they could be understood as 'more micro' and 'more macro' in orientation, they are better seen as overlapping and interconnected. The geographical/transnational is also personal and embodied, the embodied also structural.

To take the first in a little more detail: being an older man may be becoming more open to contestation. The hegemony of men may be more likely to be problematised, with frailty, disability, incontinence and other bodily leakages, dependence, death less hidden from view. Embodied experience of, effects on and social construction of the body has been unevenly present in developing debates on men and masculinities.[7] Questions of embodiment and bodily normativity seem less avoidable in addressing (men's) ageing. The hierarchy of the social over the embodied seems less hegemonic. In foregrounding embodiment, traditions from phenomenology, sexual difference and queer theory become especially relevant (Hearn and Sandberg 2009). Older men, like boys and younger men, need 're-enfleshing' (Thomas 2002), highlighting embodiment, limits of bodily facilities and normativity, frailty, dying and death, loss of bodily control in social analysis, and fragmentation of embodied standpoint knowledge (Jackson 2001, 2003).

On the second point, men's generational power in families and communities has been widely overtaken by major national, international, global and transnational forces. This is not a distant phenomenon but happens and is experienced locally, in several ways. First, global processes have political economic effects, such as restructuring of work through transnational corporations' policies. The individual autonomous older man has been superseded by not only the (patriarchal) nation, but also (patriarchal) transnational organisations. Second, there are spatial effects. While national boundaries can be rigid for some people, globalisation involves movement of people, and greater cross-cultural family and social relations for older men. Such contacts have positive implications for some, yet transnational ageing brings many complications, such as disputes between legal traditions, and parallel development of transnational legal processes. Third, globalisation processes provide contexts for personal experience. Re-formations of older men's identities occur through personal relations within globalising contexts. Increased availability of images of older men from mass media, ICTs and travel produce more contradictory global influences, for use in becoming particular 'types of older man'. This is not only an analytical, but also an emotional, lived, fictive issue.

Intersectional analyses of ageing and men thus raise many issues: blurring of age categories; recognising an age-set of older older men; differences, fracturings

---

7   Interestingly, in the first published use of the term, hegemonic masculinity, by Connell in 1979 in the paper, 'Men's bodies' (republished in *Which Way is Up?* in 1983), the focus was on the social construction of the body in boys' and adult men's practices.

and ambivalences amongst older men; sexualities and queer old age; embodiment of older men, as in frailty and disability; and transnationalisations. Yet older men are not only older men; and different paradigms of ageing, disability and embodiment may suggest quite different understandings of the same people and situations.

Neglect 2: Virtuality, 'Virtual Men'

The spread of information and communication technologies (ICTs) has brought time/space compression, instantaneousness, asynchronicity, reproducibility of image production, the creation of virtual bodies, blurring of 'real' and 'representational', wireless portability, globalised connectivity, and personalisation (Hearn 2006). Intersectionalities operate *within* the virtual; they are also produced and reproduced *by* the medium of the virtual. Virtuality can itself also be seen as conducive to multiplicity, and vice versa (DeLanda 2002). And then perhaps more controversially, virtuality can itself be understood as a social division or intersection. Just as class or ethnicity are not 'things' but are social relations, so too is virtuality a social relation, between embodiment *in situ* and in representation. Virtuality is a form of sociality, as is ethnicity or gender. Bodily absence, or apparent absence, in virtuality, though not historically new, is part of contemporary form and transformation of the social.

Virtuality makes (some women and) men dispensable, and yet also creates potential for extensions and reinforcements of men's power. It offers potentials for reformulations of social space and public domains, with positive, negative and contradictory effects. ICTs offer the possibility of more open, democratic, diverse networking and community-building of sexual minorities and dissident sexual communities, including those suffering/surviving the damage of dominant sexualities and sexual violences. At the same time, ICTs are means of oppressing others directly and virtually. They have been hugely successful in the historical promotion of pornography, trafficking and sexual exploitation of women, supplying encyclopaedic information on prostitution, and reorganising sex trade operations (Hearn and Parkin 2001). The 1990s were a time of major change in the sex trade: the annual number of hardcore pornographic video rentals in the US increased tenfold 1985–2001; in 1997 there were about 22,000 websites with free-of-charge pornographic content, by 2000 about 280,000 (Hughes 2002). Live interactive video conferencing facilitates buying live sex shows, in which men can direct the show, with real-time communication shot from multiple angles. The 'real'/bodily and the 'representational'/textual converge; sexual commodification proceeds apace. Interplays of virtualities, surveillances, and (cyber)sexualities mediated by new technologies constitute historical changes with contradictory implications for men and women (Hearn 2006). These are likely to bring new forms of virtual neo-colonial exploitation alongside direct non-virtual neo-colonialisms, as in use of ICTs to facilitate the global sex trade. The sex trade is a major institutional force in constructing men's sexualities and violences, and severely limiting moving towards gender equality (Jeffreys 2008).

ICTs not only act as media for sexualities and sexualised violences, but increasingly can be constitutive of them; they can in effect reconstitute sexualities, and may do so in new ways in the future. Sex is increasingly constructed in the context of disembodied social institutions, the state and large corporations, their laws, controls and ideologies. However, mediated cybersexual activity, without any payment, on one's own or with another or others, is possible in many embodied forms in the privacy of 'one's own home', as in 'DIY' Web pornography. Embodied approaches to men are complicated by contradictions in multiple virtual practices, with the paradoxical play of the embodiment of the virtual, and the virtuality of embodiment. These possibilities are ever more at hand, are likely to increase, and exert effects on what sexuality *is*, with sexual categories likely to become defined, blurred, in complex ways, in relation to technologies, including lifelike techno sex dolls or sex robots. ICTs and virtuality can have profound embodied forms and implications, including for the construction of men. Technologies can be enacted in relation to men's sexualities and sexual violences, in which men act as producers and consumers of virtuality, represent women in virtual media, and are themselves represented, even made dispensable (Hearn 2006). Virtualisation presents sites for contestations of hegemony in bodily presence/absence of men, whether in creating virtual bodies of women, or of men themselves.

Neglect 3: Transnationality, Transnational Men

Understandings of hegemony need to move away from the notion of a fundamental outlook of a given 'society', nation and the nation-state to the growing importance of the transnational. Social analysis has been strongly nation-based, with many analyses framed by methodological nationalism. Recent critical research on men has moved towards more international, transnational and global perspectives, away from the focus on the Western world and individual nations, and towards the South and transnational processes (Connell 1993, 1998, Ouzgane and Coleman 1998, Pease and Pringle 2001, Cleaver 2002, Morrell and Swart 2005). There is also concern with more precise specifications of men's individual and collective practices within gendered globalisations or glocalisations. Recent applications of the concept of hegemony to men and masculinities have pointed to the growing importance of moves from a focus on 'society' and nation and towards transnationalisations and transnationality, as an '*extension of the social*'.

Yet transnationality is a strongly neglected arena of intersectionality. First, transnationality concerns relations between nationalities, and thus nations. Second, it highlights intersectionalities with and between nationality, language, culture, location, movement, mobility, but also across these boundaries. Third, transnationality may involve the metamorphosing of boundaries, national and other (Hearn 2004b). Thus transnational categories are becoming defined in more complex ways, with more blurrings in interrelations with other social categories, intersectionalities, and the deconstruction, transnationalisations and transformulation of those categories – hence trans-sectionalities, as with hybrid categories that are more than the sum of, say, gender/race/languages. Furthermore, transnationality, like virtuality, can be seen as a social division or intersection itself, just as real as age or class. Transnationality also often incorporates the virtual and those intersectionalities highlighted there.

Transnationality and transnationalisations take many forms and have many implications for men and gender relations (Zalewski and Parpart 1998, Hearn and Parkin 2001, Hearn and Pringle 2006). Key issues include migration, information and communication technology, transnational corporations' gender-segregated labour forces; almost total dominance of men at top levels of transnational corporate management, militarism, arms trade and international organisations; global finance and masculinisation of capital market trading floors and business media; sexualisation of women in global mass media; internationalisation of the sex trade; gender segregation of international sports industries; energy, water, transport, environment (see Esplen and Greig 2008). A key example of the impact of transnationalisation is the importance of managers in transnational organisations for the formation and reproduction of gender orders in organisations and societies. However, transnationalisation is perhaps the most acutely contradictory of processes, with multiple forms of absence for both men in power and those dispossessed through, for example, forced migration. Multiple forms of transnationality, as an example of trans-sociality, and different transnationalisations problematise taken-for-granted national and organisational contexts, and men therein, in many ways.

The focus in earlier work on patriarchy was largely on the national, societal or cultural context, rather than what lies between and beyond. Limiting patriarchy or hegemony to a *particular* society, nation or culture is increasingly problematic. Debate on hegemony has also largely been framed in terms of a given society, yet there is now greater recognition of moves from a single society outlook towards transnational hegemonies. Global transformations and regional restructurings are part of the changing hegemony of men. Historical shifts to transnational patriarchies or transpatriarchies (Hearn 2009) are indicative of complex transnational intersectionalities.

Moves to transnational patriarchies offer the potential for processes of extension of some men's transnational intersectional power, both individual and collective. This may take the form of non-responsibility, of surveillance and disruption, of loss of expected security/privilege – from individual men to state to transnational institutions. Processes of recouping of men's power may also take place, within transnational movements and formation of transnational social, cultural spaces. Despite some obvious critiques, the concept of patriarchy persists, with historical shifts to transnational patriarchies, or transpatriarchies, which encompass intersectional gender power relations.

Concluding Remarks

Understanding men and intersectionalities demands engagement not only with class, ethnicity, racialisation, and sexuality but also with age(ing), disability, embodiment, virtuality, and transnationality. While age(ing) and disability are relatively neglected, the two dimensions of virtuality/bodily absence and transnationality expand current conceptualisations of intersectionality. Together these three divisions and intersections problematise, challenge or reinforce the gender hegemony of men. Each of these neglected intersectionalities presents reinforcements, challenges and contradictions to hegemonic categorisations of men, by: ageing/death; virtual (dis)embodiment, and disconnection from or transcending nation, respectively.

There are important connections between these neglects, and the men and masculinities implicated: social processes across and between arenas, such as the pervasiveness of men's violences; forms of re-engagements with 'absent' bodies; links across the economic, the political and the cultural; possibilities for both extensions and subversions of men's power. More specifically, there may be diverse and challenging intersections between ageing, virtuality and transnationality for men. Some older transnational men may be disabled, dying, or transnationally dispossessed, as with some ageing male stateless refugees, or dispensable through virtualisation, their bodies redundant: the powerless antithesis of hegemonic men/masculinity. Alternatively, older transnational men may represent the embodiment and extension of patriarchal power, as with ageing transnational billionaires, stateless in a different sense. Men's power may be extended transnationally, through use of ICTs, as in the control, perhaps sexually violent control, over the real, or virtualised, bodies of others, or in their own 'cyborg-ageing' through aids and adaptations. Combinations and intersections of ageing, virtuality and transnationality may produce not just new forms of hegemonic masculinity, but new possibilities for extending or subverting the hegemony of men. The ageing, virtual, transnational man is an unfamiliar, perhaps 'queer', creature, hardly a man at all – simultaneously alive yet dying, embodied yet virtual, cosmopolitan yet without voice.

Charting the particular, changing forms of rigidities and movements of and around the taken-for-granted social category of men can be a means of interrogating the possibility of abolition of 'men' as a significant social category of power; such a prospect brings together materialist theory and queer politics.[8]

---

8   The issue of bringing together materialist positions and queer perspectives is also addressed by Lykke in this volume.

Bibliography

Aboim, S. 2010. *Plural Masculinities*. Farnham: Ashgate.

Arber, S., Davidson, K. and Ginn, J. (eds) 2004. *Gender and Ageing: Changing Roles and Relationships*. Maidenhead: Open University Press.

Calasanti, T. 2005. Ageism, gravity and gender: experiences of ageing bodies. *Generations*, Fall, 8–12.

Carrigan, T., Connell, R.W. and Lee, J. 1985. Towards a new sociology of masculinity. *Theory and Society*, 14(5), 551–604.

Cleaver, F. (ed.) 2002. *Masculinities Matter! Men, Gender and Development*. London and New York: Zed.

Collinson, D.L. and Hearn, J. 1994. 'Naming men as men: implications for work, organizations and management'. *Gender, Work and Organization*, 1(1), 2–22.

Collinson, D.L. and Hearn, J. 2005. Men and masculinities in work, organizations and management, in *Handbook of Studies on Men and Masculinities*, edited by Kimmel, M., Hearn, J. and Connell, R.W. Thousand Oaks, CA: Sage, 289–310.

Connell, R.W. [1979]1983. Men's bodies, in *Which Way Is Up?* Sydney: Allen & Unwin, 17–32.

Connell, R.W. 1993. The big picture: masculinities in recent world history. *Theory and Society*, 22(5), 597–623.

Connell, R.W. 1995. *Masculinities*. Cambridge: Polity.

Connell, R.W. 1998. Men in the world: Masculinities and globalization. *Men and Masculinities*, 1(1), 3–23.

Connell, R.W. and Messerschmidt, J. 2005. Hegemonic masculinity: Rethinking the concept. *Gender & Society*, 19(6), 829–59.

Crenshaw, K.W. 1989. Demarginalizing the intersection of race and sex: a Black feminist critique of antidiscrimination doctrine, feminist theory and antiracist politics. *University of Chicago Legal Forum*, 138–167.

Crenshaw, K.W. 1991. Mapping the margins: intersectionality, identity politics, and violence against women of color. *Stanford Law Review*, 43, 1241–99.

Davis, A.Y. 1981. *Women, Race & Class*. New York: Vintage.

DeLanda, M. 2002. *Intensive Science and Virtual Philosophy*. London: Continuum.

Donaldson, M. 1993. What is hegemonic masculinity? *Theory and Society*, 22(5), 643–57.

Esplen, E. and Greig, A. 2008. *Politicising Masculinities: Beyond the Personal*. Brighton: Institute of Development Studies, University of Sussex.

Hanmer, J. 1990. Men, power and the exploitation of women, in *Men, Masculinities and Social Theory*, edited by Hearn, J. and Morgan, D. London and New York: Unwin Hyman/Routledge, 21–42.

Hearn, J. 1987. The Gender of Oppression: Men, Masculinity and the Critique of Marxism. Brighton: Wheatsheaf; New York: St. Martin's Press.

Hearn, J. 1992. Men in the Public Eye: The Construction and Deconstruction of Public Men and Public Patriarchies. London and New York: Routledge.

Hearn, J. 1995. Imaging the aging of men, in *Images of Aging: Cultural Representations of Later Life*, edited by Featherstone, M. and Wernick, A. London: Routledge, 97–115.

Hearn, J. 1996a. Deconstructing the dominant: making the one(s) the other(s). *Organization: The Interdisciplinary Journal of Organization, Theory and Society*, 3(4), 611–26.

Hearn, J. 1996b. Is masculinity dead? A critique of the concept of masculinity/ masculinities, in *Understanding Masculinities*, edited by Mac an Ghaill, M. Buckingham: Open University Press, 202–17.

Hearn, J. 1998. Theorizing men and men's theorizing: men's discursive practices in theorizing men. *Theory and Society*, 27(6), 781–816.

Hearn, J. 1999. Ageism, violence and abuse: theoretical and practical perspectives on the links between child abuse and elder abuse, in The Violence Against Children Study Group *Children, Child Abuse and Child Protection: Placing Children Centrally*. John Wiley: London, 81–96.

Hearn, J. 2004a. From hegemonic masculinity to the hegemony of men. *Feminist Theory*, 5(1), 49–72.

Hearn, J. 2004b. Tracking 'the transnational': Studying transnational organizations and managements, and the management of cohesion. *Culture and Organization*, 10(4), 273–90.

Hearn, J. 2006. The implications of information and communication technologies for sexualities and sexualised violences: Contradictions of sexual citizenships. *Political Geography*, 25(8), 944–63.

Hearn, J. 2008. Sexualities future, present, past ... Towards transsectionalities. *Sexualities: Studies in Culture and Society*, 11(1), 37–46.

Hearn, J. 2009. Patriarchies, transpatriarchies and intersectionalities, in *Gender and Intimate Citizenships: Politics, Sexualities and Subjectivity*, edited by Oleksy, E. London: Routledge, 177–92.

Hearn, J. and Collinson, D.L. 1994. Theorizing unities and differences between men and between masculinities, in *Theorizing Masculinities*, edited by Brod, H. and Kaufman, M. Newbury Park, CA: Sage, 97–118.

Hearn, J. and Collinson, D.L. 2006. Men, masculinities and workplace diversity/ diversion: power, intersections and contradictions, in *Handbook of Workplace Diversity*, edited by Konrad, A., Prasad, P. and Pringle, J. London: Sage, 299–322.

Hearn, J. and Parkin, W. 1993. Organizations, multiple oppressions and postmodernism, in *Postmodernism and Organizations*, edited by Hassard, J. and Parker, M. London/Newbury Park, CA: Sage, 148–62.

Hearn, J. and Parkin, W. 2001. Gender, Sexuality and Violence in Organizations. London: Sage.

Hearn, J. and Pringle, K., with members of CROME. 2006. *European Perspectives on Men and Masculinities: National and Transnational Approaches.* Houndmills and New York: Palgrave Macmillan.

Hearn, J. and Sandberg, L. 2009. Older men, ageing and power: Masculinities theory and alternative spatialised theoretical perspectives. *Sextant: Revue du Groupe Interdisciplinaire D'Etudes sur les Femmes et le Genre*, 27, 147–63.

Hockey, J. and James, A. 2003. *Social Identities across the Life Course.* New York: Palgrave Macmillan.

hooks, b. 1984. *Feminist Theory: From Margin to Center.* Cambridge, MA: South End Press.

Howson, R. 2005. *Challenging Hegemonic Masculinity.* London: Routledge.

Hughes, D. 2002. The use of new communication and information technologies for the sexual exploitation of women and children. *Hastings Women's Law Journal*, 13(1), 127–46.

Jackson, D. 2001. Masculinity challenges to an ageing man's embodied selves: struggles, collusions and resistances. *Auto/Biography*, 9(1&2), 107–15.

Jackson, D. 2003. Beyond one-dimensional models of masculinity: a life-course perspective on the processes of becoming masculine. *Auto/Biography*, 11(1&2), 71–87.

Jeanes, E., Knights, D. and Yancey Martin, P. (eds) 2010. *Handbook on Gender, Work and Organization.* New York: Wiley Blackwell.

Jefferson, T. 2002. Subordinating hegemonic masculinity. *Theoretical Criminology*, 6(1), 63–88.

Jeffreys, S. 2008. The Industrial Vagina: The Political Economy of the Sex Trade. London and New York: Routledge.

Kimmel, M.S. and Messner, M.A. (eds) 1989. *Men's Lives.* New York: Macmillan/Maxwell, 1st edition. [8th edition 2009].

Larsen, J.E. and Christensen, A.-D. 2008. Gender, class, and family: men and gender equality in a Danish context. *Social Politics: International Studies in Gender, State and Society*, 15(1), 53–78.

Lorber, J. (ed.) 2005. *Gender Inequality: Feminist Theories and Politics.* 2nd ed. Los Angeles: Roxbury.

Lykke, N. 2010. Feminist Studies: A Guide to Intersectional Theory, Methodology and Writing. New York: Routledge.

McCall, L. 2005. The complexity of intersectionality. *Signs: Journal of Women in Culture and Society*, 30(3), 1771–800.

Meekosha, H. 1990. Is feminism able-bodied? Reflections from between the trenches. *Refractory Girl*, August, 34–42.

Meekosha, H. 2006. What the hell are you? An intercategorical analysis of race, ethnicity, gender and disability in the Australian body politic. *Scandinavian Journal of Disability Research*, 8 (2–3), 161–76.

Morrell, R. and Swart, S. 2005. Men in the Third World: postcolonial perspectives on masculinity, in *Handbook of Studies on Men and Masculinities*, edited by Kimmel, M., Hearn, J. and Connell, R.W. Thousand Oaks, CA: Sage, 90–113.

O'Brien, M. 1984. The commatisation of women: patriarchal fetishism in the sociology of education. *Interchange*, 15(2), 43–59.

Ouzgane, L. and Coleman, D. 1998. Postcolonial masculinities: introduction. *Jouvert: A Journal of Postcolonial Studies*, 2(1), 1–10.

Pease, B. and Pringle, K. (eds) 2001. *A Man's World? Changing Men's Practices in a Globalized World*. London: Zed.

Spivak, G. 1988. *In Other Worlds: Essays in Cultural Politics*. New York: Routledge.

Thomas, C. 2002. Reenfleshing the bright boys: Or how male bodies matter to feminist theory, in *Masculinity Studies and Feminist Theory*, edited by Kegan Gardiner, J. New York: Columbia University Press, 60–89.

Walby, S. 1986. *Patriarchy at Work*. Cambridge: Polity.

Walby, S. 1990. *Theorizing Patriarchy*. Oxford: Blackwell.

Whitehead, S. 1999. Hegemonic masculinity revisited. *Gender, Work and Organization*, 6(1), 58–62.

Whitehead, S. 2002. *Men and Masculinities*. Cambridge: Polity.

Williams, F. 1989. *Social Policy: A Critical Introduction. Issues of Race, Gender & Class*. Cambridge: Polity.

Zalewski, M. and Parpart, J.L. (eds) 1998. *The 'Man' Question in International Relations*. Boulder, Colorado: Westview.

Chapter 6

Exposures and Invisibilities: Media, Masculinities and the Narratives of Wars in an Intersectional Perspective

Dubravka Zarkov

Various forms of violence against men – and especially sexual violence – in contemporary wars increasingly challenge feminist dichotomies of omnipotent violent masculinities and vulnerable femininities. Multiple vulnerabilities of specific groups of men in wars seem to be both ever more visible and carefully tucked away from the public eye. The media play a significant role in both exposing and invisibilising sexually violated male bodies.

In this chapter, I will conduct an intersectional analysis of two cases of sexual violence against men that will be taken as examples of the extremes of media exposures and invisibilities. The first is the almost total invisibility of sexual violence against men during the war through which the former Yugoslavia disintegrated, in the local (and the international) media. 'Almost total' indicates that some information about the violence did appear, primarily in the local printed press.[1] The second example is the high exposure of sexual torture of Iraqi men in the Baghdad prison Abu Ghraib, in American (and international) media – on TV, in the press and on the Internet.

It is worth noting that, in general, sexual violence against men – be it in peace or war – has traditionally appeared only very, very rarely in the media. So, I ask, if media invisibility has been the rule, why was this rule followed in the case of the former Yugoslavia and broken in the case of Abu Ghraib? It is also important to stress that sexual violence against men is not the most topical issue in feminist scholarship. Abu Ghraib has changed this too, and this raises a further question: Why has an otherwise marginal topic become so highly visible in this case?

In this chapter, I will offer a few possible answers to these questions by comparing the cases of the former Yugoslavia and Abu Ghraib. I will not focus on the media narratives *per se* (by analysing specific texts or visual images). Rather, I will focus on the *meanings of the exposures and invisibilities of the violated male bodies* in the media, and in selected scholarship from feminist, queer, black and masculinity studies.

---

1 I will focus here on the Croatian media only, and thus also on the war as it affected Croatia. For a detailed study of the media in both Serbia and Croatia see Zarkov (2007).

I will ask two sets of questions. Firstly: what the media invisibilities and exposures of sexual violence against men mean; under what conditions they appear; and what remains in the dark when the spotlight is turned onto some of the violated male bodies and their violators. After that I will turn to the questions of what is exposed and what remains invisible in studies of the violence in Abu Ghraib and its media representations; and what those (in)visibilities tell us about feminist epistemologies and the politics of gender and war. My answers to those questions will point to the need to de-centre gender as an analytical category, in favour of an intersectional perspective.

Exposures and Invisibilities in the Media: The Meanings of Violence

To answer the first set of questions, I will compare the relative invisibility of the sexually violated male bodies in the Croatian media and the high visibility of the sexually violated male bodies in Abu Ghraib in the US media. To do so, I will first reflect on the contexts within which the violence and its representations took place. After that I will engage in the discussion about their meanings, paying specific attention to the differences and similarities of representational strategies in the two cases.

The Context of Croatia: Building-the-Nation-State War

The Croatian press wrote about sexually violated male bodies in the midst of a war. Between 1991 and 1995, the former Socialist Federal Republic of Yugoslavia disintegrated as the result of a violent war that placed its Republics (the constituent parts of the Federation) in very different situations. The Croatian nationalist discourse argued that Croatia had been victimised within Federal Yugoslavia, and claimed the right to create an independent nation-state. This nation-state-building process needed the new country to define both its geographical borders and its symbolic boundaries; it needed to specify who belonged to it and who did not.

Central to this belonging was ethnicity. Ethnicity had become the primary mode of being long before the actual war started. Already in the mid-1980s, political discourses systematically referred to people, places, territories, as well as values, traditions and cultures as 'Croat', 'Muslim' or 'Serb'. As the war progressed, violent practices of expulsion that were later named 'ethnic cleansing' ensued. Violent expulsions and sexual violence against women were committed by all parties in the war, and sexual violence against women was particularly notorious in the context of imprisonment in the war camps.

It is less well known, however, that men too were assaulted sexually, in quite a systematic way, especially in the war camps; and that *men of all ethnic backgrounds* were among both the victimisers and the victimised.[2] However, sexual violence against men was hardly visible at all in the public sphere, including in the media. An examination of the main Croatian daily and the main weekly newspaper for the period between summer 1992 and summer 1993 identified just over 100 texts about various forms of war violence (murder, expulsion, destruction), about 30 texts specifically on rapes of women, and only four texts about sexual violence against men. Thus, both the daily and the weekly wrote about war violence against the general population rather regularly (every few issues, that is, for the daily, every few days), and about sexual violence against women less regularly but still systematically. But they clearly avoided writing about sexual violence against men. Furthermore, while the texts about war violence against the general population and women were often extensive editorial and journalist pieces with first-hand witness statements, extending over a number of pages and accompanied by a number of photos, the four texts where sexual violence against men was mentioned were either taken from the foreign press or were parts of reports on the work of international organisations. Finally, sexual violence against men was only mentioned in a few short lines.

Interestingly, the four texts from the 1992–1993 period all had two very specific patterns: firstly, in all four the victims and the perpetrators were named ethnically – by use of personal names that the readers would recognise as ethnic, by specifying the ethnicity of the victims and perpetrators, by specifying the place of origin in ethnic terms, or by a combination of these. Secondly, all male victims of sexual violence were defined as 'Muslims', and all male perpetrators as 'Serbs' (by any of the means mentioned above). In other words, in the selected Croatian daily and weekly, 'Croat' men were significantly absent from the narratives of male-to-male sexual violence, either as victims or as perpetrators.

The *overall invisibility* of sexual violence against men in the Croatian press and the *selective visibility* of the ethnicised victim and perpetrator indicate that ethnicity is a crucial factor in representation. But we cannot fully comprehend the relevance of ethnicity without understanding its intersectional relationship to masculinity and heteronormativity. Before I turn to those relationships, I will discuss the context within which the photos of Abu Ghraib became public.

The Context of the USA: Defending-Democracy-and-Civilisation Wars

The American media also wrote about sexually violated male bodies in the midst of wars: the 'war on terror', and the wars in Afghanistan and Iraq. Unlike the nation-

---

2   See the UN Reports (1994) and Bassiouni et al. (1996). The Reports note that imprisoned men were forced to assault or mutilate each other; were forcefully arranged in explicitly sexual poses with each other; were assaulted by foreign objects and mutilated by the prison guards while alive and often left to bleed to death; or were mutilated after death. Mutilation mostly meant that prisoners were forced to bite or cut off each other's genitals, or that guards would cut off prisoners' genitals.

state-building war of Croatia that produced a new country, the US wars have been about the self-(re)definition of the already existing country and about its symbolic and geo-political (re)positioning. Within the US, these wars have been defined as the struggle of the so-called 'freedom-loving world' and its people against a world that is supposedly full of primitivism, violence and religious backwardness. The symbolic geographies of these wars have separated America and the rest of the 'free' and 'democratic world' from the 'ticking bomb' (Hannah 2006) of the Muslim world and its terrorism. Furthermore, those symbolic geographies have very specific histories, two of which are crucial for the contemporary self-definition of the US. One is the history of slavery and racism, and another is the history of religious intolerance and its relation to secularism.

Jared Sexton and Elizabeth Lee (2006) and Avery F. Gordon (2006) argue that the contemporary 'war on terror' and the torture in Abu Ghraib have to be understood within a specific US history of racism, which extends from slavery to contemporary prison systems and incorporates a routine of 'racialised sadism' that '…has a history exactly co-extensive with the history of imprisonment in the US, which is itself co-extensive with the national history' (Gordon 2006: 48). Judith Butler (2008) points to the relationships between Christianity, secularism and modernity in the West and the US specifically. Christianity's religious exclusiveness and intolerance has largely framed discourses and violent practices towards all those who adhere to different kinds of spirituality and faith (including Native Americans). The very distinction between 'civilisation' and 'primitivism' that has defined US colonial and other violent practices towards the rest of the world has been marked by Christianity as a 'civilised/civilising' project – allowing for further de-humanisation of the racialised Other. Throughout Western history, there has rarely been a greater, a more significant, religious Other of Western Christianity than Islam. In this respect, the 'war on terror' has only utilised to the extreme the Orientalist discourses that already existed, collapsing the image of 'the terrorist' with that of 'the Muslim/Arab man'. But as Butler argues, Western secularism is embedded in Western religiosity, and in order to contest it, it has to re-animate it continuously. Thus, the Other is different both because he/she is religious, and because his/her religion is continuously re-cast as 'childish, fanatic or structured according to ostensibly irrational and primitive taboos' (Butler 2008: 14).

These histories inform contemporary US struggles for global hegemony, and as such they inform the representational strategies of the US media. Since the 'war on terror' and the wars in Afghanistan and Iraq started, many thousands of US soldiers have been killed[3] and maimed, and unconfirmed tens of thousands of the local population have suffered the same fate. But very few of those deaths and injuries have been visible in the US media. Ever since the dead US soldiers were dragged through the streets of Mogadishu, Somalia (in October 1993), the American press has had a total blackout of images of dead or injured American

---

3   As of January 2010, over 4,000 US soldiers have died in Iraq and about 1,000 in Afghanistan.

soldiers and civilian contractors and shies away from showing images of the casualties caused by US forces.[4] So, when CBS News, *The New York Times* and the *Washington Post* published the stories and photographs from Abu Ghraib, the media exposure of the abused bodies of Iraqi men, and even more so of their US prison guard torturers, went against the grain of the usual US media practice. There must be a reason for such a striking 'exceptionalism'. In the following section, I will address these reasons by comparing the meanings of the invisibilities and visibilities of sexually violated male bodies in the Croatian and US media.

Mediated Meanings: The Body of the Other Man, and the Projects of the Self

In the context of the Croatian nation-state-building war, ethnicity marked the 'Serbs' and the 'Muslims' as redundant for the Croatian national project, as 'surplus life' (Duffield 2007) that can be gotten rid of, physically as well as symbolically. Physical violence is, therefore, at the same time an outcome of privileging ethnicity as the marker of difference and an act of defining the violated person as the ethnic Other. However, as I stated earlier, while the primary motivator of violence is ethnicity, the particular forms of violence are intersectionally informed by gender and heteronormativity. To make it explicit, in this case ethnicity and not gender (or masculinity) can be described as the 'master-category' (compare Bereswill and Neuber in this volume (69f)).

Dominant notions of manhood – in that part of the world, as indeed in many others – define 'proper men' as both powerful and heterosexual. Without either power or heterosexual virility, men are not seen as 'proper men'. In this context, the man who is raped can hardly be seen as powerful, and the man who rapes the other man puts his, and the other's, heterosexuality into question. Thus, while in the context of the war ethnicity becomes a *primary difference*, this difference is constituted through the notions and practices of masculinity, power and heteronormativity.

This constitutive intersectional relationship of ethnicity, masculinity and heteronormativity is the key to the *selective visibility* of sexually violated men. If Croatia was to become the land of Croats, then Muslim and Serb men were *inconsequential* to Croatia's symbolic Self. It is their ethnic Otherness that allows for their exposure as violated, or violators. The absence of Croat men from the narrative of male-to-male rape indicates that media representations do not just assume that Croat, Muslim and Serb men have different ethnicities, but that these ethnicities are constituted through intersections of different masculinities and sexualities.

---

4   In February 2009 the Obama Administration lifted the 18-year-old ban on photographing the return of a soldier's remains in a coffin, conditional on the approval of the dead soldier's family. However, the relaxation of the rule does not apply to photos of dead and injured soldiers, and regional military commanders still have considerable power to evict journalists who dare to disobey.

To summarise, it is clear that in the Croatian press both the victim and the perpetrator of male-to-male violence are the Other. The Self is totally absent from the picture. Furthermore, while the representational strategy of the media clearly shows that Otherness is crucial in making both the victim and the perpetrator visible, this selective visibility is still situated in the context of overall silence and the invisibility of the violated male body – four texts and not a single photo during a one-year period.

The American press has had a similar pattern of representation only in one respect: when it comes to the visibility of the *victim* of violence. If we are to assume that this pattern indicates similar meanings, then the high exposure of the male Iraqi victims of sexual torture tells of the Iraqi Otherness to the American national Self. Furthermore, while in the Croatian media ethnicity is the primary marker of Otherness, in the case of Abu Ghraib Otherness is defined primarily through intersections of Islam and race. Religion is here not just any Islam, but a particularly imagined violent, threatening, backward kind of Islam that is linked to a particular kind of patriarchal masculinity, the history of which stretches from Orientalism to 'the war on terror'. Being a Muslim, in this context, is not just a racialised category in which the colour of a person's skin becomes one aspect of everything that defines the 'Arab-cum-Muslim world' in the Western imagination: it is a specific, civilisational category that functions in the context of an Islamophobic 'war on terror'.

The patterns of representations in the Croatian and the US media differ in one significant respect: the visibility of the perpetrator who is not the Other, but presumably the Self. In the case of Abu Ghraib, the visible perpetrator of sexual violence was not just the male US prison guard but the female guard as well. If we follow the same logic of representation used in the Croatian press – where the violator was the Other – can we assume that the perpetrators of sexual torture in Abu Ghraib are also rendered as the Other of the American nation, rather than its Self? The discourse of 'a few bad apples' indicates that this might be the case. It represents an attempt to separate these 'few bad apples' from the 'healthy tree' of the military and the nation. As such it is also discursively, and ideologically, defined as a military that does not use torture. So, the discourse of 'a few bad apples' allows for the individual perpetrators to be publicly exposed while the military as an institution and the practice of torture as institutionalised, and national(ist), racist, Islamophobic and homophobic ideologies that sustain, justify and organise those institutions and practices remain hidden. Thus, the prison guard both *is* and *is not* the Self: it is the Self-Gone-Astray, one that can be purged from the national body as a diseased extremity, leaving this body healthy and intact. In a perverse way, the Self-Gone-Astray serves to strengthen the belief in the righteousness and purity of the nation – a nation that is capable of self-criticism and self-healing.

In this respect, it is interesting to reflect on the meanings of the high visibility of the female prison guards among the perpetrators. Firstly, it is worth asking whether their visibility is an indication that the woman soldier is still the Other of the American military, and thus, at least to some extent, the Other of American national Self – an argument feminists put forward long ago (e.g. Enloe 2004). The representation of Lynndie England as the main female torturer that reduces her participation in violence to a feminine-dupe role seems to indicate a similar position: the refusal to include the female, militant, violent subject in the symbolic body of the military and the nation. There are, however, a few other things to consider. Firstly, Lynndie England posing in the photos of torture with thumbs up and smiling – often referred to as 'bizarre', or in the *New York Times* as 'a symbol of abuse' – defines her very explicitly as a misfit and deviant, someone hardly recognisable as a member of the military in the way this military is self-imagined and self-defined within the American national project. Her femaleness becomes one of the main explanatory factors of her bizarreness, maintaining the masculine subject as the only rightful subject of the military and the nation.

However, I would argue that the high visibility of the female torturer had yet another crucial function in the representation: it preserved the heterosexuality of the US masculine military subject. It is worth noting here that in the case of sexual violence against men in the former Yugoslavia, the UN Report indicated that some of the prisoners were raped by male prison guards. This rape – unlike the sexual torture that male prisoners were forced to perpetrate against each other – was not perpetrated in public. The dominant notions of heteronormativity would render both the rapist and the raped as homosexuals. For that reason, rape by prison guards was conducted in secret (see Loncar and Brecic 1995). In the dominant heteronormative and heterosexist context, it is difficult to imagine that a heterosexual man can assault another man *sexually*. The high presence of the female guards in the photos – or, rather, the high presence of the photos with the female guard in the media – seems to me to serve the function of reassuring the public that 'our boys' may have gone astray when it comes to treating the prisoners inhumanely, but by no means are they gay! The publicised romantic relationship of Lynndie England and Charles Graner, and their posing together on many of the photos among naked Iraqi prisoners, are supposed to indicate that he has not taken sexual – that is, *homosexual* – pleasure in the act of sexually torturing another man.

The last point to consider in comparing Croatian and US media representations is the huge difference in the overall visibility of the crimes. As already stated, sexual violence against men in the former Yugoslavia was hardly visible in the media, while the photos, texts and videos about Abu Ghraib are still available on the websites of many of the US TV broadcasters and press. I would suggest that the rationale for this difference can be found in the media construction of the master category or the *primary difference.*

In the former Yugoslavia, ethnicity was invoked as the primary difference between communities during the Second World War, during the 1980s when nationalism was steadily growing, and again during the wars of 1991–1995. However, this evocation has always had to struggle to erase shared histories, to deny that those have also been long and many. Mixed marriages, for example, posed particular problems to discourses of ethnic purity. Significantly, ethnic groups never lived in the segregation that existed in societies where differences have been much more racialised and much more absolute, as they were, for example, in colonised societies and during slavery or Apartheid. Furthermore, dominant notions and practices of femininity and masculinity and of heteronormativity have functioned as unifying factors across the lines of ethnic belonging. Thus, I would argue that the representational strategies of the media – while producing ethnicity as a primary difference – also carried an underlying assumption that lines demarcating boundaries of ethnicity often remained blurred and permeable. This meant that exposing the vulnerabilities of the Other always carried a danger of unwitting exposure of the Self. As the Self and the Other are mutually productive, the symbolic worlds they inhabit create the framework of, and place restrictions on, what can be made visible and how. Thus, I would argue that the representational strategies of the Croatian media rested on the assumption that *ethnic groups* in the former Yugoslavia had been *inhabiting the same symbolic world and had, within that world, shared the same notions of gender and sexuality;* and that this assumption of the shared world precluded public exposure of too many violated male bodies, too many masculine vulnerabilities.

In the case of the US, I would propose that assumptions about religious and racialised differences, *as well as* about differences in gender and sexuality, between an American and an Iraqi are constructed as much more fundamental, much more absolute. I argue that Americans and Iraqis are perceived – in the eyes of the American media – as inhabiting *totally different worlds* and that for this reason, exposure of the violated male body of the Other, of Iraqi men, is not seen as threatening the construction of the American Self.

How are we to understand and study the relationships of 'primary differences' in the Croatian and US wars – that is, ethnicity, religion and race, on the one hand, and gender and sexuality, and heteronormativity, on the other hand; and how have these relationships been studied? I turn now to these questions.

Exposures and Invisibilities in Scholarship: The Meanings of Analytical Categories

As stated in the introduction to this chapter, sexual violence against men is not the most topical issue in feminist scholarship. It has been present within black studies and postcolonial studies, and within prison studies, but within conflict and war studies men as victims of *sexual violence* did not exist as a research focus before the mid-1990s.[5]

Abu Ghraib has changed this, leading to the proliferation of scholarship. Unlike sexual violence against men in ex-Yugoslavia, which continues to receive relatively limited academic attention (but see Jones 1994, 2001, 2002, 2004, 2009, Zarkov

---

5   For the victimisation of men see Bourke (1996a, 1996b) and Peteet (2000), and for sexual violence against men in refugee and torture studies see Van Tienhoven (1993) and Zawati (2007).

1997, 2001, 2007, Loncar and Brecic 1995, Loncar et al. 2009, Carpenter 2006), sexual torture in Abu Ghraib has generated a substantial amount of scholarly work in a variety of disciplines (see Fallahi et al. 2009, Hannah 2006). Within media studies, many authors have analysed the representational strategies of the US (and other) TV and press, or looked at the similarities between media discourses and those of the Bush administration.[6] Feminist, queer, black and masculinity studies have followed several (interrelated) directions.

The early feminist reactions to Abu Ghraib were a kind of (self-)reflection in the light of the role of female torturers and their representation in the media. These early reactions to the torture in Abu Ghraib mainly focused on the *presence of a female torturer* and the consequences of that presence *for feminism* and/or *for women in and around the military*, sometimes to the extent that the torture and the tortured have been pushed to the margins of the analysis.[7] Feminist 'innocence', 'disdain' and 'disbelief' ruled when it came to understanding the role of the women prison guards. Zillah Eisenstein (2004), for example, persistently casts them as 'non-agentic' performers – engaged in 'gender swapping and switching' as 'decoys' who leave the 'masculinised/racialised gender in place', who only 'look like masculinist empire builders' but are actually just 'mimicking men'. Cynthia Enloe (2004) uses the violence in Abu Ghraib almost entirely in order to look at women as victims, discussing experiences of sexual violence and harassment of women soldiers by male soldiers within the US army, the violence of US male soldiers against their female partners at home, and the sexual violence of male soldiers against women in the vicinity of US military bases. When addressing the violence perpetrated by the female prison guards Enloe, too, seems to see them as pawns of men:

> *Choreographing* the women's guards' *feminized roles* so that they could act as ridiculing feminized *spectators* of male prisoners might have been imagined to intensify the masculinized demoralization. Dominant men trying to *utilize* at least some women to act in ways that undermine the masculinized self-esteem of rival men is not new. (Enloe 2004: 99) [my emphasis]

Similarly, Alexandra Murphy (2007: 26) argues that 'the behavior in the Abu Ghraib photographs parodies the sexual humiliation *traditionally inflicted upon the female body*' [my emphasis] and further states:

> While the prisoners' racial and religious identities *may* mark them out as "other" to the ethnic "same" of the American soldier – thus situating them as bodies to be subjugated – these identities do *not* play the major role in the process of acting-out the subjugations. (Murphy 2007: 32–33) [my emphasis]

---

6   See Tucker and Triantafyllos (2008) and Major (2008).
7   See for example Ehrenreich (2004), Eisenstein (2004), and Enloe (2004).

Such analyses show just how much Western feminism is still locked in the production of femininity as sexual vulnerability and masculinity as aggressive and inviolable; and in sustaining the idea that sexual and war violence are not just perpetrated by men, but are *essentially masculine*. But the violence in Abu Ghraib shows quite the opposite: women prison guards have participated in the American hegemonic, racist, Islamophobic, homophobic, violent projects of the 'war against terror' and occupation of Iraq *as in their own project*, not the project into which they have merely been manipulated or forced to join. They have used their own 'informed agency' (Butalia 2001), their own concept of the Other, to perpetrate violence, much like the male prison guards.[8] In reflecting on a decade of feminist struggles around women's human rights in the light of Abu Ghraib, Rosalind Petchesky (2005) has challenged such views and called for a serious rethinking of an analytical and political apparatus for feminists to use in addressing and redressing sexual violence in wars. The 'rights of the body', Petchesky argues, obviously matter for men too.

I would add that the violence in Abu Ghraib and the politics of its media representation in the US pose a series of challenges to contemporary feminist thinking about gender, as well as about war and the military. Those challenges are both epistemological and political. Epistemologically, the production of feminist knowledge has to let go of the centrality and primacy of gender as difference and as an analytical tool. In other words, however important gender may be, it is *only one – among many* – organising principles of social life, only one of many analytical categories. It does not have a 'natural' primacy in social relations. Rather, as Anne McClintock (1995) said long ago and Ann Stoler more recently (2009), gender intersects with other social relations in contradictory and conflictual ways, and its place and power depends on the *specific context* within which it operates.[9] In Abu Ghraib, gender is there – together with notions of sexuality and assumptions of heteronormativity – *to help produce the primary difference*: racialised Muslimness, into which the Iraqi prisoners in Abu Ghraib have been locked.[10]

In a different context the relationship between gender, sexuality, Islam and race may be very different. We see this from the chapter by Kira Kosnick (121f)

---

8   See for example Sarkar and Butalia (1995), Jeffery and Basu (2001), Bacchetta and Power (2002).

9   See also Phoenix (137f) and Ferree (55f) in this volume. The question of the primacy of gender is also discussed controversially by Mechthild Bereswill and Anke Neuber (69f) in this volume.

10   See Valerie Smith (1998) for an intersectional analysis in the specific context of US press representations of the inter-racial rape of women; Laurel S. Weldon (2005) for an application of intersectionality in comparative studies of welfare states; and Leslie McCall (2005) for a study of wage differences through an intersectional perspective. While acknowledging the huge contribution of intersectional analysis to feminist theorising, these authors at the same time call for further thinking about *how* notions, practices and structures of gender are positioned towards other social relations of power, and *how* those relationships can be studied empirically.

in this volume. Kosnick shows how the context of migration and asylum-seeking positions the 'migrating [or even the fleeing] Turkish subject' as a living proof of German enlightened tolerance towards homosexuality, and of Turkey's pre-modern, homophobic aptitude. This representation functions in this specific context – despite, and against both the homophobia and the xenophobia of German society and heteronormativity of its immigration policies. Kosnick calls such representation an 'intersectional visibility', arguing that feminists have to start looking beyond gender, at other differences and the contexts within which they make a difference.

Moreover, politically, feminism has to face the fact that in the contemporary global world marked by violent, militarised, neo-liberal capitalism, racialised Islamophobia has become the dominant platform from within which the West redefines itself and its enemies discursively.

A number of recent analyses of the torture in Abu Ghraib firmly situate the 'war on terror' within the histories of slavery and racism, colonialism and American imperialism, and the historical dynamics of the Western project of modernity.[11] But in many of these studies Islamophobia seems to be subsumed under racism. For example, in her comparative analysis of photographs of lynching in the US and the photos of Abu Ghraib, Liz Philipose (2007: 1066) states that '...the Muslim detainee is *blackened* in a regime of visibility in which blackness is the marker for the abject or nonhuman ...The photographs exhibit and simultaneously produce visible *racialized* difference for the viewer' [my emphasis]. Philipose further states: 'In an effort to quell white racial anxiety, war and the torture that accompanies it produce new racialised regimes of looking that deploy *old racisms* for new political ends' (Philipose 2007: 1067) [my emphasis] (see also Steele 2006, Richter-Montpetit 2006). What these emphases on race fail to note is that it is not just any racism, but the *specific context of Islamophobic wars* that marked the sexual torture in Abu Ghraib and its representation.

The absence of any consideration of Islamophobia in the analysis of the sexual torture in Abu Ghraib and the collapsing of that specific difference into racism has produced a discomfort that has been expressed explicitly by some authors (Sexton and Lee 2006, Gordon 2006). Sexton and Lee (2006) argue that scholarly framing of the Abu Ghraib torture through the images of lynching may lead to the appropriation of blackness as a metaphor for the suffering of Iraqi prisoners, thus rendering the specific history of slavery and contemporary imprisonment of black men and women politically marginalised.[12] An important warning has also come from Elizabeth Dauphinee (2007), who argues that the 'recirculation of imagery'

---

11   Among others, see Steele (2006), Richter-Montpetit (2006), Philipose (2007), Murphy (2007), Nusair (2008), Youngs (2006), Butler (2008), Razack (2003, 2004), and collections edited by Riley, Mohanty and Pratt (2008) and Alexander and Hawkesworth (2008).

12   Jennifer C. Nash (2008: 8–9) makes a similar argument in her critique of the use of intersectionality in feminist theory. She argues that black women have become the ultimate

of the violated Iraqi men not only separates ethically the image from the torture, but erases the specificity of the individual experience of pain by turning the image into a symbol, a 'representative example' (albeit in the political struggle against torture or US hegemony).[13]

In conclusion, I wish to return to the significance of the context: context is crucial not only for acts of torture and their media representations, as two interrelated, specific modes of violence, but also for their analysis. It is the context of the specific wars in Croatia and Abu Ghraib that produces the primary differences between the victimisers and the victimised. In the case of the former Yugoslavia, ethnic difference was the crucial generator of violence as well as the product of violence. In the intersection with ethnicity, shared notions of masculinity, sexuality and heteronormativity have, on the one hand, been decisive for the kind of sexual torture of men, and on the other hand, prevented high media visibility of sexually violated male bodies (albeit of the Other Man). In the case of Abu Ghraib, racialised Islamophobia generated the actual torture and its media exposure, while the intersections with femininity, masculinity and norms of heterosexuality have further underlined racialised Muslimness as primary difference, and have helped strengthen it in such a way that the exposed tortured body of the Other Man has not been able to destabilise the heteronormative, white, Christian/secular masculinity of the US Self.

Thus, sexual violence against men and its representations are the modes of producing ethnicity and Muslimness in Croatia and the US respectively, as much as the modes of producing specific sexualities, masculinities and femininities. In the context of wars, through violence and its representations, we have learned what it means to be a Croat, Serb or Muslim man, an American wo/man or an Iraqi man, in *specific geo-political times and spaces*. In this respect, the war in the former Yugoslavia was not so much a war between ethnic groups as a war that produced ethnic groups. And 'the war on terror' is not so much a war against 'Muslim terrorism' as a war that produces Muslimness-as-terrorism. Gender and sexuality are crucial for this process of production, but their place in this process is neither fixed nor given. Contemporary feminist scholarship thus always has to search for the place of gender in the analysis anew, always in relation to other categories. Equally, studies of contemporary wars have to analyse ethnicised, Islamised, racialised, homosexualised, gendered violence against, and by, both men and women – always anew, always embedded in the specific contexts, linked to the specific practices of violence. In both of those fields we have to remember that different groups of women and men are exposed to violence in different ways, and that their exposure to violence and the exposure of that violence before the eyes of the public do not always tell the same story.

'intersectional subjects' whose role is 'to provide a theoretical value added' but whose actual, lived experiences and diversities are often erased in the process of theorising.

13   Susan Sontag (2004) has also pointed to the ethical implications of photographs of torture.

Bibliography

Alexander, K. and Hawkesworth, M.E. (eds) 2008. *War and Terror: Feminist Perspectives*. Chicago: University of Chicago Press.

Bacchetta, P. and Power, M. (eds) 2002. *Right Wing Women: From Conservatives to Extremists Around the World*. New York and London: Routledge.

Bassiouni, M.C. et al. 1996. *Sexual Violence: An Invisible Weapon of War in the Former Yugoslavia*. International Human Rights Law Institute, Occasional Paper, 1. Chicago: DePaul University.

Bourke, J. 1996a. *Dismembering the Male: Men's Bodies, Britain, and the Great War*. Chicago: University Of Chicago Press.

Bourke, J. 1996b. Fragmentation, Fetishization and Men's Bodies in Britain, 1890–1939. *Women: A Cultural Review*, 7(3), 240–50.

Butalia, U. 2001. Women and Communal Conflict: New Challenges for the Women's Movement in India, in *Victims, Perpetrators or Actors? Gender, Armed Conflict and Political Violence*, edited by Moser, C.O.N. and Clark, F.C. London & New York: Zed Books, 99–113.

Butler, J. 2008. Sexual politics, torture, and secular time. *The British Journal of Sociology*, 59(1), 1–23.

Carpenter, C. 2006. Recognizing gender-based violence against civilian men and boys in conflict situations. *Security Dialogue*, 37(1), 83–103.

Dauphinee, E. 2007. The Politics of the Body in Pain: Reading the Ethics of Imagery. *Security Dialogue*, Special Issue on Securitization, Militarization and Visual Culture in the Worlds of Post 9/11, 38(2), 139–55.

Duffield, M. 2007. *Development, Security and Unending War. Governing the World of Peoples*. Cambridge: Polity Press.

Ehrenreich, B. 2004. *What Abu Ghraib Taught Me*. Available at: http://www.alternet.org/story/18740/ [accessed: 20 June 2010].

Eisenstein, Z. 2004. *Sexual Humiliation, Gender Confusion and the Horrors at Abu Ghraib*. Available at: http://www.awid.org/eng/Issues-and-Analysis/Library/Sexual-Humiliation-Gender-Confusion-and-the-Horrors-at-Abu-Ghraib/(language)/eng-GB [accessed: 22 June 2010].

Enloe, C. 2004. Wielding Masculinity inside Abu Ghraib: Making Feminist Sense of an American Military Scandal. *Asian Journal for Women's Studies*, 10(3), 89–102.

Fallahi, C., Austad, C.S., Leishman, L., Gendron, M. and Wood, R. 2009. Gender Differences in the Perception of Prisoner Abuse. *Sex Roles*, 60(3–4), 261–68.

Gordon, A.F. 2006. Abu Ghraib: imprisonment and the war on terror. *Race & Class*, 48(1), 42–59.

Hannah, M. 2006. Torture and the Ticking Bomb: The 'War on Terror' as a Geographical Imagination of Power/Knowledge. *Annals of Association of American Geographers*, 96(3), 622–40.

Jeffery, P. and Basu, A. (eds) 2001. *Resisting the Sacred and the Secular: Women's Activism and Politicized Religion in South Asia*. Delhi: Kali for Women.

Jones, A. 1994. Gender and ethnic conflict in ex-Yugoslavia. *Ethnic and Racial Studies*, 17(1), 115–34.

Jones, A. 2001. *Genocide and Humanitarian Intervention: Incorporating Gender Violence*. Available at:http://www.jha.ac/articles/a080.htm [accessed: 20 June 2010].

Jones, A. 2002. Gender and genocide in Rwanda. *Journal of Genocide Research*, 4(1), 65–94.

Jones, A. (ed.) 2004. *Gendercide and Genocide*. Nashville: Vanderbilt University Press.

Jones, A. 2009. *Gender Inclusive: Essays on Violence, Men, and Feminist International Relations*. London: Routledge.

Loncar, M. and Brecic, P. 1995. *Characteristics of Sexual Violence Against Men During the War in Croatia and Bosnia-Hercegovina*. Paper to the conference Engendering Violence: Terror, Domination, Recovery. Zagreb, 27–28 October.

Loncar, M, Henigsberg, N. and Hrabac P. 2009. Mental Health Consequences in Men Exposed to Sexual Abuse During theWar in Croatia and Bosnia. *Journal of Interpersonal Violence*, 20(10), 1–13.

Major, M. 2008. *Following the Flag: Nationalism, the News Media, and Abu Ghraib*. Paper to the American Political Science Association Conference, Boston, 28–31 August.

McCall, L. 2005. The Complexity of Intersectionality. *Signs: Journal of Women in Culture and Society*, 30(3), 1773–1800.

McClintock, A. 1995. *Imperial Leather: Race, Gender and Sexuality in the Colonial Contest*. London: Routledge.

Murphy, A. 2007. The Missing Rhetoric of Gender in Responses to Abu Ghraib. *Journal of International Women's Studies*, 8(2), 20–34.

Nash, C.J. 2008. Re-Thinking Intersectionality. *Feminist Review*, 89(1), 1–15.

Nusair, I. 2008. Gendered, racialized, and sexualized torture at Abu Ghraib, in *Feminism and War: Confronting U.S. Imperialism*, edited by Riley, R.L., Mohanty, C.T. and Pratt, B.M. London: Zed Books, 179–93.

Petchesky, R. 2005. Rights of the body and perversions of war: sexual rights and wrongs ten years past Beijing. *International Social Science Journal*, 57(2), 301–18.

Peteet, J. 2000. Male gender and rituals of resistance in the Palestinian Intifada: a cultural politics of violence, in *Imagined Masculinities. Male Identity and Culture in the Modern Middle East*, edited by Ghoussoub, M. and Sinclair-Webb, E. London: Saqi Books, 103–26.

Philipose, L. 2007. The Politics of Pain and the Uses of Torture. *Signs: Journal of Women in Culture and Society*, 32(4), 1047–71.

Razack, S. 2003. Those Who 'Witness the Evil'. *Hypathia*, 18(1), 204–11.

Razack, S. 2004. *Dark Threats and White Knights: The Somalia Affair, Peacekeeping, and the New Imperialism*. Toronto: University of Toronto Press.

Richter-Montpetit, M. 2006. *Empire, Desire and Violence: A Queer Transnational Feminist Analysis of the Torture of Detainees in Abu Ghraib*. Paper to ISA Annual Meeting, San Diego, California, 22 March.

Riley, R.L., Mohanty, C.T. and Pratt, B.M. (eds) 2008. *Feminism and War: Confronting U.S. Imperialism*. London: Zed Books.

Sarkar, T. and Butalia, U. (eds) 1995. *Women & Right–Wing Movements: Indian Experiences*. London and New Jersey: Zed Books.

Sexton, J. and Lee, E. 2006. Figuring the Prison: Prerequisites of Torture at Abu Ghraib. *Antipode*, 38(5), 1005–22.

Smith, V. 1998. Split Affinities: Representing Interracial Rape, in *Not Just Race, Not Just Gender*, New York & London: Routledge, 1–32.

Sontag, S. 2004. Regarding the Torture of Others. *New York Times*, 23 May. Available at: http://www.nytimes.com/2004/05/23/magazine/23PRISONS. html?pagewanted=1 [accessed: 20 June 2010].

Steele, W. 2006. Strange Fruit: American Culture and the Remaking of Iraqi Males at Abu Ghraib. *Nebula*, 3(4), 62–74.

Stoler, A. 2009. Beyond Sex: Bodily Exposure in the Colonial and Postcolonial Present. *New School of Social Research*, April 2009.

Taguba Report. 2004. Available at: http://news.findlaw.com/hdocs/docs/iraq/ tagubarpt.html [accessed: 20 June 2010].

Tucker, B. and Triantafyllos, S. 2008. Lynndie England, Abu Ghraib, and the New Imperialism. *Canadian Review of American Studies*, 38(1), 83–100.

United Nations Commission of Experts' Final Report. 1994. Section IV: Substantive Findings (E.: Detention Facilities; F.: Rape and other forms of Sexual Assault), United Nations Security Council S/1994/674, 27 May.

United Nations Commission of Experts' Final Report. 1994. Annex IX – Rape and Sexual Assault, United Nations Security Council, S/1994/674/Add.2 (V), 28 December.

United Nations Commission of Experts' Final Report. 1994. Annex IX.A – Sexual Assault Investigation, United Nations Security Council, S/1994/674/Add.2 (V), 28 December.

Van Tienhoven, H. 1993. Sexual torture of male victims. *Torture*, 3(4), 133–35.

Weldon, L.S. 2005. *Rethinking Intersectionality: Some conceptual problems and solutions for the comparative study of welfare states*. Paper to the Annual Meeting of the American Political Science Association: Mobilizing Democracy, Washington DC, 1 September.

Youngs, G. 2006. Feminist International Relations in the Age of the War on Terror. *International Feminist Journal of Politics*, 8(1), 3–18.

Zarkov, D. 1997. War Rapes in Bosnia: On Masculinity, Femininity and Power of the Rape Victim Identity. *Tijdschriftvoor Criminologie*, 39(2), 140–51.

Zarkov, D. 2001. The Body of the Other Man: Sexual Violence and the Construction of Masculinity, Sexuality and Ethnicity in Croatian Media, in *Victims, Perpetrators or Actors? Gender, Armed Conflict and Political Violence*, edited by Moser, C. and Clark, F. London: Zed Books, 69–82.

Zarkov, D. 2006. Towards a new theorizing of women, gender and war, in *Handbook of Gender and Women's Studies*, edited by M. Evans, K. Davis and J. Lorber. London: Sage, 214–33.

Zarkov, D. 2007. *The Body of War: Media, Ethnicity and Gender in the Break-up of Yugoslavia*. Durham and London: Duke University Press.

Zawati, H. 2007. Impunity or Immunity: war time male rape and sexual torture as a crime against humanity. *Torture*, 17(1), 27–47.

Chapter 7

Sexuality and Migration Studies: The Invisible, the Oxymoronic and Heteronormative Othering[1]

Kira Kosnick

In feminist theorisations of intersectionality, understood as the intersecting of hierarchical axes of difference, the 'classical triad' of 'race', class and gender has increasingly been augmented with other dimensions of socio-cultural and economic inequality, including that of sexual orientation. Contemporary intersectionality paradigms differ with regard to the scope of different axes thought to be relevant (Anthias 2001, Klinger 2003, Knapp 2005, Lutz and Wenning 2001), but sexual orientation now figures fairly regularly on their lists, while heteronormativity is increasingly recognised as an important dimension of most gender regimes.[2]

However, shifting attention to different, yet related interdisciplinary terrains such as migration studies in which attention to diversity issues has increased over the past 20 years, sexuality and sexual orientation has tended to remain a topic of relatively marginal interest within the field (Castro Varela and Dhawan 2009). While class and socio-economic differences have always held an important place for migration scholars in terms of understanding 'push and pull' factors as well as differential incorporation in receiving countries, additional questions of racism and ethnic stratification emerged as scientific attention turned to 'integration' issues in the wake of labour migration to Northern industrialised countries, decolonisation and ethnic conflicts in different parts of the world. And while some (predominantly female) voices tried already in the 1980s to draw attention to the fact that much could be learned from considering gender issues in relation to migration (Morokvasic 1984, Kofman 1999), the past two decades have seen an increase of studies both in size and scope (Donato et al. 2006). In their introduction to a special issue of the *International Migration Review* in 2006, Katharine M. Donato

---

1   I would like to thank the editors for their challenging and productive comments on this chapter, from which I benefited a lot, even as I cannot claim to have done them full justice.

2   Even though some feminist theorists have already in the 1970s pushed for the recognition of heterosexuality as – in addition to binary gender norms – constituting the second central pillar of gender regimes (e.g. Rubin 1975), this acknowledgement did not filter into dominant feminist discourses until the 1990s.

and others remarked that '… gender analysis is no longer exclusively limited to the analysis of families, households, or women's lives' (ibid.: 6), and noted that migration processes as a whole are now seen (if not everywhere) as gendered phenomena. Yet, as gender concerns seem to establish their legitimacy and, in fact, indispensability for migration research, questions of non-heteronormative sexuality remain curiously marginalised (Manalansan 2006).

This chapter investigates the normative assumptions concerning sexuality that function in dominant paradigms of migration research and links them to specific empirical instances in which migrant ethnicities and 'queer' sexualities intersect. I argue that relegating issues of sexuality to the realm of the personal and local prevents any examination of how struggles around sexualities contribute to place-making practices and mobilities at different scales and across different localities. There is, however, no single logic through which hierarchies of sexuality and border-crossing migrations intersect with each other. The chapter thus discusses empirical instances in which anti-immigrant racisms and homophobia are mutually constitutive to produce different kinds of visibility, invisibility and contradiction.

(In)Visibilities

Late in 2008, a new play had its premiere in Berlin at a small theatre venue in the district of Kreuzberg, home to a large number of immigrants from Turkey and to many gay, lesbian, trans- and queer-identified residents. The title of the play was '*Jenseits – Bist du schwul oder bist du Türke?*'[3] It is based on a number of interviews with gay men of Turkish or Kurdish descent who talk about their experiences with homophobic and racist forms of classification in Germany. The title of the play names an invisibility as much as an apparent categorical impossibility: taking inspiration from the title of the famous anthology launched by the black women's movement in the United States in the 1980s, one could translate it as 'All the Gays are White, all the Turks are Straight.'[4] The linkage between sexual and ethnic-minoritarian categories of difference that produces the intersectional invisibility of queer Turks is in this case linked to contemporary dominant discourses on ethnicity, religion and sexuality in Germany; discourses that selectively produce homosexuality as a key symbol of enlightened individualism and tolerance linked to Western modernity. The latter are qualities that Muslims with a migration background from Turkey are deemed to inherently lack in these discourses – the ethnic minoritarian position is coded here as not only non-German, but as implicitly heterosexual and homophobic.

With regard to '*Jenseits*', all the more media excitement was thus produced by the apparently oxymoronic minoritarian conjunction of sexual and ethnic precarity

---

3   The first term of which translates as something like 'beyond', 'on the other side' or 'afterlife' – followed by 'are you gay or are you a Turk?'

4   I am referring to Gloria T. Hull, Patricia Bell-Scott, Barbara Smith (1982).

that the play addresses. The interviews used in the play focus not so much on invisibility but rather on the specific forms of heightened visibility experienced by gay men with migration backgrounds from Turkey in the context of representational practices in dominant German discourses. Ercan, one of the protagonists, is quoted in the play as saying:

> I am a homosexual Turk and enjoy the fruits of positive racism in Germany. Just because I'm gay I have immediately found a job, I've had lots of people around me. Many people face me full of admiration, like: Oh, he's come here to emancipate himself! Let's make a joint effort to set him free. And I think to myself: Well then, go ahead and release me!

The play was widely discussed and extremely wellreceived in the German mass media, not least because of its apparently titillating subject matter. Berlin's daily newspapers and city guide journals gave it eager and extensive coverage. The daily *Der Tagesspiegel* ran a headline that went as follows:

> **Then you're out.** In Germany they are the minority within the minority. And they actually shouldn't even exist: gay Turks are taboo. On life between tradition and new homeland.[5]

Tradition – coded as homophobic – is here firmly associated with the country and ethnicity of non-Western origin, whereas the new '*Heimat*' homeland allows for apparently oxymoronic subjects to surface. This surfacing, however, involves simultaneously their distancing from what is termed the Turkish 'community' and its alleged traditions in Germany. The play, it is interpreted, and by extension also the German press, is thus breaking a taboo – one that, as the article goes on to explain, is however specific to Turkish traditions, not to German society. Thus, even the intentionally sympathetic reporting on a play which was intended to reveal the mechanisms and consequences of dominant discourses becomes another exercise in confirming their underlying assumptions. Rendering the apparent taboo visible in this case serves the primary purpose of reconfirming Turkish difference as pre-modern homophobia: this is where a particular productivity of intersectional visibility, rather than invisibility, emerges.

Ercan's story, told in the play and subsequently retold by the newspaper, is one of initial oscillation between Turkey and Germany, self-evidently taken to represent the antagonistic poles of tradition and modernity. His oscillation is expressed through frequent national border crossings occasioned by his parents' migration paths, his childhood commitment to Islam, and the blond, green-eyed adolescent lover he first kissed when attending a boarding school in Turkey, hidden in a classroom while the other boys were watching the American TV import *Dallas*. The newspaper article ends with Ercan, now happily 'married' to a (non-

---

5   Published 4 May 2008.

immigrant) male German elementary school teacher,[6] visiting his former childhood love in Turkey. The latter is living as a peasant in a small village, married (to a woman) with four children, and is so embarrassed by his visitor he is barely able to meet Ercan's eyes. Ercan, however, is reported as still fancying his former lover, thinking him a handsome, portly Turkish man. 'There's still an Anatolian woman somewhere inside me,' Ercan giggles.

Thanks to his migration history, Ercan thus has almost succeeded in shedding his pre-modern heritage, with the help of a modern German nation-state that gives a degree of recognition and legitimacy to same-sex unions modelled on – yet carefully separated from – the heterosexual institution of marriage. His former Turkish lover, whose unusual blondness appears as a first signification of a 'Western' coding of homosexual desire, has firmly reverted to tradition with his rural peasant existence, heterosexual marriage and his procreative feats in a small Turkish village. Confirming this gap, Ercan cannot express his desire as a gay Turkish man, but is ironically constrained to instead refer to a desiring Anatolian woman that has allegedly remained inside him somewhere. Anatolia is the territorial description for the 'Asian' part of contemporary Turkey, often used as a concept to refer to folk traditions that pre-exist the creation of the modern Turkish nation-state and its explicitly Westernising modernist cultural transformations. Ercan's change of gender positions confirms that Turkish men are firmly out of reach for homosexual desires, not least because non-Western oriental 'tradition' here ultimately outweighs even the alluring pull and modernising force of *Dallas*.

In this rendition of Ercan's story, only his migration to Germany allows for secretive homosexual practices to be transformed into a liberated gay subjectivity, one that is both individualised and normalised towards the normative model of heterosexual unions, with the German state endorsing same-sex civil partnerships and granting them (some) rights previously available only to married heterosexual couples. The fact that the article speaks of marriage is significant in that this formulation conveniently ignores the factual non-equality of same-sex unions that prevails in Germany in legal terms, and at the same time instates marriage as the ultimate sign of state benevolence and social integration with regard to 'homosexuals'. The discursive visibility of the gay Turk thus serves both to cement Germany's ethnic minority from Turkey as inherently tradition-oriented and homophobic, and to implicitly erase a modern history of state-endorsed othering and violence towards those labelled as homosexuals.

---

6   Since 2001, Germany allows for so-called *life partnerships* that give a range of rights previously reserved for male–female marriage unions to same-sex couples, excluding many rights such as pension benefits, joint taxation and adoption.

Codings of Same-Sex Desire

The narrative plot above in which Turkey comes to be unambiguously associated with pre-modern homophobic repression has already been recognised as a widespread and familiar one in Western representations of 'oriental' and postcolonial queer subjects. Particularly media representations, with films such as Deepa Mehta's India-based *Fire* (1996), Ang Lee's *Wedding Banquet* (1993) and Ian Iqbal Rashid's *A Touch of Pink* (2003) have been critically analysed as paradigmatic for the association of same-sex love with Western modernity (Gopinath 2002, Castro Varela and Dhawan 2005, Needham and Rajan 2007). The affirmation of same-sex desire and commitment often goes hand in hand with the endorsement of lifestyle practices or objects coded as symbolically 'Western' in these films, as when the protagonist in Mehta's *Fire* changes into her husband's pair of jeans (see Castro Varela and Dhawan 2005: 51).

More importantly for the interest of this chapter, leaving one's biological family behind and migrating to a 'Western' country is presented as the most promising route towards living out one's non-heterosexual desires and stabilising these into an affirmative queer identity. In a *Touch of Pink* and the *Wedding Banquet*, the Western metropolitan destinations of London and New York figure respectively as libertarian social contexts in which the protagonists can live openly with their gay partners without having to confront the wrath of their South Asian respectively Chinese parents. In films such as *Lola and Bilidikid* (directed by Kutluð Ataman, 1999), situated entirely in the migration context, it is the suffocating grasp of the ethnic community stronghold that continuously produces setbacks in the Turkish-German protagonist Murat's efforts to come to terms with his sexuality. Even figures such as Murat's long-lost brother and his long-term gay Turkish-German lover fail. The latter cannot accept his desire and love as homosexual, instead harassing the former to have a sex-change operation so the two of them can move to Turkey and live anonymously like a 'normal couple'. Murat's brother finally dies a violent death. The doubly discriminated minority of Turkish-German queers depicted in the film is ravaged by homophobia and racism, unable to sustain stable identifications or minimally enduring forms of social solidarity. At the intersection of non-normative sexuality and ethnicity, nothing but tragedy seems to await those who carry the double burden of homophobia and racism. Breaking away from the 'traditional' social bonds of one's family and ethnic community background is presented as a lonely, individualised act, leading the subject to strive for emancipation through the forced renouncement of (most often) *his* non-Western 'roots'.

Against the foil of conservative family expectations, the wider 'Western' environment in which the stories unfold emerges as self-evidently progressive and tolerant *vis-à-vis* queer lifestyles and identities. In *A Touch of Pink* and the *Wedding Banquet*, the white, Western love interests of the main characters never appear to have the slightest difficulties in living 'openly' as gay, acting as stable shoulders on which their conflicted partners can and should lean.[7] Similarly, the German mass media reporting on gay Turks in Germany has no need to render its assumptions concerning the tolerance of the host society explicit: it emerges instead against the focused backdrop of Turkish 'traditional' homophobia. The heightened visibility of the queer, ethnicised and individualised subject is thus coupled with the production of invisibility regarding the history and presence of violent and coercive heteronormativity in the context of German society. It is precisely the taken-for-granted tolerance that performs the ideological labour of producing invisibility here. While Gudrun-Axeli Knapp is certainly right to state that the invisibility of norms as hegemonic achievements is not just produced through ideological labour but also through translating them into politics and the factuality of legal arrangements and institutions (see her chapter in this book), it is nevertheless important to stress how the politics of cultural struggle carried out through mass-mediated public representations prepare the ground for such translations. There is evidence, in fact, that the curious discursive conjunction of sexuality and migration in German mainstream mass media have 'structurally effective' political consequences, as when foreign citizens wanting to take on German citizenship have to pass a naturalisation test that asks about attitudes towards male homosexuality (see Castro Varela and Dhawan 2009: 113). The regulation of sexuality, closely linked to normative orders that needed to be established and normalised ideologically as well as institutionally, has long been an important element of modern state practices and their policing of state borders.

Queering Migration Research

Just as fictional accounts of queer migrations tend to present queer cross-border mobility as an individualised act of breaking away from repressive 'traditional' socialities, the focus on seemingly individual escapes from homophobic repression also prevails in the scant attention given to queer migrations in the mainstream of migration research, where such mobility has – at once predominantly and peripherally – surfaced mainly in the context of asylum issues. The attention given to those who seek asylum on the basis of their sexual orientation tends to mirror the logic of asylum regimes in that individual asylum-seekers have to make a convincing case that they face persecution in their 'traditional' countries of origin, and are thereby forced to reinstate the tradition–modernity divide in their narratives of repression in order to achieve recognition (Grewal 2005). The queer asylum-seeker thus always appears – and has to appear – as a lone figure asking the Western state for benevolent incorporation.

---

7   Such depictions continue the long-standing representational figure of the white, Western male who comes to the rescue of 'oriental' women, as in the German film *Yasemin* (Lutz 1995).

The failure of much migration research to address issues of sexual orientation in other domains of inquiry, however, should not be taken to prove the general irrelevance of such issues in these domains.[8] Quite the contrary, the reasons for this failure need to be examined in detail. While the above discussion has shown how orientalist constructions of non-Western traditions, coded as inherently homophobic, surface in narratives of migration to produce tales of individual liberation aided by the enlightened Western state, it is also necessary to consider the extent to which heteronormative assumptions and principles have implicitly structured many of the dominant research perspectives within the field of migration studies.

As Martin F. Manalansan (2006) has pointed out in his critique of sexuality and gender in migration studies, heterosexual partnerships and 'biological' parenthood still provide the primary models for thinking about migrant families, genealogies and networks of care that span across different localities. Notions of 'family unification', for example, usually take for granted that either direct biological kinship or heterosexual marriage unions provide the legitimate grounds for mobility. It is striking to note how mainstream migration research on remittances, generational change or diasporic formations relies upon heteronormative assumptions when establishing what kinds of socio-genetic affiliations and affective ties are thought to matter. Yet, researching migration and diaspora in implicitly heteronormative terms runs the risk of unwittingly underwriting gendered and sexualised assumptions about, for example, women as 'natural nurturers' who make sacrifices for biological kin (Manalansan 2006: 239), and underestimating the role of other forms of social and affective attachment. It thus becomes difficult to consider the importance and role of differential sexual desires and non-normative family formations as well as other social bonds in migration processes.

Heteronormative and gendered assumptions are not just pervasive in migration studies, they have also left their imprints on those seemingly neutral theoretical accounts that have proved highly influential in contextualising migration research within processes of globalisation and formations of late capitalist modernity. As Judith Halberstam has argued, influential theorists such as David Harvey, Frederic Jameson, Edward Soja and others have dismissed sexuality as a negligible category of analysis in their work, only to unwittingly reinstate (hetero)normative suppositions related to sexuality and sexual orientation when it comes to examining the production of contemporary spaces and temporalities in the context of globalisation (Halberstam 2005: 5). Alongside this implicit heteronormativity, sexuality and matters of sexual orientation are relegated to the realm of the personal and local in their works, seemingly irrelevant to general conversations about globalisation, transnational capitalism and migratory movements.

---

8 This is not to diminish the importance of paying attention to the fate of queer immigrants and asylum-seekers, who in many migration contexts face daunting problems and unique legal and social barriers to securing asylum. For a discussion of such barriers in the USA that employs an intersectionality perspective, see Randazzo (2005).

Yet, relegating issues of sexuality to the realm of the personal and local prevents any examination of how struggles around sexualities contribute to place-making practices and mobilities at different scales and across different localities, a crucial issue for migrants whose capacities for place-making are often shaped and constrained by histories of racialisation, deprivation and forced migrations. It shuts the door on once pioneering yet nowadays almost forgotten considerations of how kinship and sexuality might be central to the production of social and economic relationships (Rubin 1975), and on how different sex/gender regimes impact upon or might be impacted by migration. It thus also prevents us from recognising the role of the state in the production of sexual identities and the regulation of sexual practices. As Inderpal Grewal and Caren Kaplan put it in their critique of queer sexuality studies:

> Our point is that sexual subjects are produced not just by the politics of identity or social movements but by the links between various institutions that accompany these social movements. Furthermore, we need to probe these connections and circuits to see how identities are upheld or made possible by institutions linked to the state. We find it problematic that in much work on sexual identities the state seldom has a hand in enabling these identities. (Grewal and Kaplan 2001: 672)

State Interventions

Michel Foucault has been credited with shifting the terms of the debate on sexuality since the 1970s, away from the notion that sex marked some kind of natural impulse that was faced with different kinds of repressive interventions and prohibitions, towards considering discourses about sexuality as a historically specific political technology that became central to modern European state power (Foucault 1978). He argued that sex was at the heart of population control that emerged as a central concern of European governments and state officials in the eighteenth century, with the conviction that the future of society was '... tied not only to the number and the uprightness of its citizens, to their marriage rules and family organisation, but to the manner in which each individual made use of his [sic] sex' (Foucault 1978: 26). Both the disciplining of individual bodies and the regulatory control of populations hinged upon technologies of sex. Birthrates, life expectancy, health and fertility were population variables to be brought under control, making it essential for states to produce knowledge regarding the sexual behaviour and proclivities of its citizens on an individual as well as collective basis. As migrants and diasporic groups cannot escape the technologies of state power related to sexuality, the latter need to be taken into account in the contemporary study of cross-border migratory movements, populations and subjects. It cannot simply be assumed that the transformation and potential weakening of nation-states in the wake of globalisation renders such technologies less important.

In an important critique of Foucault, however, the anthropologist Ann Laura Stoler has drawn attention to the limits of his analysis, pointing out that he did not consider that the very nation-states he was referring to were simultaneously engaged in various imperial projects and used technologies that went far beyond the confines of a single population (Stoler 1995). The colonial management of sexuality was a key site in the production of racialised bodies, and Stoler has suggested that the alleged libidinal energies of the 'savage' or the colonised functioned as racialised erotic objects of knowledge in dominant Western discourses on sexuality. Stoler's critique of Foucault allows us to see sexuality and 'race' as intimately coupled, so to speak. She has drawn attention to the fact that neither state territories nor citizenship have historically marked the limits of interest in controlling sexuality, and that different historical formations of racism and colonial conquest have been closely linked to projections and injunctions concerning sexuality. Dubravka Zarkov's chapter in this volume discusses how norms of heterosexuality, ethnicity and hegemonic masculinity intersect in the perpetuation and representation of sexual violence in the context of the recent Yugoslav wars. Male victims of sexual violence in the context of war, if representationally 'visible' at all, appear as both emasculated and ethnically/nationally dishonoured: the acts of sexual humiliation and torture aim to annihilate the symbolically masculine power of the ethnic/ racialised Other (see also Zarkov 2001).

Both insights regarding the links between sexuality and 'race' are crucial for any consideration of how migrants and diasporas, moving and living across these geopolitical divides, might be understood in conjunction with normative and non-normative sexualities. Many migrant populations and diasporas, particularly those that have emerged in the wake of colonial projects, have had to contend with racialised politics of sexuality in different ways. Racial and ethnic categories have been in use to subject potential and actual immigrants to differential policies of family reunification, marriage and moral control (Cruz-Malavé and Manalansan 2002). Modern immigration regimes have generally used heteronormative standards of sexuality to regulate the entry and settlement of non-citizens (Luibhéid and Cantú 2005). Not only are those suspected of harbouring homosexual or other 'perverse' and 'immoral' tendencies sometimes explicitly barred from legal immigration (for example in the US until 1990), but heterosexual marriage and 'family' reunification continue to be among the most promising avenues for legal migration around the globe, with 'family' usually defined as the 'nuclear' unit of a heterosexual couple and its biological children. Controlling immigration has thus been crucially linked to state projects of managing and regulating the normative sexuality and reproductive behaviour of their citizens (Manalansan 2006).

Contemporary work on the transformations of technologies of state power in the wake of globalisation certainly undermine the assumption that it is possible to speak of states as singular, unified actors that represent and enforce the will of sovereign governments (Burchell et al. 1991). However, agents of nation-states and supra-state agencies continue to shape the constitution and movement of diasporas as they regulate immigration and conditions of residence, and reach out beyond geo-political borders to citizens and nationals abroad. The 'manufacture of citizenship normativized within the prism of heterosexuality' (Alexander 2005: 181) that characterises many state formations around the globe cannot be assumed to lose its power just because the social formations in question might no longer be firmly tied to the sovereign space of a single nation-state. María do Mar Castro Varela and Nikita Dhawan (2009) show how German integration debates position migrants only within heterosexual family structures,[9] while the differential treatment of same-sex, marriage-like unions in member states of the European Union reveals limits to the efforts of establishing a unified European legal area. What is more, further hopes that migrants might escape the hegemonic grip of nation-states are quick to evaporate in light of both the de-territorialised powers of many contemporary states and the neo-colonial projects that are tied to corporate interests beyond state borders (Basch et al. 1993).

For many theorists, ties to an original homeland constitute a prerequisite in order to categorise particular social groups as diasporic (Safran 1991). While the most prominent analysis of the nation as an imagined community did not pursue issues of kinship and genealogy much beyond the 'fraternal spirit' among (male) co-nationals (Anderson 1993), earlier academic work had already exposed the crucial role of normative ideas about the nuclear heterosexual family, as the nucleus of national community and gendered bearer of differential obligations with regard to its well-being and future. In his study of middle-class morality and sexual norms in modern Europe, George L. Mosse (1985) revealed how heteronormative and androcentric understandings of sexuality were central to nationalist ideologies and politics, points that have been similarly and more complexly elaborated by postcolonial and feminist theorists for other state and imperialist projects (Yuval-Davis and Anthias 1989, Mohanty and Alexander 1997, Grewal and Kaplan 1994, Stoler 1995). There is no reason to assume that the territorial 'scattering' of diaspora as an imagined community would not continue similar concerns (Gilroy 2004). Quite the contrary, diasporic anxieties around issues of preservation and temporal continuity often focus on cultural-biological reproduction, and linked to this on a need to control sexuality, particularly the sexualities (both practices and desires) of women.

A growing body of work challenges the heteronormative bent of migration but also 'race'/racialisation research, inspired by both postcolonial critique and queer theory approaches. The work of Sara Ahmed, Jacqui Alexander, Inderpal Grewal, Caren Kaplan, Encarnación Gutiérrez Rodríguez and others is notable for their efforts to reveal sexual regulation and heteronormative ordering as important dimensions of postcolonial state projects, and to discuss their implications for marginalised subject positions and practices (Ahmed et al. 2003, Alexander 2005,

---

9   While at the same time, as stated above, tolerant attitudes towards homosexuality have been positioned as a requirement for gaining German citizenship in the test the Federal State of Baden-Württemberg implemented in 2006, a test that specifically targeted Muslims, see Castro Varela and Dhawan (2009), Haritaworn et al. (2007).

Grewal and Kaplan 1994, Gutiérrez Rodríguez and Steyerl 2003).[10] Their critical re-reading of postcolonial, racialisation and gender studies theory has been expanded to include queer theory and queer political practice in the work of activist academics and intellectuals such as Jin Haritaworn, Tamsila Tauqir, Fatima El-Tayeb and Esra Erdem, who show that the association of homophobia with (Western and non-Western) tradition has had a firm place in the political repertoire of many gay and queer activists as well as academics, and in conceptions of white, Western and male homosexual identities as representing the vanguard of sexual liberation struggles around the globe (El-Tayeb 2003, Fortier 2002). Haritaworn, Tauquir and Erdem discuss forms of racism implicit in the white queer targeting of alleged Muslim (immigrant) homophobia, a move which aligns them with Western neo-imperialist state projects and right-wing groups and thus bases the 'assimilation successes' of white gays and lesbians on a deeply racist logic (Haritaworn et al. 2007). Their point, importantly, is not simply a group-based argument about racist politics thus being supported by white gays and lesbians. Sexuality and gender, they note, have become central arenas for Islamophobic discourses in Germany as well as abroad, thereby erasing both past and persisting histories of sexism and homophobia as part of Western modernity (ibid.: 192).

If one's theorising is motivated by a cognitive interest (*Erkenntnisinteresse*) that seeks to intervene in the politics of cultural struggle (not just to 'end discrimination' and seek redistributive justice between group categories, but also to change the structural mechanisms that stabilise particular power relationships), it might not always be productive to differentiate between actor-oriented theorising and society-oriented theorising, claiming for the latter a more comprehensive understanding of power dynamics and their concomitant (in)visibilities, as Knapp suggests in this volume. The complex histories of feminism and anti-racist politics suggest that 'actors', their movements and alliances are crucial in performing the work of de-naturalisation and rendering visible what has been erased or made unthinkable.

Intersections

Returning to the example of the minoritarian conjunction of sexual and ethnic precarity the *Jenseits* play addressed on and off stage, the very visibility of gay Turks in Germany in this case did not further a progressive cause of intersectional analysis. Instead, this sensationalist visibility practically foreclosed any critical engagement with the historical and normative background against which the gay Turk emerged as such a starkly outlined figure: the orientalist distancing, on

---

10   Their work, as most of them state quite explicitly, would have been unthinkable without the pioneering earlier work of thinkers and activists such as the Combahee River Collective, Audre Lorde, Gloria Anzaldúa and others (Anzaldúa 1987, Combahee River Collective 1982, Lorde 1983).

the basis of which Germany appears to distinguish itself as a country of liberal tolerance, the normative inscription of a coming-out process that forces the homosexual subject to break with any kinfolk and 'roots', culminating in the act of individual, border-crossing migration. Performing the work of de-naturalisation and rendering visible what has been erased or made unthinkable in this context requires us here to question particular visibilities, and the uses to which they are put.

Given a historical juncture at which suspected attitudes towards homosexuality can be mobilised as a litmus test in state practices of exclusion, intended to prevent the 'naturalisation' of Muslim applicants for citizenship in Germany, and form part of a mass-mediated public discourse to highlight the alleged incompatibility of Islam with democratic values increasingly claimed as 'European' as well as national (Bunzl 2005), the concomitant visibilities of ethnicised gay men as paradoxical subjects and homosexuality as inimical to Islam need to be closely examined. While some of these subjects might, as Ercan stated in the play, individually enjoy the fruits of positive racism in Germany, their sudden discursive visibility not only promotes Islamophobia and ethnicised othering at the level of cultural group classifications, but helps cement a European political order based on the exclusion of predominantly Muslim countries such as Turkey, and bringing into force laws and regulations that curtail possibilities and forms of Muslims' participation. The fruits of positive racism are thus bound to be politically toxic, as the visibility granted in these discursive mobilisations remains oxymoronic, as people who ought not to be. There is a lot at stake in trying to understand this case of intersectional visibility.

It is in this sense that I would like to finally invoke the conference that gave rise to this volume, and more particularly to the presentation of Kimberlé Crenshaw, whose work has been crucial to intersectionality debates. At the conference, a significant part of the general discussion was dominated by attempts to further the theorisation of intersectionality, so that gender studies could rightfully claim to have made a significant theoretical contribution to the scientific community. A number of well-known gender studies scholars who were present expressed their impatience with the lack of speed concerning this theorisation process. In a very different move, Crenshaw instead tried to remind the audience of the original impetus and political urgency that had led her to develop the concept of intersectionality in the first place (namely, the effort to analyse concrete circumstances of discrimination that could not be addressed without paying attention to the particular crossing of race and gender dimensions that characterised a specific labour litigation case in the United States) (see Crenshaw in this volume). And Crenshaw finally ended with the following statement, uttered not without a hint of irony: 'Intersectionality is what is done by people who are doing the doing.'

This is anything but an obvious, self-explanatory statement. What difference does the difference make, Crenshaw asked, and what is at stake when we are trying to understand diversity? What Crenshaw seemed to imply, with some disdain, was that intersectionality theory had come dangerously close to being mobilised as capital in the race for academic recognition, and to thereby neglecting the very struggles for equality and justice that had once given rise to the very concept of intersectionality.[11] Her statement can serve as an important reminder that concepts such as intersectionality are instruments for helping us think through something, that they are intended to do a certain labour, and we should stay aware of what we want that labour to be.

Bibliography

Ahmed, S. et al. (eds) 2003. *Uprootings/Regroundings: Questions of Home and Migration*. Oxford: Berg.

Alexander, J.M. 2005. *Pedagogies of Crossing: Meditations on Feminism, Sexual Politics, Memory, and the Sacred*. Durham and London: Duke University Press.

Anderson, B. 1993. *Imagined Communities: Reflections on the Origin and Spread of Nationalism* (2nd revised edition). London: Verso.

Anthias, F. 2001. The material and the symbolic in theorizing social stratification: issues of gender, ethnicity and class. *British Journal of Sociology*, 52, 367–390.

Anzaldúa, G. 1987. *La Frontera – Borderlands*. San Francisco: aunt lute books.

A Touch of Pink (dir. Ian Iqbal Rashid's, 2003).

Basch, L. et al. 1993. *Nations Unbound: Transnational Projects, Postcolonial Predicaments, and Deterritorialized Nation-States*. New York and London: Routledge and Curzon.

Bunzl, M. 2005. Between Anti-Semitism and Islamophobia: Some Thoughts on the New Europe, *American Ethnologist*, 32(4), 499–508.

Burchell, G. et al. (eds) 1991. *The Foucault Effect. Studies in Governmentality*. Chicago: University of Chicago Press.

Castro Varela, M. and Dhawan, N. 2005. Spiel mit dem 'Feuer' – Post/Kolonialismus und Heteronormativität. *Femina Politica*, 1, 47–59.

Castro Varela, M. and Dhawan, N. 2009. Queer mobil? Heteronormativität und Migrationsforschung, in *Gender Mobil? Geschlecht und Migration, in Transnationalen Räumen*, edited by Lutz, H. Münster: Westfälisches Dampfboot, 102–21.

Combahee River Collective. 1983 (originally published 1977). A Black Feminist Statement, in *This Bridge Called my Back. Writings by Radical Women of Color*, edited by Moraga, C. and Anzaldúa, G. New York: Kitchen Table Press, 210–18.

Crenshaw, K. 1989. Demarginalizing the Intersection of Race and Sex: A Black Feminist Critique of Antidiscrimination Doctrine, Feminist Theory, and Antiracist Politics. *Chicago Legal Forum*, 139–67.

---

11 For a similar concern see also the introduction to this volume.

Cruz-Malavé, A. and Manalansan, M. (eds) 2002. *Queer Globalizations: Citizenship and the Afterlife of Colonialism*. New York and London: New York University Press.

Donato, K.M. et al. 2006. A glass half full? Gender in migration studies. *International Migration Review*, 40(1), 3–26.

El-Tayeb, F. 2003. Begrenzte Horizonte. Queer Identity in der Festung Europa, in *Spricht die Subalterne Deutsch? Migration und Postkoloniale Kritik*, edited by Steyerl, H. and Gutiérrez Rodríguez, E. Münster: Unrast, 129–45.

Fire (dir. Deepa Mehta, 1996).

Fortier, A. 2002. Queer Diasporas, in *Handbook of Lesbian and Gay Studies*, edited by Richardson, D. and Seidman, S. London: Sage, 183–97.

Foucault, M. 1978. *The History of Sexuality, Vol.1: An Introduction*. New York: Pantheon Books.

Gilroy, P. 2004. It's a Family Affair, in *That's the Joint! The Hip-Hop Studies Reader*, edited by Forman, M. and Neal, M. London: Routledge, 87–94.

Gopinath, G. 2002. Local Sites, Global Contexts: The Transnational Trajectories of Deepa Mehta's *Fire*, in *Queer Globalizations: Citizenship, Sexualities and the Afterlife of Colonialism*, edited by Cruz Malave, A. and Manalansan, M. New York: University Press, 149–61.

Grewal, I. and Kaplan, C. (eds) 1994. *Scattered Hegemonies: Postmodernity and Transnational Feminist Practices*. Minneapolis: University of Minnesota Press.

Grewal, I. and Kaplan, C. 2001. Global Identities: Theorizing Transnational Studies of Sexuality. *GLQ*, 7(4), 663–79.

Grewal, I. 2005. *Transnational America: feminisms, diasporas, neoliberalisms*. Durham: Duke University Press.

Gutiérrez Rodríguez, E. and Steyerl, H. (eds) 2003. *Spricht die Subalterne deutsch? Postkoloniale Kritik und Migration*. Münster: Unrast.

Halberstam, J. 2005. *In a Queer Time and Place: Transgender Bodies, Subcultural Lives*. New York: New York University Press.

Haritaworn, J., Tauqir, T. and Erdem, E. 2007. Queer-Imperialismus: Eine Intervention in die Debatte über 'muslimische Homophobie', in *re/visionen. Postkoloniale Perspektiven von People of Color auf Rassismus, Kulturpolitik und Widerstand in Deutschland*, edited by Ha, K.-N. et al. Münster: Unrast, 187–205.

Hull, G., Bell-Scott, P. and Smith, B. (eds) 1982. *All the Women are White, all the Blacks are Men, but Some of Us are Brave*. New York: Feminist Press.

Klinger, C. 2003. Ungleichheit in den Verhältnissen von Klasse, Rasse und Geschlecht, in *Achsen der Differenz. Gesellschaftstheorie und feministische Kritik II*, edited by Knapp, G.-A. and Wetterer, A. Münster: Westfälisches Dampfboot, 14–48.

Knapp, G.-A. 2005. Intersectionality – ein neues Paradigma feministischer Theorie? Zur transatlantischen Reise von 'Race, Class, Gender'. *Feministische Studien*, 23, 68–81.

Kofman, E. 1999. Female 'birds of passage' a decade later: gender and immigration in the European Union. *International Migration Review*, 33(2), 269–99.

Lola and Bilidikid (dir. Kutluğ Ataman, 1999).

Lorde, A. (1983). The Master's Tools will never dismantle the Master's House, in *This Bridge Called my Back. Writings by Radical Women of Color*, edited by Moraga, C. and Anzaldúa, G. New York: Kitchen Table Press, 94–101.

Luibhéid, E. and Cantú, L. (eds) 2005. *Queer Migrations: Sexuality, U.S. Citizenship, and Border Crossings*. Minneapolis: University of Minnesota Press.

Lutz, H. 1995. Ist Kultur Schicksal? Über die gesellschaftliche Konstruktion von Kultur und Migration, in *Getürkte Bilder. Zur Inszenierung von Fremden im Film*, edited by Karpf, E. et al. Marburg: Schüren (Arnoldshainer Filmgespräche, Band 12), 77–98.

Lutz, H. and Wenning, N. (eds) 2001. Differenzen über Differenz – Einführung in die Debatten, in *Unterschiedlich verschieden. Differenz in der Erziehungswissenschaft*. Opladen: Leske und Budrich, 11–24.

Manalansan, M. 2006. Queer Intersections: Sexuality and Gender in Migration Studies. *International Migration Review*, 40(1), 224–49.

Mohanty, C.T. and Alexander, J.M. (eds) 1997. *Feminist Genealogies, Colonial Legacies, Democratic Futures*. New York: Routledge.

Morokvasic, M. 1984. Birds of Passage are also Women. *International Migration Review*, 18(4), 886–907.

Mosse, G. 1985. *Nationalism and Sexuality: Middle-Class Morality and Sexual Norms in Modern Europe*. Wisconsin: University of Wisconsin Press.

Needham, A. and Rajan, R. (eds) 2007. Introduction, in *The crisis of secularism in India*. Durham, NC: Duke University Press, 1–42.

Randazzo, T. 2005. Social and legal barriers: sexual orientation and asylum in the United States, in *Queer Migrations: Sexuality, U.S. Citizenship, and Border Crossings*, edited by Luibhéid, E. and Cantú, L. Minneapolis: University of Minnesota Press, 30–60.

Rubin, G. 1975. The traffic in women: notes on the 'political economy' of sex, in *Toward an Anthropology of Women*, edited by Reiter, R. New York: Monthly Review Press, 157–210.

Safran, W. 1991. Diasporas in modern societies: myths of homeland and return. *Diaspora*, 1(1), 83–99.

Stoler, A. 1995. *Race and the Education of Desire. Foucault's History of Sexuality and the Colonial Order of Things*. Durham: Duke University Press.

Wedding Banquet (dir. Ang Lee, 1993).

Yuval-Davis, N. and Anthias, F. (eds) 1989. *Woman-Nation-State*. Basingstoke: Palgrave Macmillan.

Zarkov, D. 2001. The body of the other man: sexual violence and the construction of masculinity, sexuality and ethnicity in Croatian media, in *Victims, Perpetrators or Actors? Gender, Armed Conflict and Political Violence*, edited by Moser, C. and Clark, F. London: Zed Books, 69–82.

Chapter 8

Psychosocial Intersections: Contextualising the Accounts of Adults Who Grew Up in Visibly Ethnically Different Households

Ann Phoenix

Introduction

Intersectionality is a 'bottom–up' concept in that it has arisen from observation and analysis of everyday practices and social positioning, rather than being introduced 'top–down' from any one discipline or theorist. The oft-cited 1977 manifesto of the Combahee River black lesbian collective, for example, was crafted from the experiences of black women (including their own) in relation to black men and white women. It was inductive in being grounded in, and generated from, their analyses of those experiences and political resistance to the silencing and invisibility that could arise from their gendered, racialised positioning. While the concept was named as a result of observations in the discipline of law (Crenshaw 1989, this volume), its utility for understanding the complexity of the everyday has led to its being adopted and adapted in many disciplines. This transdisciplinary accessibility also partly results because the concept caught 'something in the air' (Lutz 2009) by naming and foregrounding a perspective that had long constituted a site of political contestation over (de)racialisation of the category woman and the invisibility of lesbians and working class women in early 'second wave' feminist work (Lykke 2005).

One of the major contributions of intersectional analysis is that it has made it commonplace to recognise the importance of analysing the ways in which people are simultaneously positioned in multiple categories. Intersectionality holds the promise of theorisation and analyses that are non-essentialising and reflect the complexity of everyday life, rather than reducing it to single analytic categories that obscure the complexity of commonalities and differences in social positioning and experience. How best this can be achieved, however, remains at issue and is subject to debate. The proliferation of work both about, and drawing on, intersectionality includes numerous meta-theoretical analyses of the concept that indicate that it is particularly useful in the analysis of everyday lives and practices, hence its transdisciplinary appeal (for example Buitelaar 2006, Ludwig 2006, Prins 2006, Taylor 2009).

This chapter uses intersectionality as an epistemological and ontological tool to analyse accounts from a study of adults looking back on 'non-normative' childhood experiences produced through growing up in households which were visibly ethnically different. It employs intersectional analyses to examine the complexity of transnational family lives and experiences for four research participants. The analyses illustrate how psychosocial intersectional analyses are multilevel, able to illuminate the situated, contingent nature of (reconstructed) experience and identities and how individuals can fruitfully be understood within the specific social contexts they negotiate.

Intersectionality as a Multilevel Analytical Tool

The question of how to analyse and understand differences, which is at the heart of intersectionality, is thorny and puzzling. In attempting to keep multiple categories simultaneously in view, intersectionality is sometimes criticised for treating all differences as equivalent and, hence, interchangeable when they have different logics and operate at different levels (Verloo 2006, Yuval-Davis 2006). Intersectionality thus is used to deal with different, incoherent, theoretical concerns (Choo and Ferree 2010). This is perhaps not surprising given the complexity of attempting to analyse the intersection of different social structures while recognising that the different levels interpenetrate, but are not interchangeable. Nicola Beisel and Tamara Kay (2004) help to address the issue of how categories with different logics can be analysed as intersectional by arguing that social structures incorporate cultural resources and so are simultaneously cultural and material (and hence multilevel). This means that racialised structures, for example, are partly expressed through everyday cultural practices, whether people are complicit with, reproduce, resist or transform expectations of what it is to belong to particular racialised categories through their everyday practices. People can, and do, transform social structures through their practices (Bourdieu 1984).

Intersectional analyses are consonant with Beisel and Kay's (2004) argument that it is important to grapple with the complexity of simultaneously foregrounding structure and viewing it as open to change and modulated by culture. They help with this in two ways that are sometimes not recognised. First, analysing any level, whether macro- or micro-social, helps to contextualise other levels. This multi-level analytic potential is demonstrated in studies that use situated microanalysis of everyday practices and identity narratives. For example, Marjo Buitelaar's (2006) analysis of the accounts of a Dutch Muslim woman politician shows that examination of the ways in which she orchestrates intersectional 'I' voices in her narratives gives simultaneous insights into her social positioning as well as her identities. Similar processes can be seen in Gail Lewis's (2009) analysis of a research encounter where she, as a black woman researcher, encounters a white woman social work manager whose racist discourse evokes rage, vengeance and hatred in her. Lewis contextualises her analysis by examining the manager's intersecting social positioning and the nuanced and shifting power relations in which she is positioned and agentically positions herself. Equally, Kathy Davis (2007), starting from a different level – the analysis of the global reception of the feminist health handbook, *Our Bodies Ourselves* – discusses the multiple levels at which the book is received by situating its reception in cultural and transnational epistemological currents as well as its emotional impact. In a similar way, quantitative intersectional analyses are able to illuminate shifting constellations of commonalities and differences and so different possibilities for subjective positioning. Intersectionality can thus be viewed as fitting with psychosocial analyses by simultaneously contextualising the psychological and social.

Second, intersectionality is simultaneously epistemological and ontological. It is a social theory of knowledge in that it is predicated on the notion of knowledge as situated and so necessarily differentiated since people occupy different social positions. At the same time, knowledge is necessarily subject to change since people always occupy multiple social positions and the ways in which people are positioned change over time and according to circumstances. Knowledge is, therefore, always partial, dynamic and subject to the interplay of power relations. This epistemology constructs ontological subjects as multiple, constructed through difference, complex and non-essentialist and so subject to change. These notions, of knowledge as partial, dynamic and situated and being as multiple, complex and in process are central to intersectionality and fit with many current ways of theorising identities and social positions. This does not mean, however, that everyone who subscribes to intersectionality agrees on how to conceptualise this partial and situated knowledge and being. There is, for example, a potential contradiction between ways of constructing difference that make particular differences the focus of identities and those that refuse the making of political claims on the basis of categorical sameness (as 'we') (Gressgård 2008, Knapp 2005, Prins 2006). The tension between standpoint epistemologies, which privilege knowledge constructed from ontological experience, and the deconstruction of categorical thinking, facilitates multilevel analysis in that it requires both a focus on people's own perspectives and on social categories at different levels as well as the questioning of the appropriateness of categories in particular contexts.

The utility of intersectional analyses of empirical research means that those who eschew intersectionality have to find other conceptualisations that do similar work. Ivy Ken (2008: 152), for example, seeks to 'articulate new imagery – via a metaphor of sugar ... [to highlight] how race, class, and gender are produced, used, experienced, and processed in our bodies, human and institutional. This metaphor allows us to emphasise structural and individual forces at work in their continual and mutual constitution.' Ken's focus is on the ways in which, in particular contexts, interacting forces transform processes, in ways that are more profound than Ken considers to be captured by the notion of intersectionality. Her analogy with growing sugar cane and then digesting sugar is designed to capture the multiple, major transformations that occur in the processes and social relations of production (including racialisation, postcolonialism and gender) and of ingesting and making it part of the body. Her extended metaphor of the production, sale and use of sugar is compelling in refusing notions of intersections as just meeting and passing points. However, it loses flexibility in that sugar, baked in cakes, for example, is not reversible, separable or able to change in new ways that do not require its destruction. There have also been some earlier partially comparable metaphors that seek to do some of the same work Ken's sugar metaphor is designed to do. For example, Maria Lugones (1994) used the metaphor of separating eggs, then blending them with oil to form mayonnaise, always with the risk that they can unexpectedly curdle. A rather different metaphor has been developed by Floya Anthias(2008), who prefers the term 'translocational positionality' to move away from notions of pre-given 'groups' or 'categories', such as of gender, ethnicity and class and, instead, treats intersections as fluid, contradictory and involving social locations and processes that are broader than the social categories usually analysed as intersecting. Anthias is, however, clear that she aims to retain an intersectional framing.[1]

The sections that follow apply an intersectional and psychosocial approach to analysing accounts from adults who, as children, spent time living in 'non-normative' family situations, all of which were constituted through transnational migration (although not always for the participants themselves).[2] It attends to whether intersectional analyses can address the criticisms often made of it in terms of whether it can illuminate the inextricable linking of individual and social processes (that is, multilevel analyses). The analyses highlight the ways in which experiences and identities are situated, contingent and located (Anthias 2009, Prins 2006, Staunaes 2003).

The Study

The narrative accounts analysed below come from a UK Economic and Social Research Council Professorial Fellowship programme of work called 'Transforming Experiences: Re-conceptualising identities and "non-normative" childhoods'.[3] The fellowship was concerned with the ways in which adults from different family backgrounds re-evaluate their earlier experiences over time. It aimed to help understand the factors that produce adult citizens who lead 'normal' lives despite having childhood experiences that have received little attention and are often not recognised because they do not fit expected patterns. It focused on adults from varied ethnicised groupings who grew up in three kinds of 'non-normative' contexts: (i) serial migration, where the adults came as children from the Caribbean to Britain to rejoin parents (N=53); (ii) adults who grew up in visibly ethnically different families (N=41); (iii) 'language brokers', who sometimes interpreted

---

1   See also Ferree in this volume.

2   An intersectional approach to transnationality is also suggested by Jeff Hearn in this volume.

3   ESRC Professorial Fellowship, Award number: RES-051-27-0181. Ann Phoenix was the professorial fellow and Elaine Bauer and Stephanie Davis-Gill were research fellows on the project.

and/or translated for their parents in childhood (N=40). For groups (ii) and (iii), a few participants were interviewed outside the UK, in Australia, Italy, Sweden and the USA. Once all the individual interviews were completed, participants were invited to feedback sessions for the groups to which they recruited into the study. The discussions of seven focus group interviews were recorded after presentations of the early analyses. This chapter focuses on only one part of the study: adults who grew up in households where they were visibly ethnically different.

The interviews are thematically analysed to provide an overview of the findings. Interviews are then selected for detailed narrative analysis on the basis of the particular issues they raise and are often analysed jointly in the project team and sometimes with other groups of researchers. Narrative analysis is particularly suited to the study of non-normative lives in that, while narratives are so ubiquitous that the importance of storytelling was recognised in Aristotle's Poetics and humans have been referred to as 'homo narrans', storytelling people (Bruner 1991, Fisher 1987, MacIntyre 1984), narratives are most likely to be developed to account for the self when lives are 'interrupted' (Riessman 2002, 2008). Narrative analysis also gives insight into the culture, making it possible to analyse canonical narratives about the way life ought to be lived in the culture (Bruner 1990) and the narrative identities that are normative for a generation (McAdams 2006). Narrative analysis has been successfully deployed in several pieces of research conducting intersectional analyses (see, for example, Buitelaar 2006, Dahl and Malin 2009, Hernández 2008, Ludwig 2006, Prins 2006).

Intersectional and Multilevel Analyses of Shifting, Situated Disjunctions in Identities

Over the last two decades 'mixed parentage' has increasingly been recognised and researched as specific identities (for example, Ali 2003, Caballero et al. 2008, Ifekwunigwe 2004, Song 2009).[4] Work on 'mixed parentage' sometimes discusses, or at least mentions, that children with the same parents can have different shades of skin colour (England 2009). Julie Cunningham (1997) found that 'colorism' was reported to have had a profound effect on the 11 'light skin blacks' aged 21–59 in the USA she interviewed – all of whom had two parents who were African American. She found that several of them reported that their families contained people who ranged widely in colour. Many reported difficult experiences to do with colour during their adolescence because people seemed uncertain about who they were and because some of their own family members did not accept them. Such experiences are also reported in popular media. The Canadian actress and singer Gloria Reuben, for example, has said that her siblings were 'all different shades', which made it difficult growing up in London, Ontario, because it was

---

4   This is the case for the UK, much less so for the rest of Europe, see also the introduction to this volume.

a somewhat segregated, conservative area. Little is known, however, about the impact of growing up in a visibly mixed household, an experience that children of all ethnicised/racialised groups increasingly experience. The study of adults who grew up in visibly ethnically different households aimed to gain understandings of this experience. Most of the sample was of mixed parentage, from a variety of ethnicised and racialised backgrounds (32 of 41). However, nine of the participants either had two black or two white birth parents and had spent time in foster, adoptive or step-parent families or had parents of the same colour, but looked sufficiently different from them or their siblings for this to have been remarked on in childhood.

The participants in the study of adults who grew up in visibly ethnically different households generally told stories of coming to understandings of how others saw them through experiences of being differentially positioned in different circumstances and from family members. Their experiences were situationally specific and frequently involved disjunctions that led them to develop identities through struggle to understand the relational specificity of, and power relations involved in, their positioning. They commonly narrated a process of coming to recognise their racialised/ethnicised/chromatic positioning and, often, their households and families as unusual in being visibly ethnically different. This section presents examples from four participants who illustrate the utility of intersectionality in analyses of these issues. The quotations that follow have been transcribed to include some paralinguistic features and repetitions, and so on, in order to facilitate analysis of emotions, fluency and lack of fluency. The transcription conventions used are presented in the footnote below.[5]

Negotiating Disjunctive Situated Identities

Isaac's account highlights how growing up in two separate ethnically different households produced identities that were inextricably and complexly intersectional.

> …So I, one of the strongest parts of my identity I would say is, I–I feel I've been socialised in a predominantly white working class background, so I identify strongly with white working class lads from that background. <u>However</u> when

---

5   **Transcription conventions:**
… represents talk omitted
<u>Underlining</u> represents louder talk
Italics represents emphasis
(text inside brackets) represents a substitution for the words actually spoken
[text in square brackets] represents an explanation by the author
(.) represents a pause of less than two seconds
All participants' names used are pseudonyms

I'm outside of (area in Manchester), people think I'm, because I'm mixed race and I looked mixed race. People don't naturally associate me as connected with the white working class side of my cultural identity which to me is stronger than my mixed race identity. Because it's something I've lived with more and I think something around which I've built my identity. And as I've gotten older I've added more things to myself but the core of me, is that…

… What I did do at some point was internalise external opinions of my identity. And I learnt that via the other adults around me, within the extended white family and also within my Jamaican family. Never been black enough to be black or white enough to be white and whenever an issue or discussion would happen around mixed identity, people would say oh stop trying to make yourself special, stop (.) talking about it. They would dismiss it. So I would in some ways have to minimise anything which was, externally different to a white background. So if I'd been to my father's for the weekend I would have to minimise talking Jamaican patois or the way I would walk or the way I would move because I was obviously looking to my father for some kind of behavioural identity. When I bring that behaviour back to my mum's it was always frowned upon, or I'm sure it wasn't on a conscious level, I'm sure it was very unconscious thing because lots of my family didn't understand my experiences within my Jamaican family, outside of them. So I had an absolute definite different experience with my father at weekends, than I did when I was back with my other white brothers. (.) And yeah it's just fascinating to see how I've kind of absorbed all those experiences and I wasn't able to articulate any of these emotions, feelings, thoughts at the time. I used to explain to my older white brothers that they were er– (.) they were always in a majority. I felt I was in a majority when I was at home, within my family house but when I came out of there I was in a minority and because they were male, they were quite strong, and good looking guys they were never in a minority so they didn't understand that experience. And again I would have my identity brought into question, and get into trouble around that because people called me nigger or paki or all that ridiculous stuff that people do. (.) Yeah and that's how I learnt. ('Isaac', 40s, UK-born, of mixed parentage)

In the above example, Isaac's account illustrates one reason that intersectionality is fruitful for research analyses; intersectional thinking is an everyday heuristic device (c.f. Knapp this volume) central to the negotiation of identities. Isaac orients to negotiations of gendered/racialised/classed and familial identifications as central to the development of his identities and constructs these as relational. He talks of learning his identity by internalising what people around him thought of him and his account indicates that he also learned different cultural practices at his mother's and his father's homes. His learning about the situatedness of practices and identities was not only disjunctive between the two households in which he grew up, but between 'at home', where he felt 'in the majority' and 'out' (where he was called racist names). In racialised terms, his black and white relatives attempted to deny him black, white and 'mixed' positionings. His 'mixed' identity was, therefore, developed as a result of struggle and in resistance to his family at the same time that he both identified with his black father and continues to identify most strongly with his 'white', working class, masculine (and local) identities. This struggle and resistance demonstrates Isaac's agency in negotiating everyday practices, in producing explanations of his identities and positioning and in his reactions to racism and his resistance to racialised outsider ascriptions. Isaac appeals to the psychosocial in that he discusses unconscious processes, identifications, identities and emotions as well as societal issues represented in terms of outsider definitions of where he belongs and racism. He presents a dynamic view of himself in that, in the rest of his narrative, he recognises that both he and society have changed over time and that his experiences are geographically as well as historically located.

Isaac's account also demonstrates the now-accepted notion that siblings experience 'non-shared environments', rather than living in the same environment just because they share households (Dunn and Plomin 1990, Turkheimer and Waldron 2000). In Isaac's case an intersectional approach highlights how shared gender intersects with racialised difference to produce a complex and dynamic constellation of commonalities and differences (in addition to other differences that separate siblings' experiences). An intersectional analysis of Isaac's account thus highlights the complexity and shifting nature of his positioning and of power relations in the development of identities. It does so even though the focus of the study is on a particular aspect of racialisation; growing up in visibly ethnically different households.

First Encounters with the Puzzle of Disjunctive Positioning

The example below, from Sylvia, adds to understanding of how disjunctive experiences of being positioned differently in different circumstances help children to be meta-analytic about their positioning and identities.

> As soon as I hit the school age, there are things, there are some distinct memories so for example there was an Irish family who lived across further down the road, and a Pakistani family who lived opposite me. And the girls in the Pakistani family were good friends and we used to walk to school together but the Irish family were terrible racists and they had a dog and they used to set their dog on us to chase us up the road after school. And they didn't see any difference between me and the Caribbean family next door to me or the Pakistani family across the road. So I knew that I had things in common with those and yet the dog wouldn't be set on my white cousins when they came or the white friend I had who was further up the road, so you know that was probably from about the age of five so those sorts of things kind of set you apart from other members of your family or your peers who are white and it's all about being visibly different.

Because I wasn't like the Pakistani girls, in this Pakistani household which had, which clearly differentiated itself, my household was essentially a white Anglo-Saxon household you know. The food we ate, the language we spoke was, there was nothing that kind of set itself out as different, the only thing different was essentially the way I looked. ('Sylvia', mixed parentage, 30s)

Sylvia presents her developing understanding as akin to solving a jigsaw puzzle. She could see that the Irish family racialised her as like Caribbean and Pakistani children and viewed her as different from her white cousins and friends. Yet, she could also see that her family had different cultural practices from the Pakistani family. The disjunction between how she was treated outside the house and her family and cultural practices led her to come to the conclusion that her (mixed-parentage) visible difference from her white family set her apart from them. As with Isaac, above, her account suggests that she came to understand the situational specificity of racialisation, her family as unusual in being visibly ethnically different and herself as the source of difference. At the same time, the fact that the Caribbean and Pakistani girls were also subject to attack meant that she could see that racism did not result from her personal characteristics. The analysis of Sylvia's account requires that intersectional analysis is taken beyond the Big Three of 'race', class and gender that are most analysed (Davis, this volume). For while racialisation and gender are explicit and social class implicit, age is also highlighted in her account; it is when she becomes of school age and can walk to school with friends that she is exposed to the disjunctions that fuel consciousness of racialised identities. Sylvia also orients to issues of everyday cultural practices and household composition as central to the development of her identities and to her professed determination to have black partners so that her own child(ren) will not share her experience of growing up in a visibly ethnically different household.

Arguably, without a concept of intersectionality (however named) it would be easier to focus only on issues of racialisation and ethnicisation, which are a major focus of the research and of Sylvia's account. One of the contributions of an intersectional focus is to serve as a reminder that all social categories and identities are decentred by others (Rattansi and Phoenix 2005), highlighting the need for an approach that allows an inductive focus on what participants make relevant, both explicitly and through researcher analysis (Staunaes 2003).

Negotiating Geographical Disjunctions in Racialised Power Relations

As can be seen in the two examples above (Isaac and Sylvia), the invitation to reflect on the experience of growing up in visibly ethnically different households commonly produced accounts of disjunction and memories made salient because the participants recognised themselves to be in relatively powerless positions. Odette, in the extract below, illustrates the intersection of racialisation and geography when she moved from Nigeria, where she spent her first few years, to a rural school in the UK and experienced a shift from being more to being less powerful, valued and recognised in the racialised terms she expected.

Q: What do you remember about first coming [to the UK]?

Odette: Um, feeling very cold and umm going to school and nobody in school realising I was mixed race. Everyone thought I was black. And there was one other group (.) one other black family in the whole school and they were three sisters and they were very very dark. And people couldn't tell the difference between me and them. And, not that I particularly minded to be dark or anything but I was shocked that people couldn't tell the difference between (.) um me being mixed race and (.) now I'm extremely light skinned um I was probably a bit darker when I came then and and and then and even in my sister's class she had someone who refused to believe that her mum was white (.) (Odette, mixed parentage, moved from Nigeria).

The 'shock' that Odette recalls partly results from what Knapp (this volume) calls 'intersectional invisibility' (in keeping with Crenshaw's (1989, this volume) concerns about the invisibility of black women in jurisprudence). Her 'mixedness', which she explains was visible, and highly valued, in Nigeria, was (at the time she came) invisible in the UK context. However, part of the complexity of the example is that she was simultaneously highly intersectionally visible, but as black, not mixed. Odette's relative powerlessness here resides in her inability to be defined as she wished (since she wanted to maintain the distinction between 'mixedness' and blackness she was used to in Nigeria) and in finding that she was immediately constructed as of low status in her UK school. While Odette only mentions 'shock', and says that she did not 'particularly mind' being dark, her account is emotionally marked in that she pauses (indicated by (.)) and repeats 'and and and and' in discussing her first exposure to racialisation in the UK, suggesting that the memory puts her into a 'troubled subject position' (Wetherell 1998). Difference was at the heart of her emotional responses.

Odette's account demonstrates the socially constructed nature of categories and the geographical and historical particularities of the intersection of national and racialised identities and histories of classification. In Nigeria, she had been used to being called 'white' and to be viewed as favourably different from the local population because of her colour. The change she experienced in coming to the UK was particularly disjunctive because, as a young child, she had no conceptual framework through which to understand this conceptual paradigm shift in her social world and insufficient power to make other people accept her view. Intersectionality was central to the development of her racialised positioning in that the geographical move produced a disjunctive shift. This provides another indication of how identities are always intersectional and decentre and mutually constitute each other as well as always being marked by the macrosocial.

Agency is evident in Odette's account. She demonstrates active negotiation of her ethnicised positioning in her refusal of the positions other people constructed for her (to herself, if not to them) and her critical examination of her everyday experiences in the light of her past experiences and expectations. Her resistance to being thought 'black' at a time when it was common in the UK for people of mixed parentage to be considered black gives an insight into the impetus for racialised categorisations to change, as 'mixed' categories have over the last 30 years. It also indicates that, even though discussing these issues put Odette into a somewhat troubled subject position, this narrative is made easier, and indeed possible, by social changes that make 'mixed parentage' (however termed) a recognisable and allowable category.

Imagining Gendered/Racialised Situated Positioning

Not only is intersectional thinking part of an everyday heuristic, but it is part of the everyday imagining of liveable life and of the characteristics that produce particular identity positions. Some participants demonstrate this by invoking the hypothetical as they attempt to think through the impact of their childhood experiences.

> Charlene: I think I would have struggled ... if I had two sisters, I probably would have found it harder and less part of the family, especially. And I think at an early age you pick up the hierarchy around skin colour. You look in any book, you didn't see any black princesses, you didn't see anything like that. So if I had two sisters that maybe looked like Edwina [who is of mixed parentage] is, more fairer skin and straighter hair, I would have found it very difficult. People sort of made comparisons ... (Black woman with two mixed-parentage brothers)

The above example benefits from intersectional analyses in four ways. First, it shows how the ubiquity of intersectionality as a heuristic makes imagined commonalities and differences central to struggles for identity. Second, it illuminates shifting commonalities and differences across socially constructed boundaries. Charlene felt that she shared a sense of insiderness and belonging within her family that she feared she would not have done if she had a sister who, like her brothers, had been of mixed parentage. She bases this on her experience of how people in general compare sisters who are racialised differently and the ways in which popular culture excludes black girls but values the hair, and sometimes the skin colour, of girls of mixed parentage. She, therefore, imagined a greater sense of commonality with her mixed-parentage brothers across constructed gendered and racialised differences that she feels she would not have shared if they had been sisters. Third, it exemplifies the mutual constitution of categories in that racialisation and gender are constructed in Charlene's account as co-constituted (Lewis 2000). Fourth, she invokes relationality in that other people's reactions have an impact and produce power relations that, in this case, make the negotiation of racialised identities a painful struggle. This relationality is both direct ('People sort of made comparisons') and indirect in cultural products such as children's story books and macrosocial constructions of racialised gendered intersections that made Charlene aware of 'the hierarchy around skin colour'.

Concluding Thoughts

This chapter has drawn on four examples from a study of adults who grew up in visibly ethnically different households to highlight ways in which intersectional analyses can fruitfully illuminate the psychosocial processes involved. In analysing narrative extracts, it has demonstrated that processes of racialisation, gendering and social class differentiation are routine, mundane and implicit aspects of familial (micro), school (meso) and societal (macro) practices. The four narrative accounts go beyond the 'Big Three' categories most frequently invoked in social analyses (Davis, this volume) by making relevant age, nation, locality, historical period and household cultural practices. All these intersections foreground relationality and the participants' accounts indicate that processes are experienced emotionally, often involve struggle over power relations and are continually reworked in memory, transforming experiences as adults negotiate new identities in dynamic processes. These reconstructed memories and the simultaneous multiple positioning they involved are central to the participants' current and future identities and practices. Many participants, for example, made decisions about how to rear their own children on the basis of their reconstructions of the impact of their childhoods on their identities.

Narrative analyses are theorised as allowing the interlinking of past, present and future (Rosenthal 2006). However, they also allow access to the ways in which the imagined is consequential in the development of identities and practices. Participants' accounts of the imaginary (for example, what could/would have been if circumstances were changed) were as much intersectional heuristic devices as were reconstructions of experiences.

The stories the participants told indicate that the disjunctions they experienced in different contexts were central to the negotiation of their identities. Such disjunctions frequently provide the conditions in which narratives are developed (Riessman 2008). In each of the examples above, the disjunctions narrated included their experiences with siblings and provided support for the notion of multiplicity in sibling cultures and emotions and so of 'non-shared' sibling environments (Dunn and Plomin 1990).

Intersectionality was fruitful in helping to take forward the analysis of multi-level analyses of psychosocial complexity (c.f. Yuval-Davis 2006) and of the ways in which power differentials are organised around mutually constituted social categories. While intersectionality is not the only theoretical framework that facilitates such analyses, it is a particularly fruitful epistemological and ontological concept that serves as a heuristic for theorising and analysing the situated, complex ways in which categories are co-constitutive. It enables analyses that are conceptually and analytically rich and non-formulaic. It is also a feminist democratic theory, whose very formulation encourages good, complex analyses with possibilities for development in a range of disciplines that are fruitful in leaving open possibilities for fruitful engagement with empirical accounts (Collins 1990, 1998, Davis 2008). As Bonnie T. Dill, Amy McLaughlin and Angel D. Nieves (2007) suggest, 'intersectionality is unique in its versatility and ability to produce new knowledge...[and to lay bare] the roots of power and inequality while continuing to pursue an activist agenda of social justice.'

Bibliography

Ali, S. 2003. *Mixed-Race, Post-Race, Gender, New Ethnicities and Cultural Practices*. Oxford: Berg.

Anthias, F. 2008. Thinking through the lens of translocational positionality: an intersectionality frame for understanding identity and belonging. *Translocations: Migration and Social Change: An Inter-Disciplinary Open Access E-Journal*, 4(1), 5–20.

Anthias, F. 2009. Translocational Belonging, Identity and Generation: Questions and Problems in Migration and Ethnic Studies. *Finnish Journal of Ethnicity and Migration*, 4(1), 6–15.

Beisel, N. and Kay, T. 2004. Abortion, race and gender in nineteenth-century America. *American Sociological Review*, 69(4), 498–518.

Bourdieu, P. 1984. *Distinction*. Cambridge, MA: Harvard University Press.

Bruner, J. 1990. *Acts of Meaning (the Jerusalem-Harvard Lectures)*. Cambridge, MA: Harvard University Press.

Bruner, J. 1991. The Narrative Construction of Reality. *Critical Inquiry*, 8(1), 1–21.

Buitelaar, M. 2006. 'I Am the Ultimate Challenge': Accounts of Intersectionality in the Life-Story of a Well-Known Daughter of Moroccan Migrant Workers in the Netherlands. *European Journal of Women's Studies*, 13(3), 259–76.

Caballero, C., Edwards, R. and Puthussery, S. 2008. *Parenting 'mixed' children: difference and belonging in mixed race and faith families*. York: Joseph Rowntree Foundation.

Choo, H.Y. and Ferree, M.M. 2010. 'Practicing intersectionality in sociological research: A critical analysis of inclusions, interactions and institutions in the study of inequalities'. *Sociological Theory*, 28(2), 129–49.

Collins, P.H. 1990. *Black Feminist Thought: Knowledge, Consciousness, and the Politics of Empowerment*. Boston: Unwin Hyman.

Collins, P.H. 1998. *Fighting Words: Black Women and the Search for Justice*. Minneapolis: University of Minnesota.

Crenshaw, K. 1989. Demarginalizing the intersection of race and sex: A black feminist critique of antidiscrimination doctrine, feminist theory and antiracist politics. *University of Chicago Legal Forum*, 139–68.

Cunningham, J. 1997. Colored existence: Racial identity formation in light-skin blacks. *Smith College Studies in Social Work*, 67(3), 375–400.

Dahl, I. and Malin, T. 2009. Oral history, constructions and deconstructions of narratives: Intersections of class, gender, locality, nation and religion in narratives from a Jewish woman in Sweden. *Journal*, 3 June. Available at: http://www.nottingham.ac.uk/shared/shared_enquire/PDFs/3rd_Dhal_and_Thor_Final.pdf [accessed: 21 June 2010].

Davis, K. 2007. *The Making of Our Bodies, Ourselves: How Feminism Travels Across Borders*. Durham, NC: Duke University Press.

Davis, K. 2008. Intersectionality as Buzzword: A Sociology of Science Perspective on What Makes a Feminist Theory Successful. *Feminist Theory*, 9(1), 67–85.

Dill, B.T., McLaughlin, A. and Nieves, A.D. 2007. Future directions of feminist research: Intersectionality, in *Handbook of Feminist Research: Theory and Praxis*, edited by Hesse-Biber, S.N. London: Sage, 629–38.

Dunn, J. and Plomin, R. 1990. *Separate Lives: Why siblings are so different*. New York: Basic Books.

England, S. 2009. Mixed and multiracial in Trinidad and Honduras: rethinking mixed-race identities in Latin America and the Caribbean. *Journal*, 1–19. Available at: http://dx.doi.org/10.1080/01419870903040169 [accessed: 21 June 2010].

Fisher, W. 1987. *Human Communication As Narration: Toward a Philosophy of Reason, Value, and Action*. Columbia: University of South Carolina Press.

Gressgård, R. 2008. Mind the gap: intersectionality, complexity and 'the event'. *Theory and Science*, 10(1), 1–16.

Hernández, T.K. 2008. The Intersectionality of Lived Experience and Anti-discrimination Empirical Research, in *Handbook of Employment Discrimination Research*, edited by Nielsen, L.B. and Robert, L. New York: Springer, 325–35.

Ifekwunigwe, J.O. (ed.). 2004. *'Mixed race' studies: A reader*. London: Routledge.

Ken, I. 2008. Beyond the Intersection: A New Culinary Metaphor for Race-Class-Gender Studies. *Sociological Theory*, 26(2), 152–72.

Knapp, G.-A. 2005. Race, Class, Gender: Reclaiming Baggage in Fast Travelling Theories. *European Journal of Women's Studies*, 12, 249–65.

Lewis, G. 2000. *'Race', Gender, Social Welfare: Encounters in a postcolonial society*. Cambridge: Polity.

Lewis, G. 2009. Animating Hatreds: Research Encounters, Organisational Secrets, Emotional Truths, in *Secrecy and Silence in the Research Process: Feminist Reflections*, edited by Gill, R. and Ryan-Flood, R. London: Psychology Press.

Ludwig, A. 2006. Differences between Women? Intersecting Voices in a Female Narrative. *European Journal of Women's Studies*, 13(3), 245–58.

Lugones, M. 1994. Purity, Impurity, and Separation. *Signs: Journal of Women in Culture and Society*, 19(2), 458–76.

Lutz, H. 2009. Coexisting inequalities and other pitfalls of the debate on intersectionality. Paper given at the conference 'Celebrating Intersectionality'. 21 January.

Lykke, N. 2005. Intersectionality Revisited: Problems and Potentials. *Kvinnovetenskapligtidskrift*, 2(3), 7–17.

MacIntyre, A. 1984. *After Virtue: A Study in Moral Theory*, 2nd ed. Notre Dame, IN: University of Notre Dame Press.

McAdams, D. 2006. *The Redemptive Self: Stories Americans Live By*. New York: Oxford University Press.

Mixed-Child. (undated) *The Pulse of the Mixed Community: Our Stories, Our Experiences: Defining who we are*. Available at: http://www.mixedchild.com/ Celebrities/Celeb_Quotes/Gemini.htm [accessed: 21 June 2010].

Prins, B. 2006. Narrative Accounts of Origins: A Blind Spot in the Intersectional Approach. *European Journal of Women's Studies*, 13(3), 277–90.

Rattansi, A. and Phoenix, A. 2005. Rethinking youth identities: Modernist and postmodernist frameworks. *Identity: An International Journal of Theory and Research*, 5(2), 97–123.

Riessman, C.K. 2002. Analysis of personal narratives, in *Handbook of Interview Research*, edited by Gubrium, J.F. and Holstein, J.A. Thousand Oaks, CA: Sage Publications, 695–710.

Riessman, C.K. 2008. *Narrative Methods for the Human Sciences*. Thousand Oaks, CA: Sage.

Rosenthal, G. 2006. The Narrated Life Story: On the Interrelation between Experience, Memory and Narration, in *Narrative, Memory and Knowledge*, edited by Milnes, K., Horrocks, C., Kelly, N., Roberts, B. and Robinson, D. Huddersfield: University of Huddersfield Press, 1–16.

Song, M. 2009. Siblings in 'mixed race' families, in *Putting Sibling Relationships on the Map: A Multi-Disciplinary Perspective*, edited by Klett-Davies, M. London: Family and Parenting Institute.

Staunaes, D. 2003. Where have all the subjects gone? Bringing together the concepts of intersectionality and subjectification. *NORA*, 11(2), 101–10.

Taylor, Y. 2009. Complexities and Complications: Intersections of Class and Sexuality. *Journal of Lesbian Studies*, 13, 189–203.

Turkheimer, E. and Waldron, M. 2000. Nonshared environment: A theoretical, methodological, and quantitative review. *Psychological Bulletin*, 126, 78–108.

Verloo, M. 2006. Multiple inequalities, intersectionality and the European Union. *European Journal of Women's Studies*, 13(3), 211–28.

Wetherell, M. 1998. Positioning and interpretative repertoires: Conversation analysis and post-structuralism in dialogue. *Discourse and Society*, 9, 387–412.

Yuval-Davis, N. 2006. Belonging and the politics of belonging. *Patterns of Prejudice*, 40(3), 197–214.

PART III
Advancing Intersectionality: Potentials, Limits and Critical Queries

Chapter 9

Beyond the Recognition and Re-distribution Dichotomy: Intersectionality and Stratification

Nira Yuval-Davis

'Politics of recognition', as an alternative and/or as a complement to the socialist politics or 'politics of redistribution', to use Nancy Fraser's terminology (2000), became more and more important during the 1970s and 1980s. This was due to a variety of historical, social and political developments which saw the decline of the older socialist movement and the fall of the Soviet Union and all that it supported in global politics.

In particular, this had to do with the important role identity politics movements have played in a growing number of social fields – gender, race, indigenous people, sexuality and disability, to name but a few. Social and political theorists, such as Charles Taylor (1992) and Michael Walzer (1992), have argued that the need for recognition is one of the driving forces behind nationalist and other identity (or 'subaltern') political movements. Taylor (1992: 32) claims that the increased significance of the politics of recognition in the public sphere is an outcome of the growing importance of two supposedly contradictory assumptions – relating on the one hand to human rights and the assumption that everyone is entitled to universal dignity and equal respect, and on the other hand to individuation, which draws attention to the different unique identities of different individuals and groups.

Socialist feminists, such as Fraser (2000), Seyla Benhabib (2002) and others, have acknowledged some validity in these arguments but insist that not every claim for recognition should be respected. Unless identity politics is complemented with a politics of redistribution, the emancipatory and progressive character of such an acknowledgment can be lost.

While acknowledging the important contribution of Fraser's approach to feminist and generally emancipatory politics, the argument of this chapter is that, although it is helpful as a heuristic device to highlight some of the weaknesses as well as the strengths of identity politics, the dichotomy of recognition and redistribution politics can ultimately be misleading. The chapter goes on to suggest that the politics of intersectionality can encompass and transcend both. The binary of recognition and redistribution was also recently acknowledged as the feminist contribution to sociological stratification theory and the rethinking of class issues (Crompton and Scott 2005). For the same reasons that the chapter argues for the politics of intersectionality to replace or rather encompass that of recognition/ redistribution, it also argues for intersectionality to be accepted as the most valid contemporary sociological theoretical approach to stratification.

This contribution, therefore, endorses Leslie McCall's claim (2005: 1771) that intersectionality is 'the most important theoretical contribution that Women's Studies, in conjunction with related fields, has made so far'. The next section of the chapter discusses intersectionality, before turning to examine how this concept relates to issues of 'recognition' and 'redistribution' and what contribution it can make to sociological stratification theories.

Intersectionality

As is widely recognised, the intersectionality approach has a long history. bell hooks (1981) chose the groundbreaking 1851 claim for recognition of Sojourner Truth, an emancipated slave, *'Ain't I a woman'*, as the title of her first book, which rejected the homogenisation of women's oppression by white feminists. Sojourner Truth was speaking at an abolitionist convention and argued that, given her position in society, she worked hard, carried heavy loads and so on, but this did not make her less of a woman and a mother than women from privileged backgrounds, who were constructed as weak and in need of constant help and protection as a result of what society considered to be 'feminine' ways.

Indeed, intersectional analysis, before it was 'mainstreamed', was carried for many years mainly by black and other racialised women who, from their situated gaze, perceived as absurd, not just misleading, any attempt made by feminists and others since the start of the second wave of feminism to homogenise women's situation or oppression and especially to treat it as an analogue to that of blacks. As hooks mockingly remarked in the introduction to her book: 'This implies that all women are White and all Blacks are men.'

However, what today can be called intersectional analysis was developed at roughly the same time by several European and post-colonial feminists (for example Bryan et al. 1985, James 1986, Lutz 1991) as well. As Sandra Harding claimed when she examined the parallel development of feminist standpoint theory:

> ... [F]eminist standpoint theory was evidently an idea whose time had come, since most of these authors worked independently and unaware of each other's work. (Standpoint theory would itself call for such a social history of ideas, would it not?) (Harding 1997: 389)

This was obviously the case also with the development of intersectionality theory. My own work in the field of intersectionality (although we called it 'social divisions' then) also started in the early 1980s when, in collaboration with Floya Anthias (for example 1983, 1992), I started to study gender and ethnic divisions in south-east London and at the same time became engaged in a debate with British black feminists, organised then in OWAAD[1] on the right way to theorise what would now be called an intersectional approach. As I have argued in a recent (2006a) article, some of the basic debates we had then continue to occupy those engaged in intersectional analysis today, after it became 'mainstreamed' and came to be accepted by the UN, the EU and many other equality and equity policy organisations in many countries. Some of the differences among those who use intersectionality have resulted from the different disciplines and purposes for which it is used.[2]

I outline below the main characteristics of the intersectional approach, which I would like to apply so as to transcend in feminist and sociological theory the dichotomy of recognition and redistribution. While doing so, I recognise the validity of other intersectional approaches that may be used for other purposes, as well as the sense of discomfort that many feminists (including myself) share regarding the term 'intersectionality' itself.

Intersectionality is a metaphorical term, aimed at evoking images of a road intersection with an indeterminate or contested number of intersecting roads, depending on the various users of the term and how many social divisions are considered in the particular intersectional analysis. As will be developed a bit further below, this can vary considerably from two to infinity. In a recent lecture, Kumkum Bhavnani (2008) used the term 'configurations' as an alternative metaphor, wanting to emphasise the flowing and interweaving threads that constitute intersectionality, which she found a much too rigid and fixed metaphor. Davina Cooper (2004: 12) explains that she uses the term 'social dynamics' rather than intersectionality, because she wants her terminology to trace the shifting ways relations of inequality become attached to various aspects of social life. While agreeing with all these reservations, which are important for the theorisation of intersectionality in this chapter, I do want to retain the term; it is so widely used that it evokes an intuitive understanding of the subject matter discussed, in spite of all the reservations.[3]

---

1   Organisation for Women of African and Asian Descent, set up in 1978 in the UK, defunct today.

2   Speaking at a panel on intersectionality at the American Sociological Conference in August 2009 in San Francisco, Kimberlé Crenshaw complained that those who use intersectionality for different purposes than the legal ones for which she originally developed the intersectional analysis make unwarranted critiques of her work. She aimed to make discriminated groupings such as black women legally visible. This is a justified complaint, and I would like to make clear that my approach and development of intersectionality consists of my application of it to sociological and feminist theory and has no implied critique of Crenshaw's legal theory.

3   In this respect the term 'intersectionality' resembles another term which I use often, that of 'fundamentalism'. Members of the organisation 'Women Against Fundamentalism', of which I am a co-founder (see Sahgal and Yuval-Davis, [1992] 2001), use the term while recognising that it is misleading in some ways and is often used in a racialised and

Two main positions in relation to the intersectionality approach used in this chapter need to be clarified here. The first relates to the division McCall makes between those approaches to intersectionality that she calls intercategorical and those she calls intracategorical; the second relates to the boundaries of the intersectional approach and thus the number of social categories included in intersectional analysis.

Inter- or Intra-categories?

According to McCall, different studies which have been using intersectional approaches differ as to whether they use an intercategorical or an intracategorical approach. By intercategorical approach she means focusing on the way the intersection of different social categories, such as race, gender, class and so on, affect particular social behaviour or distribution of resources.

Intracategorical studies, on the other hand, are less occupied in the relationships among various social categories but rather problematise the meaning and boundaries of the categories themselves, such as whether black women are included in the category 'women' or the shifting boundaries of who is considered to be 'black' in a particular place and time.

I do not see these two approaches as mutually exclusive, and call for an intersectionality approach which combines the sensitivity and dynamism of the intracategorical approach with the socio-economic perspective of the intercategorical approach. As I have argued elsewhere (2006b), I consider as crucial the analytical differentiation between different facets of social analysis – that of people's positionings along socio-economic grids of power; that of people's experiential and identificatory perspectives of where they belong; and that of their normative value systems. These different facets[4] are related to each other but are also irreducible to each other. Moreover, although I consider intersectional analysis to be a development of feminist standpoint theory, I argue that there is no direct causal relationship between the situatedness of people's gaze and their cognitive, emotional and moral perspectives on life. People born in the same families, with the same socio-economic background and geographical location, can have different identifications and political views (for example, see Phoenix's (137f) investigation of mixed-heritage siblings in this volume); people can identify themselves as belonging to the same racial or ethnic collectivity and have very different socio-economic backgrounds as well as different political and normative evaluations of these identity categories; and people can share the same

---

securitised way. However, no other term among those available carries with it the implicit recognition of the subject matter of the issues discussed.

4   In my previous work (for example 2006a and 2006b), I related to these different analytical dimensions as 'levels'. The term 'levels' assumes a hierarchy, and seems to be a remnant of the old Marxist infra- and super-structural levels. I am grateful to Cass Balchin for alerting me to this.

political and value systems but come from very different backgrounds as well as memberships in identity groupings. For this reason, it is not enough to construct intercategorical tabulations in order to predict, and even more so understand, people's positions and attitudes to life.

The Boundaries of Intersectional Analysis and Intersectional Categories

To quote McCall again (2005: 1774), she argues that 'in its emphasis on black women's experiences of subjectivity and oppression, intersectional theory has obscured the question whether all identities are intersectional or whether only mutually marginalised subjects have an intersectional identity'. Indeed, Kimberlé Crenshaw (1989: 139) defines intersectionality as 'the multidimensionality of marginalised subjects' lived experiences'. Other black feminists (for example Thornton Dill 1983, Bryan et al. 1985) also remain within the triad boundaries of race, class and gender. Philomena Essed (1991) even limits it to the two dimensions of 'gendered racisms' and 'racist genderisms'. Others have added the specific categories they were interested in, such as age (for example Bradley 1996), disability (for example Oliver 1995, Meekosha and Dowse 1997), sedentarism (for example Lentin 1999) or sexuality (for example Kitzinger 1987). In other works, however, feminists have attempted to develop complete lists and included in them many more categories – for example, Helma Lutz (2002) identifies 14 categories and Charlotte Bunch (2001) 16. Floya Anthias and I (1983, 1992; see also Yuval-Davis 2006a, forthcoming), strongly argue that intersectional analysis should not be limited only to those on the multiple margins of society, but rather that the boundaries of intersectional analysis should encompass all members of society and thus intersectionality should be seen as the right theoretical framework for analysing social stratification.[5]

In *Gender Trouble* (1990), Judith Butler mocks the 'etc' which often appears at the end of long (and different) lists of social divisions mentioned by feminists and sees it as an embarrassed 'sign of exhaustion as well as of the illimitable process of signification itself' (1990: 143, see also Villas's contribution in this volume (171f)). As Fraser (1997) and Gudrun-Axeli Knapp (1999) make clear, however, such a critique is valid only within the discourse of identity politics where there is a correspondence between social positionings or locations and identifications with particular social groupings. When no such conflation takes place, Knapp finds rightly that Butler's talk

> ... of an illimitable process of signification can be reductionist if it is generalized in an unspecified way... [and] runs the risk of levelling historically constituted 'factual' differences and thereby suppressing 'differences' on its own terms. (Knapp 1999: 130)

---

5   The point that intersectionality is also suited for the investigation of privileged social positions is also highlighted by Jeff Hearn in this volume (89f).

Knapp's critique of Butler clarifies again the crucial importance of the separation of the different analytical dimensions in which social divisions need to be examined. Nevertheless, the question remains whether there are, or are not, in any particular historical condition, a specific and limited number of social divisions that construct the grid of power relations within which the different members of the society are located.

As I have mentioned elsewhere (2006a), I have two different answers to this question which are not mutually exclusive. The first one is that while in specific historical situations and in relation to specific people there are some social divisions which are more important than others in constructing their specific positionings, there are some social divisions such as gender, stage in the life cycle, ethnicity and class which tend to shape most people's lives in most social locations while other social divisions such as disability or statelesness tend to affect fewer people globally. At the same time, for those who are affected by these and other social divisions not mentioned here, such divisions are crucial and one needs to fight to render them visible, as this is a case where recognition – of social power axes, not of social identities – is of crucial political importance. Therefore, the question of how many social divisions exist in every historical context is not necessarily fixed and is a product of political struggle as well as of an analytical process.

This is linked to my second answer, which relates to what Cornelius Castoriadis called the 'creative imagination' (1987; see also Stoetzler and Yuval-Davis 2002) that underlies any linguistic and other social categories of signification. Although certain social conditions may facilitate this, the construction of categories of signification is, in the last instance, a product of human creative freedom and autonomy. Without specific social agents who construct and point to certain analytical and political features, the rest of us would not be able to distinguish them. Rainbows include the whole spectrum of different colours, but how many colours we distinguish depends on our specific social and linguistic milieu. It is for this reason that struggles for recognition always also include an element of construction, and it is for this reason that studying the relationships between positionings, identities and political values is so important (and impossible if they are all reduced to the same ontological level).

The struggle for recognition, therefore, is inherently important to any intersectional analysis. It is time, then, to turn to discuss the construction and differentiation Fraser (2000) and others make between politics of recognition and politics of redistribution.

The Recognition/Redistribution Dilemma

When Lois McNay states her case *Against Recognition* (2008), she makes it clear in her introduction that she is not against recognition in the Hegelian sense, which is crucial to the dialogical and embodied way of constructing subjectivity (see also Yuval-Davis 2010), nor against the role of recognition in identity claims in social and political struggles which have played important roles in social and political transformations. Her challenge to recognition, which I would concur with and which will be developed below, is to recognition 'as an interpretive trope for explaining the centrality of identity claims to so many significant and political struggles' (McNay 2008: 2). This idea gained major theoretical currency after Charles Taylor's book on the politics of recognition (1992; see also Walzer 1992) and brought identity politics into social and political theory.

Fraser (1997) was not challenging the notion of recognition as such, but was looking more at the ways in which demands put forward by people as collective agents for recognition of their separate identities and culture can be reconciled with a more traditional socialist concern with the redistribution of wealth in compensation of class inequities. Rosemary Crompton and John Scott (2005) claim that she is following here the Weberian differentiation between economy and culture, but actually her goal is somewhat different. She differentiates between what she calls recognition and redistribution, while grappling with the dilemmas of justice and morality in the 'postsocialist' condition. Her basic argument is that certain, but not all, collective identities which are not class identities do affect issues of unequal distribution as well as recognition. She therefore calls gender and race bivalent collectivities that cut across the redistribution and recognition spectrum, while class relates to the redistributive model and what she calls 'despised sexualities' to the social and cultural recognition model. However, I am sure she would agree that such generalisations are historically and spatially specific; they are not inherently valid in every situation and are undergoing continuous processes of contestation and change.

What is most important to note here, however, is that Fraser sets up an analytical equivalence between the collective identities on the recognition and redistribution levels. However, they operate in very different ways and, as I mentioned earlier, belong to different analytical facets of social divisions. While people can identify exclusively with one identity category, collectivity or grouping – whether as women, as black, as gays and so on – their social location is concretely constructed along multiple, if mutually constitutive, intersected categories of social power. While gaining social and political recognition of an identity grouping can positively affect, and sometimes even transform, the social location of those who identify and/or are identified as belonging to this collectivity (although often such a positive transformation affects only a dominant minority among the members of this grouping), the two cannot be equated.

While struggles for recognition often involve reification and essentialisation (or, at least 'strategic essentialism', to use Gayatri Spivak's term [1993]) the conflation of the different analytical facets can be used to cover up intersected power relations within the members of the identity grouping. Very often the promoters of particular struggles for recognition are more articulate, better educated, better connected and better resourced in other ways than other members of the grouping, and their social locations are significantly different in many ways from those of others. Thus, they need to be seen as their advocates rather than their representatives (Yuval-Davis 1994, 1997).

As McNay (2008: 8) states, 'the normative potency invested in the idea of recognition is also the source of a central weakness ... The normative "redemptive" force that resides in the ideal of mutual recognition constrains the way it is used as an analytical tool to explain how power creates unequal identities.' For this reason, an intersectional mode of analysis which differentiates between the different analytical facets of social divisions and explores their connectivity in different historical contexts is a much more systematic and generally applicable mode of analysis than the recognition/redistribution model. Such a genuinely sociological perspective – instead of a moral philosopher's – also makes it easier to deconstruct and analyse the inner dynamics of collective identity groupings.

Stratification

Stratification, or rather social stratification, relates to the differential hierarchical locations of individuals and groupings of people on society's grids of power. While traditionally, social stratification theories related to 'societies' as national societies, within boundaries of states, it is of vital importance that any comprehensive contemporary theory of social stratification should include global and regional, as well as national and local, orders of stratification, since they are continually contesting and shifting. This is, of course, true also in relation to all intersectional analyses. I find it problematic, for instance, that the construction of 'black woman' is automatically assumed, unless otherwise specified, to be that of a minority black woman living in white Western societies. The majority of black women in today's world are black women in black societies. This has major implications for a global intersectional stratification analysis, and I shall come back to this point later in the chapter.

This is not the appropriate place to survey the sociological literature on stratification. However, in the most generic terms, the two major approaches to sociological stratification used to be the Marxist and Weberian[6] ones, and in recent years a third alternative approach has been inspired by the writings of Pierre Bourdieu (for example 1984, 1997). Helma Lutz, in her presentation on a panel on intersectionality at the International Sociological Association conference in Durban (2006), argued that the Bourdieuian perspective has the potential to revolutionise intersectional analyses. I shall sum up the Marxist and Weberian approaches to stratification in the broadest and most generic terms. As Bourdieu is rather less well known, I shall describe his approach in a little more detail.

---

6   For overviews of the vast sociological literature on stratification, see for example, Devine et al. (2005), Esping-Anderson (1993), Giddens (1971), Levine (1998), Parkin (1974).

The Marxist approach to stratification locates people according to their relationship to the means of production. An important debate here has been whether this relationship is basically that of ownership, or lack of, or whether ownership itself is just a specific case of control of the means of production in a particular society. This broader definition has given rise to more nuanced Marxist analyses which recognise the power, for instance, of state managers in the former Soviet system, or – very differently – of executive managers in multinationals in which the shares are continuously traded and often no one person, family or even company holds the majority of shares.

Weberian approaches to stratification differentiate between three different kinds of stratification axes, those of economy, power (political, but also as backed by the physical) and status. Many theoretical debates have been conducted around the relationship and exchangeability between these axes, as well as the extent to which the distribution of people along these stratification axes necessarily congeals into fixed separate classes, the conflict between which is so central in the Marxist approach. Generally, however, the overall effects of people's differential stratified locations have tended to be seen as resulting in people's differential 'life chances'. In Britain, at least, this was transformed for census purposes into a list of categories based on people's occupations (Goldthorpe et al. 1980).

Bourdieu (1997) developed a 'sociology of practice' which identifies inequalities as the result of interplay between embodied practices and institutional processes, which together generate far-reaching inequalities of various kinds. His approach is based on a conceptual trinity of field (=fluid structures), capital (can be mobilised in particular fields by people with appropriate habitus) and habitus (which determines their competence to participate in fields). People's actions, then, are determined not by those people constructing themselves as belonging to a specific category but by differentiating themselves from others via tactical and strategic moves within the field (Devine and Savage 2005).

In both Marxist and Weberian analyses there is a basic differentiation between the structural and subjective understanding of stratified social power, although they differ in the ways in and extent to which the two are connected. Marx differentiates between 'class in itself' and 'class for itself' as part of the relationships between the social infrastructure and superstructure, while Weber differentiated between social classes, status groups and political parties and did not see a necessary causal relationship between them.

In Bourdieu's theoretical approach this sharp differentiation between the different levels disappears, as he sees consumption not just as the effects of class inequalities but also as part of their constructions, discussing cultural and social forms of capital as well as economic capital. Although in his earlier writings he still gave priority to the economic, this tended to disappear in his later work. The distribution of the different classes (and class fractions) runs from those who are best provided with both economic and cultural capital to those who are most deprived in both respects. The habitus is the relationship between the capacity to produce classifiable practices and works and the capacity to differentiate and appreciate these practices and products (taste). This is where the represented social world, the space of lifestyle, is constituted and where both practices and products embody a system of distinctive signs. The habitus is necessity internalised and converted into a disposition that generates meaningful practices and meaning-giving perceptions. Different conditions of existence produce different habitus. In this way Bourdieu (1984: 10) aimed at transcending

> the opposition between the vision which we can indifferently label realist, objectivist or structuralist on the one hand and the constructivist, subjectivist, spontaneist vision on the other. Any theory of the social universe must include the representation that agents have of the social world and, more precisely, the contribution they make to the construction of the vision of that world and consequently, to the very construction of the world.

This constructionist perspective is of crucial importance when considering the relationship between intersectionality and stratification. By allowing both production and consumption to structure social stratification in his theory and by treating class 'boundaries' as linguistic constructions, Bourdieu avoids the 'problem' of the apparent refusal of 'objective' classes to act and feel as they 'should', which affects both Marxian and Weberian approaches to class and stratification (Devine et al. 2005). Some of his formulations can be seen as intersectional analysis, although, as Helma Lutz (2006) has pointed out, he did not acknowledge his debt to feminist theory.

Lutz points out that although Bourdieu mentions gender as an important aspect of the class habitus throughout his work, it is only in his late work that he analyses 'masculine domination' (2001) as a special case of social inequality. Masculine domination is for him 'the paradigmatic form of symbolic domination' (Bourdieu and Wacquant 1996: 208), division and subordination being its most important characteristics. Bourdieu argues that the persistence of male domination is a result of the continuous deception of the symbolic violence of the gender order. The dominant gender order is a product of the habitus as much as it is a symbolic order, inflated, safely guarded and recognised as legitimate male power while misconceiving/disguising symbolic violence. Masculine domination is a concept that basically functions because of a 'compliance of actors'; men *and* women reproduce this interplay of incorporated structures on the individual and the institutional level.[7]

This concept is of particular interest because Bourdieu elaborates in great detail how a physical order becomes a social and symbolic one, and the issue of 'embodiment' has been central to feminist theory, especially through the work of Elizabeth Gross (1993) and others who were influenced by the work of Spinoza.[8]

---

7   See also Mechtild Bereswill's and Anke Neuber's contribution in this volume (69f).

8   The issue of embodiment is also addressed by Paula-Irene Villa (171f) and Jeff Hearn (89f) in this volume.

One implication of this is that the fate of social classes, understood as collectivities constituted through practices of social classification, becomes more contingent than ever on the historical vicissitudes of the discourse of social class. This issue will be revisited later as, while I am overall sympathetic to such an intersectional construction of stratification, I find the Bourdieuan equation between social collectivities and categorical locations along axes of power problematic.

The Bourdieuan perspective brings into question not only to what extent issues of culture, space and subjectivity are important for theorising stratification, but also how these issues should be incorporated. Intersectionality analysis, however, addresses other forms of 'symbolic power' than that of masculinity, such as those of race, ethnicity, nationality, ability, sexuality and so on, and especially the relations between them. While the Bourdieuan triad of field, capital and habitus provides an analytical tool in which such a comprehensive and inclusive intersectional analysis can be carried out, at least on the micro level, the original prioritisation in Bourdieu's writings of class differences as foundational in stratification analysis continues to prevail even when culture, and even later, the power of masculinity, become part (and in the case of the latter, not a very integrated part) of Bourdieu's analytical model.

Intersectionality as Stratification Theory: An Outline of a Conclusion

In this final section of the chapter I would like to outline a very general and work-in-progress framework of the way/s I would like to see intersectionality inserted and accepted as a sociological stratification theory.

As elaborated above, I suggest that the differentiation Fraser and others draw between recognition and distributive differences needs to be encompassed in an intersectional analysis that would be sensitive to the differential constructions of the same social category as an intersected social location and as a mode of social identification. Collective identities such as 'despised sexualities' (to use Fraser's expression) might be accepted and 'recognised' in certain social and historical contexts, but these identities can not only prevent people from gaining access to particular jobs but also endanger their lives in others. Moreover, as Henriette Gunkel (2010) has shown in her study of South Africa, homosexuals of different racial, class, age and cultural backgrounds can be treated in very different ways in the same society.

The emphasis on the shifting and contested nature of the different axes of power in specific social situations and the location of individuals and groupings along these axes are characteristic to the intracategorical approach to intersectionality mentioned earlier in the chapter. In this respect, the Bourdieuan perspective is conducive to the intersectional framework that I would like to promote as a stratification theoretical analysis. However, although focusing on everyday life, on subjectivities, on nuanced and minute alterations might be important for what Crompton and Scott (2005) call the 'case study approach to stratification', it becomes problematic when we try to shift the focus towards a more generic and global overview which is necessary to reach some valid observations avoiding the distortions of the ethnocentrist gaze. In some of my other works (for example 1994, 2007) I have discussed the problematics of the feminist truism of 'the personal is political'. This is too often interpreted not only as a statement concerning the political nature of intimate relationships but also as if valid politics needs to be based on personal experience. It is for this reason that I have promoted transversal dialogues that cross borders and boundaries and involve people with different situated gazes (but within common normative boundaries) as the only epistemological basis of what Patricia Hill Collins (1990) calls 'approaching the truth'.

My argument is that an intersectional approach to stratification would require a mode of analysis which combines case and variable analysis and would be sensitive to situated contexts, but which would also not fall into the relativist trap that prevents comparative judgement.

McCall's intercategorical comparative research methodology on the structural level has to be supplemented with intracategorial comparative research that would explore how these different analytical dimensions are connected or not in different situated gazes of people with differential identities and normative political views. In other words, we have to interrogate the assumptions of both case and variable methodologies, reject the naturalisation of any constructions of social divisions, and challenge the prioritisation of any of them, such as class or gender.[9] This might create complex, multi-layered methodologies which would require cooperation between researchers with similar approaches but in different locations, but the political economy of European research is already moving in this direction and at least we should be able to make use of it for the purpose of appropriate intersectional stratification studies.

Bibliography

Anthias, F. and Yuval-Davis, N. 1983. Contextualizing Feminism: Gender, Ethnic and Class Divisions. *Feminist Review*, 15, 62–75.

Anthias, F. and Yuval-Davis, N. 1992. *Racialized Boundaries: Race, nation, gender, colour and class and the anti-racist struggle*. London: Routledge.

Benhabib, S. 2002. *The Claims of Culture*. Princeton: Princeton University Press.

Bhavnani, K. 2008. *The shape of water*. Paper presented at the University of East London, Centre of Narrative Studies Series.

Bourdieu, P. 1984. *Distinction: a Social Critique of the Judgement of Taste*. London: Routledge & Kegan Paul.

---

9   The question of priority of certain categories is addressed by Bereswill and Neuber (69f) as well; also, Dubravka Zarkov (105f) arrives at a similar result in her more empirical investigation (all in this volume).

Bourdieu, P. 1997. *Cultural Theory: Critical Investigations*. London: Sage.

Bourdieu, P. and Wacquant, L.J.D. 1996. *An Invitation to Reflexive Sociology*. Chicago: University of Chicago Press.

Bradley, H. 1996. *Fractured Identities: The changing patterns of inequality*. Cambridge: Polity Press.

Bryan, B., Dadzie, S. and Scafe, S. 1985. *The Heart of the Race: Black women's lives in Britain*. London: Virago.

Bunch, C. for the Center for Women's Global Leadership. 2001. *A women's human rights approach to the World Conference against Racism*. Available at: www.cwgl.rutgers.edu/globalcenter/policy/gcpospaper.html [accessed: 21 June 2010].

Butler, J. 1990. *Gender Trouble: Feminism and the subversion of identity*. New York: Routledge.

Castoriadis, C. 1987. *The Imaginary Institution of Society*. Cambridge: Polity Press.

Collins, P.H. 1990. *Black Feminist Thought*. New York: Routledge.

Cooper, D. 2004. *Challenging Diversity*. Cambridge: Cambridge University Press.

Crenshaw, K. 1989. *Demarginalizing the Intersection of Race and Sex*. Chicago: University of Chicago Press.

Crompton, R. and Scott, J. 2005. Class analysis: beyond the cultural turn, in *Rethinking Class: Culture, identities and life styles*, edited by Devine, F. et al. London: Palgrave Macmillan, 186–203.

Devine, F., Savage, M., Scott, J. and Crompton, R. (eds) 2005. *Rethinking Class: Culture, identities and life styles*. London: Palgrave Macmillan.

Devine, F. and Savage, M. 2005. The cultural turn, sociology and class analysis, in *Rethinking Class: Culture, identities and life styles*, edited by Devine, F. et al. London: Palgrave Macmillan, 1–23.

Esping-Andersen, G. (ed.) 1993. *Changing Classes: Stratification and Mobility in Post-Industrial Societies*. London: Sage.

Essed, P. 1991. *Understanding Everyday Racism: An interdisciplinary theory*. Newbury Park, CA: Sage.

Fraser, N. 1997. *Justice Interruptus*. New York: Routledge.

Fraser, N. 2000. Rethinking Recognition. *New Left Review*, 3, 107–20.

Giddens, A. 1971. *Capitalism and Modern Social Theory: An analysis of the writings of Marx, Durkheim & Max Weber*. Cambridge: Cambridge University Press.

Goldthorpe, J. H., Llewellyn, C. and Payne, C. 1980. *Social Mobility and Class Structure in Modern Britain*. Oxford: Clarendon Press.

Gross, E. 1993. Bodies and Knowledges: Feminism and the Crisis of Reason, in *Feminist Epistemologies*, edited by Alcoff, L. and Potter, E. London: Routledge, 187–216.

Gunkel, H. 2010. *The Cultural Politics of Female Sexuality in South Africa*. London: Routledge.

Hancock, A. 2007. When multiplication doesn't equal quick addition: examining intersectionality as a research paradigm. *Perspectives on Politics*, 5(1), 63–80.

Harding, S. 1991. *Whose Science Whose Knowledge?* Ithaca: Cornell University Press.

Harding, S. 1997. Comment on Hekman's 'Truth & Method: Feminist Standpoint Theory Revisited'. *Signs*, 22(2), 382–91.

hooks, b. 1981. *Ain't I a Woman?* Boston: South End Press.

James, S. 1986. *Sex, Race & Class*. London: Centerpress, Housewives in Dialogue Series.

Kitzinger, C. 1987. *The Social Construction of Lesbianism*. London: Sage.

Knapp, A. 1999. Fragile foundations, strong traditions, situated questioning: critical theory in German-speaking feminism, in *Adorno, Culture and Feminism*, edited by O'Neill, M. London: Sage, 119–41.

Lentin, R. 1999. Constitutionally excluded: citizenship and (some) Irish women, in *Women, Citizenship and Difference*, edited by Yuval-Davis, N. and Werbner, P. London: Zed Books, 130–44.

Levine, R. F. 1998. *Social Class and Stratification: Classic statements and theoretical debates*. Lanham, Maryland: Rowman & Littlefield Publishers.

Lutz, H. 1991. *Migrant women of Islamic background – images and self images*. *MERA*: Working Papers, 11.

Lutz, H. 2002. *Intersectional analysis: a way out of multiple dilemmas?* Paper to the International Sociological Association Congress, Brisbane, July.

Lutz, H. 2006. *Can intersectionality help?* Paper to the International Sociological Congress, Durban.

McCall, L. 2005. The Complexity of Intersectionality. *Signs*, 30(3), 1771–1800.

McNay, L. 2008. *Against Recognition*. Cambridge: Polity.

Meekosha, H. and Dowse, L. 1997. Enabling citizenship: gender, disability and citizenship in Australia. *Feminist Review* 57, 49–72.

Oliver, M. 1995. *Understanding Disability: From Theory to Practice*. London: Macmillan.

Parkin, F. (ed.) 1974. *The Social Analysis of Class Structure*. London: Tavistock.

Sahgal, G. and Yuval-Davis, N. (eds) 1992/2001. *Refusing Holy Orders: Women and Fundamentalism in Britain*. London: Virago; WLUML.

Skeggs, B. 2004. *Class, Self, Culture*. London: Routledge.

Spivak, G. 1993. *Outside in the Teaching Machine*. London: Routledge.

Stoetzler, M. and Yuval-Davis, N. 2002. Standpoint Theory, Situated Knowledge & the Situated Imagination. *Feminist Theory*, 3(3), 315–34.

Taylor, C. 1992. *Multiculturalism and 'the Politics of Recognition'*. Princeton: Princeton University Press.

Thornton Dill, B. 1983. Race, class & gender: Prospects for an all-inclusive sisterhood. *Feminist Studies*, 9(1), 131–50.

Walzer, M. 1992. *Spheres of Justice: A defence of pluralism and equality*. New York: Basic Books.

Yuval-Davis, N. 1994. Women, Ethnicity and Empowerment. *Feminism and Psychology*, 4(1), 179–97.

Yuval-Davis, N. 1997. *Gender & Nation*. London: Sage Publications.

Yuval-Davis, N. 2006a. Intersectionality and feminist politics. *European Journal of Women's Studies*, 13(3), 193–209.

Yuval-Davis, N. 2006b. Belonging and the politics of belonging. *Patterns of Prejudice*, 40(3), 196–213.

Yuval-Davis, N. 2007. Human/Women's rights and feminist transversal politics, in *Transnational Feminisms: Women's Global Activism and Human Rights*, edited by Ferree, M.M. and Tripp, A.M. New York: New York University Press, 275–95.

Yuval-Davis, N. Forthcoming. *Intersectional Politics of Belonging*. London: Sage.

Yuval-Davis, N. 2010. Theorizing Identity: Beyond the 'us' and 'them' Dichotomy. *Patterns of Prejudice*, 44(3), 261–280.

Zeitlin, M. 1974. Corporate ownership and control: The large corporation & the capitalist class. *American Journal of Sociology*, 79(5), 1073–1119.

Chapter 10

Embodiment is Always More: Intersectionality, Subjection and the Body[1]

Paula-Irene Villa

In everyday life we always live, act, feel and think in a bodily-somatic mode of being. Starting from this rather trivial statement, I suggest that we need to think through the concept of intersectionality from the *somatic* side of social life. In order to do so, I will present some conceptual-theoretical musings on subjectivation, its failure and the bodily dimension, illustrated by some examples taken mainly from the subculture of Argentine tango. The point is to discuss the pros and cons of intersectionality when trying to sociologically understand the linkage between discourse and its norms, on the one hand, and embodied practices on the other. As I see it, intersectionality risks the reproduction of an old reductionist flaw in social theory, that is, the search for order as characteristic of the 'macro' level and its somewhat determinant projection onto the praxeological level. To put it differently: embodiment as part of any social practice shows that 'doing' is *necessarily* more and thus other than the *incorporation* of theoretically and analytically defined central social categories – however many categories there might be.[2] This by no means disregards the necessity and importance of intersectional perspectives. But it seems important to recall that *categories* of difference and inequality follow their categorical or structural logic and that action follows its own practical logic, including its corporeal dimension. Each of these logics relies heavily on the other, that is, they are co-constitutive, but they are not the same and cannot be reduced to one another. Thus, I argue that we should not lose sight of the inconclusive nature, instability and (also theoretical) constructedness of categories, and I argue that one main reason for this need lies in the somatic aspect of concrete social action.

1   I am extremely grateful for informative and inspiring discussions with Nina Degele, Sabine Hark, Gudrun-Axeli Knapp, Sybille Küster, and the students who took my intersectionality course in the summer term 2009 in the Institute of Sociology at LMU Munich. I further thank the editors of the present volume for very helpful comments, questions, and hints without which central arguments in this chapter would have been much more superficial.
    2   Jeff Hearn, in this volume (89f), also investigates the matter of embodiment.

The Failure of Persons When It Comes to Being Subjects

In order to conceptualise persons, individuals and subjects I concentrate on a post-structuralist perspective, while at the same time challenging the main line of thought within ongoing (Neo)Foucauldian approaches as increasingly prominent in gender studies right now.

Following Judith Butler (2001), who relies heavily on Foucault but also on Althusser and Lacan when thinking the subject, concrete persons never equal a subject (Butler 2001: 15–16). In her writings, Butler clearly differentiates between subjects and individuals, the former being sort of neat and orderly intelligible discursive positions, the latter somewhat untidy complexities. Subject positions are expressed in socially recognised and valid titles such as woman, manager, father, gay, sociologist, etc., which factually are heavily constituted by norms. Following Butler, and this leads me to my core argument, concrete persons do not directly embody norms, but norms rather regulate the conditions under which concrete actions by concrete persons can be intelligible, that is, normal:

> A norm is not the same as a rule, and it is not the same as a law. A norm operates within social practices as the implicit standard of *normalization*. [...] Norms may or may not be explicit, and when they operate as the normalizing principle in social practice, they usually remain implicit, difficult to read [...]. The norm governs the social intelligibility of action, but it is not the same as the action it governs. [...] The norm governs intelligibility, allows for certain kinds of practices and action to become recognizable as such [...]. (Butler 2004: 41–42)

This means that persons can only be socially acknowledgeable and recognisable[3] insofar as their actions 'follow' the implicit, surely diffuse norms contained in social categories such as woman, German, migrant, elite, etc., which themselves are materialisations of core social structures of inequality and/or difference such as gender, class, sexuality, race (etc.?). In other words: we necessarily act *as* someone. We act as a man, as an academic, etc. Concrete, empirical individuals are not only *subjected* to social titles in order to gain any kind of social visibility and thus recognition, but are equally *enabled* in a very fundamental way by the adoption of these discursive positions. We all have to live up to the apparently clean-cut titles provided by tidy discourse in order to achieve any kind of agency and identity. Entitlement is the key concept here: we are supposed to act *not* as persons or individuals in the endlessly complex meaning of the word, but always in the name of a subject position. We speak, talk, act, and are recognised *as* someone.[4]

So far the norm, the ideal – one might even say, the ideological stance. But of course, we are all always so much more than the position defined by discourse and

---

3 I use the term 'recognition' here in the philosophical sense as developed in critical social theory (Honneth and Fraser 2003).

4 For a more lengthy examination of these issues, see Villa (2006, 2010).

institutionalised by organisations, such as, for example, in my case when writing this text, science and academia. Real-life persons are – compared with discursive order – a mess: untidy, complex, fuzzy, multilayered, dynamic. A quite vivid example of the tension between subject positions on the one hand and empirical individuals on the other is the struggle for women in science to become 'subjects that matter'. This example also illustrates the normative, even ideological framing of factual subject positions: the hegemonic idea concerning 'the scientist' is that it is not he or she, but rather an 'it' – something neutral regarding ethnicity or race, age, sexuality, etc. Modern science relies on the idea of the scientific subject as a mere embodiment of intellect, genius, hard work, devotedness, etc. In other words, scientists are or rather have been implicitly and explicitly thought of as 'incarnations' of objective neutrality. This, of course, is not only valid for scientists as core subjects of modernity, but applies to *all* versions of central subjects of modernity: citizens, consumers, workers, bureaucrats, members of organisations, politicians, etc. All modern subjects are, following the interlocked and genuinely modern discourse of rationality, equality, freedom, meritocracy, etc., 'neutral' subjects.

But as extensive feminist analysis in many fields has clearly shown, all these positions are actually gendered since they are based on the modern discourse and construction of the universal as male and woman/female as the gendered and sexualised particular 'other'. To put it more bluntly: 'female scientist' has been and partly still is an oxymoronic position, a contradiction in terms. To be a woman is to be a gender, which according to normative traditions (and institutionalised policies of exclusion) probably cannot be reconciled with being a scientist.[5] We experience this kind of logic even nowadays, after the various waves of feminism and women's movements, after the institutional inclusion of women in academia, and after many and varied (more or less) successful programmes targeting women scientists on all levels, for example in the current political debates regarding women and science in Germany. In the public debates evolving about how to increase the numbers of women in academia, especially at the higher levels, women are addressed as mothers and policies are designed in order to respond to the needs of mothers within academia. Universities come up with child-care programmes or the infamous 'dual career couple services'. Thus, women are repeatedly essentialised (as mothers). As the body of intersectional analysis shows, the category of woman is not enough in order to understand the complex structural forces and logics which constitute concrete experiences. This stands true for any person, be it a working woman who 'turns out to be' black as well as or a white foreign minister in Germany who is also gay. And it certainly applies to women in science. The current German debate on the 'lack of women' in professional elites (for example academia) implicitly, but effectively, addresses white, middle-class, heterosexual, non-migrant (etc.) women. It does so by effectively invisibilising

---

5   This, of course, is a very abbreviated account of one of the core issues of modernity concerning gender – and other 'othernesses'. For more thorough accounts consult Harding (2008), Honegger (1992), and Schiebinger (1989).

any inequality or class issues as well as any reference to ethnicity/race or sexuality. The policies mentioned, such as 'dual career couple' offices or the focus on child-care institutions for women scientists, quite inevitably address a heterosexual, middle-class, white/German subject.[6]

Intersectional perspectives are extremely important in just this sense: they address the complexity of individual social positions which can – when seen from the practical side – never be reduced to just one axis or aspect. While this insight is surely undisputed within the debate around intersectionality, I think it is important to remain sensitive to the practical or experiential foundation of the issue. In other words: the dynamics of intersection emerge from the complexity of experiences.[7] I will come back to this point later in the chapter.

Is Seeing Believing? Tango Subjects

A further – rather picturesque and quite clear – example of the exceedingly complex dynamics of practice are those crazy, feverish, addicted, somewhat bizarre tango dancers we see in flyers and ads for touring tango shows or for tango lessons. Many images show subject positions which we can quite obviously analyse as embodiments of intersectional subjects:[8] tango men and tango women are, evidently, never only women or men. They are extremely stereotypical Argentine – that is, exotic, passionate, different, raw – genders: Argentine tango is normatively coded as passionate, intensive, sensual, authentic, raw and as 'other'. Its otherness lies, if we are to believe the iconographic and semantic discursive coding, in its Argentine origins, its 'Argentinicity'. Argentina is imagined as an origin, and as such as an exotic, primitive, somewhat irrational, mystical place – untouched by modernism and its discontents such as rationality, political change, cultural antagonisms and

---

6   The same can be said of the recent public debates on demography and fertility rates in Germany. When we look closer, the main 'problem' turns out to be not that not enough children are being born in Germany, but rather the 'quality' of the offspring: the well-trained, middle- and upper-class, German women were/are not having the babies the economic and political elites longed for.

7   See also Phoenix (137f) and Ferree (55f) in this volume.

8   Due to copyright issues, I unfortunately cannot include illustrations. You might want to spend some entertaining moments browsing the web for tango images. Search for 'tango argentino', and your search engine will come up with hundreds, even thousands of images which are variations on the same theme: a male–female couple in a more or less close embrace, she in a red (or otherwise sassy) dress which shows much of her skin, and wearing high-heeled shoes. He will most probably be pictured in a more or less formal suit, sometimes wearing a hat. She is likely to be held by him, leaning in or even close to falling, or wrapping one of her legs around him. She will in most cases be looking up to him or turning away from his upper body – but doing so from a bodily position inferior to his. Correspondingly, he will in most cases be or seem taller than her, often bending over her from above.

social movements.[9] One of the main modern diseases Argentina seems free from is feminism or, to put it more mildly, the political issue of gender equality.[10] Thus, tango comes along as the culture of pure, raw, almost savage gender struggle in its most authentic forms: man hunting and/or seducing woman, woman apparently resisting but wanting to give in. In my experience as a dancer, teacher and scholar of tango, this phantasm, the pureness of gender struggle within stereotypical gender roles, is what attracts so many people all over the world to tango. The promise tango makes, its seductive call, is the intensity of archaic heterosexual gender roles beyond all kinds of intellectual, political and social complexities. In my view, this promise is a norm – a norm in a post-structuralist, Butlerian sense: unachievable, but nonetheless constitutive for concrete embodied actions.

So far, so well known and so Foucauldian-Butlerian. From what I have said so far, one might be tempted to think of tango dancers as somatic embodiments of these phantasmic discourses. One could analyse the concrete doing – the dancing, the use of space at tango-related venues, the dressing of the body, the interactions on and off the dance floor, dancing lessons and workshops, etc. – as determined by the described norms. To put it more generally: one could sociologically describe persons, the individual or the self as an effect of norms. The self would be a representation of a subject.

Mind the Gap: Practice and Norms

But real, empirical subjection doesn't work this way. I *am* not a scientist – not always, not fully, not definitely. Nor *am* I a mother – not always, not fully, not definitely. And also in tango, people constantly fail to live up to the subjects they should be – and thus quite often complain about frustration, dullness, anxiety, unexpected emotions, etc.[11] At the same time, tango people are quite aware of the gap between norms and experience in tango. This cleavage is one of the main topics in all dimensions of tango culture: any tango talk touches sooner or later on the issue of how to relate to the 'otherness' of tango. Doing tango, thus, is experienced as different from what images and stories say about tango. The practical 'doing' is *known* to be different from what is knowable. One can go further: the gap between discourse and experience is one of the main drives in keeping the tango scene alive and dynamic. It's a constitutive element of a 'post-

---

9   Linda Supik has pointed out that the concepts 'primitive' and 'natural' may not be accurate since, and I fully agree here, the symbolism surrounding tango is heavily related to urbanism and a playful engagement with 'artificiality'. I would nevertheless want to insist on an underlying fantasy of 'Argentina' as the 'other' of Europe in a postcolonial sense. Thanks again for the helpful and inspiring comments by the editors!

10   For a brilliant analysis of tango as cultural product and practice in the context of economic, and political transnational circulation, see Savigliano (1994).

11   For a more extensive discussion of the failure within subjection as exemplified within the culture of Argentine tango, see Villa (2009).

traditional' community (*Gemeinschaft*) which is neither defined by written rules or norms nor based on hereditary traditions. In other words: what and who tango is must be constantly negotiated, and these negotiations are as somatic as they are verbal. Interestingly, these negotiations deal – implicitly – with what in theory is often done away with: the etc. and the 'supplement' (Derrida 1983: 244–82). What are the 'core', meaning the characteristic and defining, features of tango and what are those which are 'add-ons' or even contaminations of the core? And further: how to deal with experiences which systematically differ from the hegemonic norms and images? Are they evidence of a lack of training and knowledge? Or are they accepted as the normal experience, the 'real thing' in comparison with the idealised normative images? These questions keep the tango scene 'going', simply because they can never be silenced by clear and stable answers. One attempt at definition necessarily leads to further questions and further unstable concepts – the meaning slips. As I have discussed elsewhere (Villa 2009, 2010), the constant questioning of what people do when they do tango is not only part of what people do when they do tango (that is, all tango dancers are involved in 'tango talk', be it by discussing styles, places, history, local scenes, music, partners, outfits, journeys, movements, sensual experiences, etc. or by commenting on the many images and wordings related to tango which circulate in the media) but also part of the knowledge tango dancers produce and rely on.

But, as I have myself done in earlier sociological examinations of tango, social theory tends to overlook this complex logic of praxis by focusing on normative discourses or structures. As I stated before, this is no failure in itself. But it becomes a problem when both dimensions are mingled. I hope that the tango experience I have briefly sketched here illustrates the logic of any praxis. And thus it is the disturbing 'reality' that challenges (any) categories. In order to pin down what are believed to be the main dimensions of social order – in parts of intersectional theory the trinity of race, class, gender – the 'etc.' is a kind of theoretical rhetoric which, while acknowledging the complexity of practices and experiences, at the same time tends to do away with it.[12] This provocative remark takes me back from the dance floor to theory.

The Quest for Categories – A 'Will to Knowledge'?

The examples of the oxymoronic position of women scientists and of the gap between discourse and practices in tango suggest the following. On the discursive level intersectionality makes a great deal of sense, and in fact I have worked on the amalgamation of gender, class and ethnicity/nationality/regionalism within tango myself (Villa 2002). But the question is whether the categories we use and have to

---

12   For the ('German') insistence on the structural perspective, see Klinger (2003) and Knapp (2005). Soiland (2008) and the responses by Knapp (2008) and others discuss exactly this point.

use in order to work with the concept of intersectionality are useful when looking at practice. Do we see what happens in practice, in the intersubjective micropolitics of everyday action, when we put on the intersectionality spectacles? Can we describe the complex 'doing' of people by using the admittedly complex and interlocked categories that the intersectionality framework offers? Or do we again reduce the factual complexity and particularity of practice in favour of a selected number of categories that we assume are 'the' core dimensions of modern social structure (such as the consensual trinity of gender, class, and race), and by doing so reproduce the flaw so many approaches within (feminist) gender studies have critically pointed out, that is, the blindness to factual complexity and its normative dimensions due to the attention paid to hegemonic norms? These are my main questions. And they haunt, as I see it, the recent debate around intersectionality since this debate tends to do away with the fluidity and shifting nature of practical action by going into the 'etc.' mode. Anything which does not fit into the three central – or canonised – categories of race, class and gender is banned by the kind of magical 'etcetera'. And where we use as many as 13 categories (Lutz and Wenning 2001): would even these be enough to describe the specific logic of action? Wouldn't it make more sense to use the intersectional approach in a processual and thus stronger political sense, meaning that we look at how exceedingly complex interactions are gendered, racialised, (hetero-)sexualised, classed?

I pose these questions so sharply for two reasons. First, I am not so naïve as to suppose that historical (economic, political and social) structures (of domination) are one thing and concrete action by persons something quite different. On the contrary, following authors such as Bourdieu, Butler, Goffman, and Foucault I am deeply convinced that social structures constitute and frame social action – and that at the same time, social action produces and simultaneously shapes social structures. These processes are deeply marked by power, dominance and social inequality (as, for example, gendered), that is, not all actions produce the same structural effects, and not all structures affect all actions to the same extent. But when thinking about this inherent co-constitutional nexus between structures and action, it strikes me as extremely important to preserve and explore the differences between these two logics. We cannot describe social structures by reconstructing concrete actions, and we cannot reconstruct actions as simple materialisations of structures. This, as I have already stated, might sound somewhat trivial and simple. And I'd agree with this judgement. Nonetheless, it seems extremely important to think through the complex entanglement of structure and action, and it seems to me extremely important to do so within the framework of intersectionality. Otherwise, gender and feminist theory will once again have to face the problem of exclusion by reductionism. Even worse, by a reductionism that believes itself to be universal, neutral, and all-inclusive. We've been there before. Am I that name? Am I that category? Is what I do and experience visible in 'high theory'? As Leslie McCall (2005) has pointed out, the 'anti-categorical' move within intersectional approaches is an attempt to deal with precisely this problem.[13] But the anti-categorical critique risks being marginalised within intersectional theory.

My second issue with the questions posed is that I (simply) want to highlight the aspects that have been mentioned, especially concerning the German debate around intersectionality. While there is a considerable and inspiring body of work done by American, British and many other international colleagues in which the complex dynamics of intersectional analysis are dealt with critically (especially regarding qualitative empirical designs), there are rather few such designs within the German context (Degele and Winker 2009). Although there are positions which do formulate a critical stance on the insistence on definite categorical structures (Lutz and Wenning 2001, Walgenbach 2007), interestingly, the 'German' (as in German language) debate on intersectionality focuses on social theory (as in 'macrosociology') – on 'Gesellschaftstheorie' (cf. Klinger 2003, Knapp 2005, 2008). This is by no means 'wrong', or even a problem in itself! But I would insist that within this debate, there is a lack of sensitivity towards the reductionist move implied by the consensual trinity class/race/gender, and there is a lack of sensitivity towards the semi-autonomous, complex logic of action. The latter is somewhat shaded by the 'will to know' (Foucault) what modern society is all about in terms of structure.[14]

A Programmatic Proposal: Failure as Structure

In order to think through the complex intersections (sic!) of intersectional structures and 'fuzzy' actions, I suggest using a conceptual framework which at least keeps both dimensions and their differences visible. Therefore, I turn again to Butler's conceptualisation of subjection and try to give it a somatic twist, which in my view is crucial.

There is a systematic failure built into the nexus between subjects and persons. When taking a closer (sociological) look at the processes of subjection, we see the constant failure of concrete persons when they aim at *being* a subject. Since the specific regulative norms of specific subjects are dynamic, contested and opaque and since we are always, at any time, much more than the specific subject position we aim at, subjection – as coherent, unambiguous, stable, and intelligible embodiment of a subject position – necessarily fails. Persons are excessive compared with subjects. There is an excess of complexity, of emotions, of needs and yearnings, an excess of biographical experiences. The repressed, barred traces of who we might be, who we were, and who we might want to be haunt any process of subjection. That which is excluded doesn't disappear, nor can it be

---

13   See also Ferree in this volume (55f).

14   Although arguing from a different angle, Gressgard (2008) formulates a similar critique. She points out the necessity of thinking through the issues of complexity and multiplicity in order to avoid the pitfalls of reductionism.

mourned as lost. As Butler argues, relying here on Freud's concept of melancholia, the abjected and excluded must remain barred but present. We might and must live up to subject positions, but in the end we can never make it – at least in the strong sense of the concept meaning stability, coherent identity, and adequacy. We must always stumble over what is excluded from the often narrow socially acceptable places offered by discourses. Thus, persons fail to become subjects.

To sum this first part up: Subjection in this Butlerian-Foucauldian framework is the highly ambivalent process any real-life person has to engage in, in order to become socially recognisable. There is simply no other path that leads to agency. The destination is, again always ideally, to embody a subject. That is, not to become, but to *be* a sociologist, a man, a mother, a straight. But, alas, this never works out as it should.

Mimesis – Failure by Doing at its Performative Best

Embodiment is always fragile and transitory, never done. If subjects imply regulative norms, they even more so imply regulative norms of embodiment. To inhabit a subject position is to embody a title. To be a man or a woman, for example, necessarily means to have a male or female body. This might sound trivial, but there is much historical and empirical evidence that the embodiment of gender is extremely complex, fragile and, above all, never fully achieved. Ethnomethodological work tells us a lot about the endless effort it takes to be socially recognisable as a man or woman (Garfinkel 1967, Hirschauer 1989): the constant care of the body implies plucking and shaving, clothing and mimicking, nipping 'n tucking, sporting and dieting, styling and showing. And so forth. There is always more to do and things to be done differently, that is, concrete bodies are necessarily always somehow 'too' something: too fat, too slim, too tall, too loud, too aggressive, too shy, too soft, too strong, too round, too square, too pale, too dark, too… Further, ongoing empirical research as well as theoretical reflections on the 'intersectional' logic of 'doing difference' tells us much about the complexity of everyday action (West and Fenstermaker 1995).

This, again, is quite evident in the context of tango – however, as in many studies with transsexual people, the 'evident' and seemingly 'extreme' forms of body manipulations and other somatic strategies are examples of what everybody does, except that the main part of such strategies usually occurs within half-conscious routines based on lifelong socialisation processes. For individuals, doing exotic tango-gender or doing normalised-white-German-sociology-professor-gender, or whatever subject, implies a constant embodiment. Thus, the body as 'a representative of the social, as a symbol and indicator of status and subjectivation' (a formulation used by the organisers of a panel at a recent conference) is only partly plausible. Bodies equally indicate the failure of 'the social' on the individual level. Or at least, they indicate the complexity, fragility and constructedness of sociality.

Again, there are many ways of theorising and researching embodiment. Rather than running through them all, I'd like to continue the line of thought so far by adding a somatic aspect to the idea of subjectivation.

The concept of 'performative mimesis' might prove useful for this purpose. Mimesis is a traditional concept, mainly used in aesthetics and philosophy (Gebauer and Wulf 1992, Horkheimer and Adorno 2003, Metscher 2003). In recent years there has been growing interest in the specific social dimension of mimesis. Authors such as Gunter Gebauer and Christoph Wulf (1992, 2003), anthropologists and social theorists, and also Butler (1995: 149) have been musing on the force of the concept.[15] What does mimesis mean in this horizon? Mimetic acts, to paraphrase Gebauer and Wulf, are practical actions which to some extent 'imitate' or 'copy' a previous act. The movement of my arm when writing is a copy of another movement of an arm as seen maybe in a friend, in a movie, on stage, in a dream. Bodily references to previous worlds are necessarily mimetic. We have an image of Heidi Klum as a female subject and try to copy her (if we want to, that is). We see a successful colleague in a meeting and try to be like him as part of our own process of subjection – to talk as convincingly as he does, to smile as confidently, to dress in the same matching manner, maybe even to eat the same stylish food in order to match the milieu. Tango dancers try to look as in the images, move as the other dancers at the venue do, imitate the spin their teacher just showed them. But, and this is as obvious as it is often ignored, a movement is never an exact copy of another. This is a characteristic aspect of mimetical acts – they are never 'mimicry' or mechanical replications, but rather corporeal acts which, while relating to acts, meanings, images outside of the concrete act necessarily vary, shift, re-create, and (re)produce meaning. Arguing again from the dance floor: the image of the 'passionate' embrace as seen in the tango image functions as a sort of 'original' beyond the concrete moves of a dancing couple on the dance floor, and in their shared implicit effort to be/move/feel/look *as* or like the image, the moves actually done and experienced by the concrete couple alter the image since the persons, the context, and the situation differ from the iconographic image. Thus, mimetic acts are 'variation' (Gebauer and Wulf 1998: 13), and they are necessarily so:

> Their similarity is found in their variation; this is typical of mimetic acts. There is no uniform theoretical principle which would make it possible to identify them as actions of the same type. They always occur in a new situation, and never produce the same results. The reasons for these unavoidable variations are the range of the action situations, the fact that they involve the body, the genesis of the action which is different in every case, the absence or the impossibility of drawing up more precise rules governing the performance [...] Signatures are the same: each individual has a characteristic, authentic and recognizable signature,

---

15   For detailed discussions of Butler's use of mimesis, see Bell (1999: 85–112) and Möhring (2001).

> but no-one ever signs their name twice in exactly the same way. (Gebauer and Wulf 1998: 13–14)

Due to the singularity of each situation and each person in specific situations, copies are never a 1:1 blueprint. Rather, mimetic efforts of resemblance (*'Anähnlichung'*) necessarily vary the copied gesture. And exactly this is its performative dimension. Whenever we try to be like or as – let's say the woman, the scientist, the father, the straight, the male tango dancer – we necessarily create new meanings and embodiments for these 'titles'. The novelty might be barely perceptible, ever so microscopically small, but it's there nonetheless.

This is even more so since bodies never are objects, at least not only. Real bodies in real social life are not 'things', they are not static entities but ongoing transformation. Embodiment is always embodiment as social process, expanding over time and space, and including the many layers of individual social existence in ever-specific shades. Images are bodies, dehumanised flesh is a body.[16] But otherwise, in the realm of the social, we act and encounter processes of embodiment. And embodiment is never static and never monothematic. Whenever we see each other or interact in intersubjective face-to-face situations, we do embodiment. We see not only a sociologist, but old or young, pretty or not, woman or man or whatever, we see class and sexuality, etc. And we act in this way too. Embodiment is *per se* intersectional in its form, and due to its mimetic dimension it exceeds any categorical frame. This is especially obvious and yet not fully taken into account within empirical research on embodiment, and less so within debates on subjection. Whatever picture you may want to look at, whatever praxis you may cast your empirical gaze on: you'll never find *the* subjected body. You'll never find *the* embodied subject as in the Black, the Woman, the Tango dancer. Rather, you'll find complex embodiments. And this complexity is not dealt with by framing it in intersectional terms.

In Lieu of Conclusion: Don't Believe the Hype

Intersectionality, as I see it, is a notion that has its roots partly in the analysis of empirical experiences, of practices. This might be traced back to the legendary speech by Sojourner Truth (Truth 1851, see also hooks 1981) in which she challenges the hegemonic and largely unquestioned notion of 'Woman' within the (white, mainly middle and upper class, bourgeois) First Women's Movement in the USA by referring to her experiences as a former slave, mother, and black person.[17] References to one's own experiences, which exceed the political categories (subject

---

16   For a profound critique of 'body' as object, see Horkheimer and Adorno (2003: 266–68).

17   For a discussion of Truth's 'truth' within the debate on intersectionality, see Brah and Phoenix (2004).

positions) of a given time, have been a major force for the increasing complexity of feminist practices *and* theory, be it regarding material/economic conditions, race or ethnicity and nationality matters, or be it sexuality. Obviously, Crenshaw's starting point in her foundational text (Crenshaw 1989) is exactly the impossibility of adequately framing concrete experiences of marginalisation, discrimination, and violence (Crenshaw 1994) by using only one category. They do not even 'fit' in two categories, at least if used in separated, parallel analyses:

> My objective there [in Crenshaw 1989, P.–I.V.] was to illustrate that many of the experiences Black women face are not subsumed within the traditional boundaries of race or gender discrimination as these boundaries are currently understood, and that the intersection of racism and sexism factors into Black women's lives in ways that cannot be captured wholly by looking at the women race or gender dimensions of those experiences separately. (Crenshaw 1994, without page)

I am convinced that this applies to far more categories than those dealt with in these lines, that is, not 'only' to race and gender:

> I should say at the outset that intersectionality is not being offered here as some new, totalizing theory of identity. Nor do I mean to suggest that violence against women of color can be explained only through the specific frameworks of race and gender considered here. Indeed, factors I address only in part or not at all, such as class or sexuality, are often as critical in shaping the experiences of women of color. My focus on the intersections of race and gender only highlights the need to account for multiple grounds of identity when considering how the social world is constructed. (Crenshaw 1994, without page)

At the same time, I am convinced that it will not do to either add categories to the analysis of experience or subtract them, nor to end the 'arithmetics' of categories by reducing them to those which some consider the core categories of social structures. The force of the concept of intersectionality – which it undoubtedly still has and which is much needed, especially within the quite ethnocentric, colour-blind and heteronormative German gender studies context – is to seriously account for the concrete complexity of both norms/structures and practices. No one is ever only a gender. No gender norm is ever solely gender-related. No class position is untouched by gender or race issues. And so forth. The (admittedly trivial) example of Argentine tango reveals that gender in tango is always, inevitably, necessarily heteronormative, marked by normative constructions of 'alterity' (Argentinian), and it is marked by class in complex ways. But it also shows that on the practical level, in which mimetical processes of embodiment play a crucial role, categories such as sexuality, gender, class, 'race' or ethnicity, etc. constitute corporeal practices, they do not determine them. Experiences necessarily exceed the categorical conditions they are embedded in.

In my view, the 'etc.' we all know from theoretical, political, and everyday discourses is much underrated. The analysis of embodiment processes – in tango or wherever – can make quite clear that the etc. is *necessary*. We'll never get rid of it, and trying to do so might be a dominant move, a move that tries to enthrone a certain kind of orderly theoretical analysis as more adequate than the fuzzy logic of concrete action. Discourse is order – at least as far as we know it and for sure in modernity, even in its high, post- or reflexive forms.[18] Social theory tends to reproduce this orderly ambition by searching for those categories which *really* make a difference. And although I am quite sceptical about whether this is the correct way of doing social theory, especially feminist social theory, it might work on the so-called macrolevel, that is, the level of discourse itself, of social structures and historical processes of the *longue dureé*.

But on the level of embodiment, intersectionality is only partly helpful. As long as it's used as a heuristic framework, as a kind of reminder to keep the complexity and intersection of many constituent categories in mind, it is extremely helpful. But when related to the analysis of interactions, especially in its somatic dimensions, I suggest that we need to de-ontologise the categories which constitute social structures in order to processualise them. This would mean looking at how the exceedingly complex bodily practices are interpreted by the actors themselves within these categories. How do people make sense of their own practices within specific social settings, and by which categories do they do so? How are practices thereby gendered, racialised, sexualised, or classed? If we skip over this complex – and often enough ideological – transition, the theoretical framework of intersectionality might obscure the necessary fragile, instable, slippery nature of what we in practice believe is ontologically given. This is why I again argue that we should not forget what intersectionality was or could be about according to McCall (2005): a critical stance on categories, even an anti-categorical move.

As a feminist sociologist with a considerable affinity with queer positions and coming from a migration background, I know there is always much more that matters than what we see. Dealing with processes of embodiment – rather than with *the* body – makes this perfectly clear as well. I hope that the hype of intersectionality will not become an intersectional*ism* which objectifies complexity for the sake of order and orderly theory.

Bibliography

Bauman, Z. 2005. *Moderne und Ambivalenz*. Hamburg: Hamburger Edition.
Bell, V. 1999. *Feminist Imagination: Genealogies in Feminist Theory*. London: Sage.

---

18 I rely on the work of Zygmunt Bauman (2005), and his analysis of modernity as a historical era and of modern theory.

Brah, A. and Phoenix, A. 2004. Ain't I A Woman? Revisiting Intersectionality. *Journal of International Women's Studies*, 5(3), 75–86.

Butler, J. 1995. *Körper von Gewicht. Die diskursiven Grenzen des Geschlechts.* Berlin: Berlin Verlag.

Butler, J. 2001. *Psyche der Macht. Das Subjekt der Unterwerfung.* Frankfurt a.M.: Suhrkamp.

Butler, J. 2004. *Undoing Gender.* New York: Routledge.

Butler, J. 2009. *Die Macht der Geschlechternormen.* Frankfurt a.M.: Suhrkamp.

Crenshaw, K. 1989. Demarginalizing the Intersection of Race and Sex: A Black Feminist Critique of Antidiscrimination Doctrine, Feminist Theory and Antiracist Politics. *University of Chicago Legal Forum*, 139–67.

Crenshaw, K. 1994. Mapping the Margins: Intersectionality, Identity Politics, and Violence Against Women of Color, in *The Public Nature of Private Violence*, edited by Fineman, M.A. and Mykitiuk, R. New York: Routledge, 93–118. Available at: http://www.wcsap.org/Events/Workshop07/mapping-margins. pdf [accessed: 20 June 2010].

Degele, N. and Winker, G. 2009. *Intersektionalität. Zur Analyse sozialer Ungleichheiten.* Bielefeld: Transcript.

Derrida, J. 1983. *Grammatologie.* Frankfurt a.M.: Suhrkamp.

Garfinkel, H. 1967. *Studies in Ethnomethodology.* Malden: Blackwell Publishers.

Gebauer, G. and Wulf, C. 1992. *Mimesis: Kultur – Kunst – Gesellschaft.* Reinbek b. Hamburg: Rowohlt.

Gebauer, G. and Wulf, C. 1998. *Spiel – Ritual – Geste. Mimetisches Handeln in der sozialen Welt.* Reinbek b. Hamburg: Rowohlt.

Gebauer, G. and Wulf, C. 2003. *Mimetische Weltzugänge.* Stuttgart: Kohlhammer.

Gressgard, R. 2008. Mind the Gap: Intersectionality, Complexity and 'the Event'. *Theory & Society*, 10(1), without pages. Available at: http://theoryandscience. icaap.org/content/vol10.1/Gressgard.html [accessed: 20 June 2010].

Harding, S. 2008. *Sciences from Below: Feminisms, Postcolonialisms, and Modernities.* Durham, NC: Duke University Press.

Hirschauer, St. 1989. Die interaktive Konstruktion von Geschlechtszugehörigkeit. *Zeitschrift für Soziologie*, 18, 100–18.

Honegger, C. 1992. *Die Ordnung der Geschlechter. Die Wissenschaften vom Menschen und das Weib.* Frankfurt a.M.& New York: Campus.

Honneth, A. and Fraser, N. 2003. *Redistribution or Recognition? A Political-Philosophical Exchange.* New York: Verso.

hooks, b. 1981 *Ain't I a Woman? Black Women and Feminism.* Boston, MA: South EndPress.

Horkheimer, M. and Adorno, Th.W. 2003 (Original English 1944, German 1969). *Dialektik der Aufklärung. Philosophische Fragmente.* Frankfurt a.M.: Suhrkamp (Th. W. Adorno Gesammelte Schriften, Bd. 3).

Klinger, C. 2003. Ungleichheit in den Verhältnissen von Klasse, Rasse und Geschlecht, in *Achsen der Differenz. Gesellschaftstheorie und feministische*

Kritik II, edited by Knapp, G.-A. and Wetterer, A. Münster: Westfälisches Dampfboot, 14–48.

Knapp, G.-A. 2005. 'Intersectionality' – ein neues Paradigma feministischer Theorie? Zur transatlantischen Reise von 'Race, Class, Gender'. *Feministische Studien* 23(1), 68–81.

Knapp, G.-A. 2008. Kommentar zu Tove Soilands Beitrag. querelles-net, 26. Available at: http://www.querelles-net.de/index.php/qn/article/view/695/703 [accessed: 20 June 2010].

Lutz, H. and Wenning, N. 2001. Differenzen über Differenz. Einführung in die Debatten, in *Unterschiedlich verschieden. Differenz in der Erziehungswissenschaft*, edited by Lutz, H. and Wenning, N. Opladen: Leske & Budrich, 11–24.

McCall, L. 2005. The Complexity of Intersectionality. *Signs: Journal of Women in Culture and Society*, 30(3), 1771–1800.

Metscher, Th. 2003. *Mimesis*. Bielefeld: Transcript.

Möhring, M. 2001. 'ein nackter Marmorleib'. Mimetische Körperkonstitution in der deutschen Nacktkultur oder: wie lässt sich eine griechische Statue zitieren? in *Zitier-Fähigkeit. Findungen und Erfindungen des Anderen*, edited by Gutenberg, A. and Poole, R.J. Berlin: Erich Schmidt Verlag, 215–33.

Savigliano, M. 1994. *Tango and the Political Economy of Passion*. Boulder, CO: Westview Press.

Schiebinger, L. 1989. *The Mind has no Sex? Women in the Origins of Modern Science*. Cambridge: Harvard University Press.

Schroer, M. 2001. *Das Individuum der Gesellschaft. Synchrone und diachrone Theorieperspektiven*. Frankfurt a.M.: Suhrkamp.

Soiland, T. 2008. Die Verhältnisse gingen und die Kategorien kamen. *Intersectionality* oder Vom Unbehagen an der amerikanischen Theorie. *querelles-net*, 26. Available at: http://www.querelles-net.de/index.php/qn/ article/view/694/702 [accessed: 20 June 2010].

Truth, S. 1851. *Ain't I a Woman?* Available at: http://en.wikipedia.org/wiki/Ain't_ I_a_Woman%3F. [accessed: 20 June 2010].

Villa, P.-I. 2002. Tanz die Leidenschaft! Argentinischer Tango zwischen Phantasma, Anrufung und Herzklopfen. *Berliner Debatte Initial. Zeitschrift für Sozialwissenschaftlichen Diskurs*, 13, 111–19.

Villa, P.-I. 2006. Scheitern – Ein produktives Konzept zur Neuorientierung der Sozialisationsforschung, in *Sozialisation und Geschlecht. Theoretische und methodologische Aspekte*, edited by Bilden, H. and Dausien, B. Opladen/ Farmington Hills: Barbara Budrich, 219–38.

Villa, P.-I. 2009. 'Das fühlt sich so anders an.' Zum produktiven 'Scheitern' des Transfers zwischen ästhetischen Diskursen und tänzerischen Praxen im Tango, in *Translationen*, edited by Klein, G. Bielefeld: transcript, 105–22.

Villa, P.-I. 2010. Subjekte und ihre Körper. Kultursoziologische Überlegungen, in *Kultursoziologie. Paradigmen – Methoden – Fragestellungen*, edited by Wohlrab-Sahr, M. Wiesbaden: VS, 251–275.

Walgenbach, K. 2007. Gender als interdependente Kategorie, in *Gender als interdependente Kategorie. Neue Perspektiven auf Intersektionalität, Diversität und Heterogenität*, edited by Walgenbach, K., Dietze, G., Hornscheidt, A. and K. Palm. Opladen: B. Budrich, 23–65.

West, C. and Fenstermaker, S. 1995. Doing Difference. *Gender and Society*, 9(1), 8–37.

Chapter 11

Intersectional Invisibility: Inquiries into a Concept of Intersectionality Studies

Gudrun-Axeli Knapp
[translated by Rebecca van Dyck]

In her text 'The Intersectionality of Race and Gender Discrimination' (Crenshaw 2000), the American law professor and human rights activist Kimberlé Crenshaw states that neither the gendered aspects of racist discrimination nor the racist implications of gendered discrimination have been adequately apprehended within the human rights discourse. She calls this blind spot intersectional invisibility. My contribution introduces Crenshaw's principal arguments, in particular her concept of intersectional invisibility, which she reflects primarily against a background of anti-discriminatory policy. Subsequently it will be demonstrated how the idea of intersectional invisibility has been taken up in American social psychology. At issue here are interdependencies and interferences on the level of social perception and categorisation of individuals and groups, social-psychological processes producing visibility and invisibility, and their dependence on differently combined constructions of group membership. This example from the area of social psychology shows how disciplinary specialisation can promote the transdisciplinary discussion on intersectionality. In this case it is research on social cognition and stereotyping which supplements Crenshaw's considerations and lends them a social-psychological accent. At the same time, however, foreshortenings of this particular approach become visible. I comment on these from a subject-theoretical and social-theoretical perspective in an interim summary. My central question in the following is, whether and how the concept of intersectional invisibility can be made useful for multi-level approaches to societal complexity. I argue that our understanding of intersectional invisibility could be advanced by a socio-historically informed view of societal formations that obstruct insight into power relations and the forms of dominance which shaped their historical constitution. However, parallel to justifying the relevance of a social-theoretical conceptual framework, it becomes evident that the intersectional perspective not only expands the horizon of social analysis, but undermines the possibility of establishing connections with established forms of social theory and theories of society without major revisions (Knapp 2008). Conversely, it becomes equally evident that attempts to elaborate an intersectional perspective in terms of a theory of society make it impossible to be satisfied with a 'groupist' (Brubaker

2007) understanding of social 'categories' (for a controversial discussion on the problematics of this, see Querelles-Net Forum 2008). This has consequences for the conceptualisation of intersectional invisibility.

Forms of Denaming: Intersectional Invisibility – Over-inclusion – Under-inclusion

Crenshaw uses the term intersectional invisibility to describe the systematic suppression of differences within discriminated groups (intra-group difference) through the common concepts of racist and gender discrimination. Her text 'The Intersectionality of Race and Gender Discrimination', the first version of which was drawn up for the Expert Group Meeting on Gender and Race Discrimination held in Zagreb, Croatia, in 2000, formulates a guideline intended to allow the practical identification of the interactive effects between the two forms of discrimination. The specific problems of racially marginalised women would become invisible if they were either regarded as being subject to sexual or racist discrimination, a problem that is symptomatic in the field of politics and jurisdiction. According to Crenshaw, this twin problem of over-inclusion and under-inclusion develops within the context of such obscurations, and nowhere is this more evident than in the question regarding intra-group difference.

Crenshaw uses the term 'over-inclusion' to describe the occasion on which a problem or a condition that is particularly or disproportionately visited on a subset of women is simply claimed as a women's problem. This leads to an inadequate analysis of the problem, with the consequence that recommendations for political action are also insufficient. As an example she mentions the discourse on the trafficking of women, which is absorbed within the gender framework without addressing the fact that the probability of becoming a victim of women traffickers is greater for certain groups of women than for others. The parallel term 'under-inclusion' refers to the process in which particular subsets of women experience a problem that is not seen as a gendered problem in an ethnicised form of articulation, as the gender-related aspect is completely masked by the ethnic framing and/or because it does not reflect the experience of women from the dominant groups in society, according to the contours of which sexual discrimination is defined. In her text, Crenshaw sketches a provisional framework which is meant to enable people affected by multiple forms of discrimination to develop a language to describe their own experiences.

Who is (In)Visible? The Advantages and Disadvantages of Intersectional Group Membership

In North American psychology, the concept of intersectional invisibility has been elaborated with a discipline-specific accent. In their article 'Intersectional

Invisibility: The Distinctive Advantages and Disadvantages of Multiple Subordinate-Group Identities', the social psychologists Valerie Purdie-Vaughns and Richard P. Eibach (2008) argue that membership in several subordinated groups makes a person 'invisible' compared with those who only belong to one subordinate group. The first category includes, for example, heterosexual female members of an ethnic minority, gay/bisexual male members of an ethnic minority,[1] *white* lesbian/bisexual women, and many more. *White* gay men, *white* heterosexual women, or heterosexual male members of an ethnic minority represent the latter category. Purdie-Vaughns and Eibach substantiate this suggestion with the aid of cognitive social psychology, prejudice and stereotype research. In doing so they are particularly interested in how psychological biases in the perception of others interact with cultural interpretation patterns and ideologies. In their view, androcentric, ethnocentric, and heterocentric ideologies contribute to the fact that people with multiple subordinate identities are perceived as non-prototypical members of their respective 'identity group'. These persons then experience what Purdie-Vaughns and Eibach call intersectional invisibility. There are references to Crenshaw's considerations on intersectional invisibility as well as to the concepts of over-inclusion and under-inclusion; however, Purdie-Vaughns and Eibach concentrate on intersectional invisibility as an effect of cognitive prototype formations that ground social perception and govern economies of attention. Differentiating discussion of approaches to multiple discrimination, Purdie-Vaughns and Eibach link the invisibility of non-prototypical members of groups to a specific mixture of the advantages and disadvantages experienced by people with 'intersectional identities'.

The authors spell out their underlying idea by listing both the advantages and the disadvantages of intersectional invisibility in various constellations of identity. The advantages include, for example, that relative invisibility can lead to people being less likely to experience active forms of discrimination and oppression than the visible members of a group. They illustrate this by citing an example from the television series *Six Feet Under* in which two approximately 50-year-old women go on a thieving spree convinced that they will not be caught, because women of this age are 'invisible'. A further example relates to the frequently documented relative invisibility of female homosexuality and, in comparison with male homosexuality, the lesser degree of interest in prosecuting it. From this social-psychological perspective, the androcentric tendency of viewing men as prototypical members of a group leads to subordinate men being more frequently exposed to active forms of oppression than subordinate women. Like Crenshaw, and partly drawing on her argument, the authors distinguish between historical invisibility, cultural invisibility, political invisibility, and legal invisibility.

---

1   For a different theoretical perspective on the intersectional (in)visibility of gay men of an ethnic minority see Kosnick in this volume.

Summary: Desiderata and Questions

Both of these texts, each of which productively uses and goes beyond disciplinary specialisation, show desiderata which I will specify in the following. However, I am well aware that one cannot expect all aspects to be elaborated in a working paper on anti-discriminatory policies (Crenshaw 2000) or in a programmatic essay in the field of social psychology (Purdie-Vaughns and Eibach 2008). The desiderata concern: 1) the understanding of the cultural order of modernity and the diverse logics of constructing difference; 2) the question of how to relate theories of intra-subjectivity with conceptual architectures of inter-subjectivity; and 3) the need to advance a more complex understanding of society and societal structures.

The first problem relates to the conceptualisation and situating of difference in the cultural order of modernity. The strong emphasis on the construction of group identities in both texts, understandable though this is from the perspective of the respective problem (discrimination/prototypicality), leads to an overly narrow analysis not only regarding societal structures but also regarding cultural orders. What has been focused on, and this is evident with Purdie-Vaughns and Eibach, are only the category-based typifications and markers. In feminist scholarship, however, it is well known that the androcentric structure of the symbolic order does not exhaust itself in the marking of differences and hierarchies, but culminates in the androcentric standard itself remaining unmarked and being universalised as unmarked, as for instance in the concept of the human being or the person. Purdie-Vaughns and Eibach elide this central point of androcentrism, although they make reference to this concept. The non-marking of the dominant general is the perfection of an utterly effective abstraction and exclusion mechanism of modernity. Feeding on the pathos of departicularisation, it represents both the condition and the medium of universalisation. One of the central dialectics of enlightenment and modernisation is the simultaneous and uncanny dynamic of de-particularisation on the one hand and the radicalisation of difference and exclusion on the other. Against the background of established universalisms, constructions of the '*Besonderen – Minderen – Anderen*' (the Particular – Inferior – Other [Knapp 1987]) are no longer what they were under pre-modern conditions. The absent marking of the 'human being' hinders assigning the privilege that is hidden within this general to societal forms of domination, social power relations and specific groups. The invisibility constituted by means of this form of hegemonic departicularisation cannot be subsumed by the designation 'intersection', as it is related to group categories. Similar problematics are negotiated in the 'critical whiteness' debate, according to which only 'black' or 'people of colour' are accounted for with categories of 'race', while '*white*' people usually remain unmarked.[2] Each of the implied relations, however, has to be contextualised and historicised: as is widely known, National Socialist policy not only involved an increasing self-ethnicisation of the 'German nation' (Küster 2007). In the evolutionist and eugenic dispositif of the

---

2   See also the introduction to this volume.

'race struggle', this self-ethnicisation was also associated with a self-racialisation of Germans as members of the 'Aryan race', which celebrated itself as the master race in contrast to Jews, Slavs, and the non-white 'races'. Multi-level analyses need to address the complexity, unevenness and contradictory character of such cultural constellations and the options they offer for establishing differences and legitimating exclusion. In doing so we have to take into account the alternating relations and construction logics of: 1) the unmarked general and the marked particular (for example, *'Der Mensch und sein Weib'*/Man and his woman); 2) the marked difference between particular A and particular Non-A (for example, man = non-woman), constructed in terms of identity logic and thus producing relations of standard and deviation; 3) the marked simple difference between particular A and particular B (for example, man/woman); and 4) the situative-flexible 'nitty-gritty of everyday talk', which also operates with sub-stereotypes. Much research needs to be conducted regarding the cultural-symbolic forms in which interferences between different social categorisations (for example, class, nationality/ethnicity/race, sexuality) can either show themselves or become invisible within and across contexts and in each of the four modes of construction mentioned.

The second desideratum concerns questions regarding relations between intra-subjectivity and inter-subjectivity. Are there phenomena of intersectional invisibility at work in the self-understandings of subjects? Here I am thinking of forms of denying or suppressing one's membership in multiply discriminated or privileged social categories which may accompany inter-subjective forms of being made over-visible or invisible. What is being addressed is, among other things, the problem of perception, experience, and the problem of how to deal with discrimination, whose inclusion could considerably augment *both* approaches to intersectional invisibility. One of the most painful aspects of multiple discrimination is the uncertainty of not exactly knowing why and on what basis one is being treated 'like that': because I'm a woman, because I'm black, because I'm a black woman, because I am the way I am? One of the individual coping strategies in dealing with discrimination could be the *intrapsychic* production of intersectional invisibility in the form of suppression or denial, sealing oneself off from the mortifying perception of oneself as the victim of multiple derogation, disrespect, and ignorance. On the other side, on the side of those who are multiply privileged, cognitive and affective denaming, oppressing and rationalising the privilege virtually belongs to the psychic and political perpetuation of the status quo. From a social-psychological point of view, what opens up here is a broad field of intrasubjective and intersubjective 'affect policies': it ranges from ignorance and cool indifference and the selective admission of the thought of privilege (for instance, being a man in contrast to being a woman, but not being a native German in contrast to being an immigrant) to the affect-laden defence of the perception barrier that prevents one from even considering one's own privileged position, let alone thinking it through. There is an 'inner bond' between the two sides of intersectional invisibility – the suppression of multiple discrimination and the suppression of multiple privilege – that shapes political culture and the way people treat each other. Work on such forms of complementary intersectional invisibility is a key for social learning processes and policies of alliances. When being discriminated against is not named and discrimination is not recognised we have, once again, a 'problem without a name' (Friedan 1966).

However, one could direct the question of self-relations, which are referred to by the popular concept of 'identity' in the Anglo-American discussion (Siems 2007), in the opposite direction: Does it even make sense to extend the concept of intersectionality to include relations, processes and dynamics of intra-subjectivity? (For a critical treatment of this, see Rendtorff 2008.) Do psychodynamic approaches to subjectivity not preclude, at least to a certain degree, a category-based concept of 'identity', that is, literally sameness/being at one with oneself, in terms of theory architecture? A concept that comes close to a reified understanding of membership categories, which cannot be completely avoided even by means of multiplication and hybridisation? A concept that poses difficulties in particular with respect to questions of class membership (Skeggs 2004)? A concept that, moreover, only narrowly agrees with those variations of social psychology and political psychology oriented towards the dynamics of conflict that, tying in with psychoanalysis, lend themselves as an extension of or alternative to cognitive and interactionistic approaches and that play a certain role in German-language feminist theory? What forms of intersectional invisibility are even imaginable in the self-relations of subjects if one takes into account that internal and external forms of societalisation (*Vergesellschaftung*) are not congruent (Becker-Schmidt 1990)? Might the concept of identity not be a useful but ultimately deceptive and impromptu bridging of the gap, separating as well as mediating the constitutional logics of subjectivity and societal objectivity?

In short: one arrives at different social-psychological problematics and insights using the approaches of cognitive psychology together with sociological and social-psychological social identity research, which appear to dominate in the English-speaking discussion on intersectionality, in preference to a social psychology oriented towards the psychodynamics of conflict, for whose view of subject constitution gender and desire are more fundamental than, for instance, the categories of nationality or class. The latter categories influence experience and self-perception in a different way than the distinctions between self and other rooted in the earliest intimate relationships, which are contained in intimate and highly cathexed relationships of dependence and affection. Does the respective specific entrenchment of the distinctions in the genesis of the subject have an influence on the forms of its topicalisation (*Aktualisierung*) in one's self-awareness as well as in intersubjective relationships in adult life? How do intersectional aspects influence forms of topicalisation? In this context, what is the effect of the phenomenon of deferred psychic action (*Nachträglichkeit*), the fact that we cannot evoke antecedent experiences 'as such', but only against the background of current horizons of experience and interpretation? If we incorporate 'deferred action', we are dealing with different temporal structures than those presumed in developmental psychological experiments on the infantile significance of gender and race categories or in interactionist approaches to identity-construction. The question, which I can only pose but not answer here, is to what extent the diverging perspectives (of intra- and intersubjective processes, conflict dynamics and social cognition) mutually exclude each other, or whether it is possible to make them useful for one another. I advocate further efforts in the latter direction.

A desideratum from a sociological perspective is that the underlying concepts of structure are not elaborated in the texts presented above – a problem shared by many contributions to the debate on intersectionality. The discussion on intersectionality and intersectional invisibility would undoubtedly also benefit from a clearer differentiation between phenomena of power disparity/power conflicts, forms of domination/dominance, forms of governmentality, structures of inequality, and forms of discrimination. Even if one analytically concentrates on discrimination and inequality within and between social groups (mostly understood in terms of relative privilege/deprivation, the relative positioning of groups in a stratification structure) from a sociological point of view, the question arises how this making of differences is shaped by and also shapes overarching societal and cultural constellations: How are specific categories of human beings embedded into a societal constellation, and how does the form of their incorporation and their action under these conditions influence their positioning in the system of inequality? Are 'categories' of people always 'groups', and if so, in what sense?

In order to be able to approach such questions in a comprehensive way, I am convinced that this requires the conceptual differentiations mentioned above. In order to be able to grasp the conditions of the reproduction of complex forms of inequality and domination in modern society, we furthermore need a more decisive engagement with social theory/theories of societalisation/theories of society (these are the connotations of the German term *Gesellschaftstheorie*). But this is easier said than done, for there is no *Gesellschaftstheorie* as such. There are various theoretical traditions with different notions of the social, of societalisation and of society whose respective ability to connect to questions of intersectionality differs accordingly. I myself strive to sound out possibilities of societal analysis by critically drawing on feminist revisions of Adorno and Horkheimer and on theories of societalisation put forward by Max Weber and Michel Foucault. And I gain much from theory discussions and research in the historical disciplines, including the Anglo-American tradition of historical sociology. Looking at the criteria deriving from critiques of earlier forms of macrosociology and social theory, I think that a complex theory of society should make it possible to take into account phenomena of societal differentiation/modernisation as well as the historically shifting forms of domination, power relations and inequality. And it should also be able to grasp the specific form assumed by capitalist societalisation 'before any particular stratification' (Adorno 1990, Knapp 2009). The question that I would like to pose in the following section relates to the possibilities and limits of transferring the concept of intersectional invisibility into a broader sociotheoretical horizon.

Obstructed Insights – Mediations of Domination

When considering sociotheoretical options, one can make a rough distinction between two main tendencies that diverge in particular on the level at which they focus on forms of societalisation: social theories which are oriented towards action theory primarily or exclusively make reference to social actors and their practices with respect to the sociostructural and discursive conditions of their action, as well as to society as a configuration of institutions with regulated practices. Here, the concept of societalisation accentuates the historically generated formation of relationships of communication, exchange and interdependence between (individual and collective) social actors and the ways they are institutionalised, understood and legitimated.

Analyses oriented towards social theory in a stricter sense of theories of society include an overlying level of construction. In addition, they focus on the historical differentiation of society into subsystems, specialised spheres of practice, sectors, or fields of societal reproduction and their relationships to one another. Accordingly, here the concept of societalisation refers not (only) to forms of the inclusion of actors or social groups in the social life process and institutional settings, but to the relations of communication, exchange, interdependence, and regulation between societally differentiated spheres of practice, functional sectors or subsystems. What is examined is how the different spheres of societal reproduction are themselves societalised (*vergesellschaftet*), that is, how are they interconnected and dependent on each other, and how the type and developmental dynamics of their relationships to each other affect structures and processes in the respective sub-systems. Which spheres of practice are to be included, and from what perspective their relationship to one another is conceptualised, is decided in the respective approaches. Economy, state, household-economy/family/intimacy, and the relationship between law, science, and religion are among the central areas for an understanding of the forms of differentiation and societalisation in modern society. The most frequently discussed question is how one can analytically do justice to the complexity of mediations without reverting to deterministic or functionalistic perspectives or, in the case of Marxist theories, misleading and reductionist constructions of base–superstructure relations.

I suspect that issues of intersectionality and thus intersectional invisibility are easier to negotiate within the framework of action-theory-based social theories, which make it possible to refer to persons and group categories. However, their translation into a conceptual architecture based in a stricter sense on a theory of society comes up against characteristic difficulties that need to be more precisely illuminated.

Let us first examine the more general question of how the invisibility of social relations or relations of dominance can even be conceived of in sociology and social theory, and in a second step translate it into the question of whether it may be useful to apply this to the problematics of intersectional invisibility. I distinguish between the thematisation of invisibility in social theory in a stricter sense (that is, theories of the social) and a theory of society perspective as developed in the early Frankfurt School, which has been taken up and revised by feminist theorists. Both make it possible to specify characteristic conceptualisations of invisibility that suggest different forms of critique and de-reifying thought.

The becoming and making invisible of social relations of power, domination, and inequality and their interferences has been connected with different concepts. The forms in which becoming invisible can take place range from naturalisation and normalisation to the reification of the social. In all cases it is about the production of an appearance of immediateness, that is, an appearance of ontological givenness, authenticity or naturalness, that obscures insight into the actual sociocultural character of phenomena. The approaches to this problem taken up in more recent work in gender studies include, for example, Mary Douglas's thoughts on 'socially structured forgetting' (Douglas 1991) and the social constructivism put forward by Peter Berger and Thomas Luckmann (1969), who pursue the objectification of social relationships and take up Marx's thoughts on alienation and reification, which they address in terms of a sociology of knowledge (Knorr-Cetina 1989).

The method of historicising reconstruction suggested in these approaches is one of the preferred methods of de-reifying critique. Thus, using an understanding of intersectional invisibility that has been expanded in this way, in the relation of class and gender in the German context one could, for instance, reconstruct how, in the course of its becoming hegemonic and established, the ideal of the breadwinner-housewife-family's origin in the bourgeois (*bürgerlich*) classes becomes increasingly invisible. With the normalisation, naturalisation, politicolegal institutionalisation, and establishment of these gender roles and concepts of the family, what also becomes invisible is how extensively the material conditions of the possibilities of this form of marriage and family remain bound to a specific form of positioning in the structure of inequality and to systems of welfare-state security. This generalised normative model, at least for West Germany, only briefly became a cross-class lived reality after the Second World War. This fact is misappropriated in contemporary theories of 'detraditionalisation'. In this respect, references to 'detraditionalisation' are less about an appropriate diagnosis of social transformation and more about overgeneralising the circumstances that prevailed in West Germany in the 1950s and 1960s, by projecting them back into the nineteenthcentury. And this usage is also about denaming the genuinely modern and class-specific origin of this family form and gender roles. Historically speaking, the gradual invisibility or socially structured forgetting of the class origin of the breadwinner-housewife model not only occurs on an ideological level. What became a hegemonic norm is also made invisible in the course of its translation into policy and into the factualities produced by decisions of those in power. In government policy, the breadwinner-housewife model served as a point of orientation in a variety of ways, for instance in the areas of social legislation, family legislation, education policy, and occupational safety legislation. It is not only cast into structurally effective decisions by conservatives, but also by representatives of the labour movement and the unions, who base their demands for a 'breadwinner's wage' and their ideas of social advancement on this ideal. In German-speaking regions, the norm of the breadwinner and the housewife enters social institutional regimes, their functions, and time economies in numerous ways at the turn of the twentieth century. In West Germany after 1945, it is essentially reinforced by post-war political decisions. Today, however, these institutional regimes, which have been generalised in the process of German unification, are as a rule no longer perceived as hegemonic cross-class structurings of gender relations but as neutral institutional facts (for example, half-day schools, the bifurcation of the vocational training system, etc.) and rationalised as practical constraints (*Sachzwänge*). Helga Krüger and her associates have empirically investigated the 'coagulated force of history' (Marcuse) materialising therein and formulated it theoretically as an 'institutional approach' in feminist theory and gender research (Krüger 2008, Becker-Schmidt and Krüger 2009, Knapp 2009; on the two variants of organised modernity in Eastern and Western Germany, see Doelling 2003).

The historical reconstruction of mediations of class and gender (that have become invisible) in the sense described is an important form of de-reifying critique. In the following, it will furthermore be shown how the becoming invisible of societal relations of power, dominance and inequality are conceived in social theory, or more precisely in the Marxist critique of political economy and the variants of (feminist) social theory critically referring to the earlier Frankfurt School. In this case, beyond socially structured forgetting and the associated forms of naturalisation and ontologisation, what is involved are objectified reversals (*Verkehrungen*) in societal relations and their function in the production of invisibility or societal unconsciousness.

With Marx, the fetish character of the commodity and the invisibility of the non-contractual element in the exchange of equivalents on the market represent the specific forms of making mediations of dominance invisible in the unfolding bourgeois, capitalist society. While 'the specific social relations of men …that assumes for them the phantasmagoric form of a relation of things' is manifested in the fetish form of the commodity (Marx MEW 23: 86), the ideology of the exchange of equivalents between labour and capital constitutive for liberal bourgeois society denames the coercive processes of 'original accumulation', from which, in the genesis of modernity, the transformation of the possession of the means of production into capital and the form of wage labour and labour capacity develop as a commodity that is free in two senses: free from the means of production and free from feudal restraints, thus free and forced to sell one's labour. The concealment of disparate initial conditions and of the mechanisms of their continued progression assists the belief in equality and the meritocratic form of the legitimation of inequality that comprise the ideological putty in modern society. At the same time, however, the claim to and possibility of equality and justice in modern societies are sustained even in their reversal.

Marx's considerations, which reflect the socioeconomic developments of his time, are based on an emphatic concept of expanded societalisation in modern (European) industrial capitalism, in whose course – he assumes – an increasing and ultimately politicisable discrepancy between socially produced wealth and its private appropriation by and availability to a few develops. As problematical as these prognoses and developmental assumptions may be in terms a teleology of history, Marx's thoughts on commodity fetishism and the non-equivalent exchange of equivalents provide an important impetus to help us understand the specific character of societalisation in the emerging capitalist society.

Other founding fathers of sociology reflected the heightened form of societalisation in industrial-capitalist society of the nineteenth century: Emile Durkheim with respect to the increasing division of labour and growing societal interdependence as 'organic solidarity', and Weber as the 'iron cage' taking on a life of its own due to economic-technical rationalisation and bureaucratic administration. Authors belonging to the early Frankfurt School, namely Adorno and Horkheimer, critically address motifs from Marx, Weber, and Durkheim and emphasise the dialectics of individualisation and societalisation in bourgeois capitalist society and the dominance of the general over the particular that increasingly permeates it. Society is manifested as an objectified context of reciprocal dependence permeated by instrumental dominance and identity thinking that sets itself up behind people's backs as an unintended, systemic consequence of their action. The capitalistic logic of utilisation (*Verwertung*) that lends this constellation its special dynamics has taken on a momentum of its own with respect to its protagonists; the occurrence seems to be irrational, crisis-laden, and no longer controllable, even for those in positions of power (Adorno 1966). The current transnational economic and ecological crises lend these thoughts a frightening actuality.

I mention this strong idea of societalisation as an increasingly irrational dominance of the general over the particular in order to illustrate the extent to which such a historically founded understanding of societalisation departs from and, indeed, has to distance itself from the idea of societies as systems of group-based hierarchies, as put forward in the Anglo-American discussion on intersectionality, for example by John Sidanius and Felicia Pratto (1999).

At issue here is the understanding of the specific form of *sociability/ societalisation* in capitalist society and, at the same time, the structurally intrinsic difficulty of doing so. This is what Adorno means when he speaks of the necessity of understanding mechanisms of societalisation prior to any particular forms of stratification which would address questions of class, race and gender in a more narrow sense, for example by asking about empirically measurable social positions and related distributions of economic, social and cultural resources.

Against the background of Marx's conceptualisation of invisibility as an objectively necessary appearance (*objektiv notwendiger Schein*), as a reversal and obscuration of insight into the historically specific character of society/ societalisation which the different variants of a critical social theory have taken up, what becomes clear is not only the subcomplex layout of a group-hierarchical model of society and social relations of dominance. What also becomes visible is how strongly this idea of societalisation is oriented towards the relation of capital and labour and the forms of surplus value and commodity exchange that developed in capitalist modernity, and is thus subcomplex in another respect and not sufficient for understanding modern society. Thus, the aspect of the functional differentiation of societal spheres of practice, which plays the primary role in modernisation theories, would, for instance, have to be much more decisively taken into account without lapsing into the reverse extreme of exaggerating the functional and criterial autonomy of the respective subsystems. This problem, common in systems theoretical approaches, arises from underestimating the dominance, power relations and inequality which permeate the forms of sectoral and institutional differentiation as well as the interrelation between different spheres of practice. Furthermore, as symptomatic one-sidedness, it must be stated that the issue of the historical mediation of patriarchalism/andrarchy/ androcentrism and capitalism and the embedding of gender relations in all aspects of the process of societal reproduction and transformation is not sufficiently taken into account. It was feminist theory that placed these questions on the agenda in the first place, and gave them the weight they deserved. Thus, a threefold opening came into play: Firstly, feminist theory extended the focus of social theory/theory of society beyond questions of 'labour' to include issues of generativity and sexuality. To use Ursula Beer's words, it is a question of the relation between the 'form of economic subsistence' (*Wirtschaftsweise*) of a society and the 'population strategy' (*Bevölkerungsweise*), which comprises generative reproduction and the associated policies of the regulation of the population (Beer 1990). In European modernity, this regulation of the population takes place within the framework of national statehood and is historically accompanied by heterocentric, ethnocentric and racist ideologies, which legitimise and rationalise processes of inclusion and exclusion, exploitation and even extermination. Secondly, the concept of labour itself is extended. From a feminist point of view, it evidently has to include all forms of societally necessary work in order to be able to determine its conflict-laden clustering in different phases of social development. These issues are at stake in the care debate, for example (Lutz 2007). In this context, Regina Becker-Schmidt has also made the fruitful suggestion that theory and empirical research should investigate the differently composed 'work ensembles' of certain social groups, the way in which different and often contradictory forms of work were, still are and have to be combined (Becker-Schmidt 2002). Yet the feminist agenda forces open the handed-down horizon of theories of societalisation in capitalist modernity not only because of the expansion of the understanding of material and generative reproduction, but also because of the specific significance accorded to issues concerning the symbolic order and cultural processes for the analysis of gender relations as a particular structure and as a structure which is itself mediated by other forms of social relationships. While 'pushing the boundaries' of former social theory in these three dimensions undoubtedly opened up new paths for feminist theorising, at the same time it became evident that such an expansion of perspectives on society can be better associated with the issues of 'work' and 'generativity' than with 'sexuality'. In the handed-down framework of social theory, 'sexuality' is viewed in a way that is only oriented towards generative reproduction and thus implicitly heteronormative, and tends to functionalistically focus on the regulation of sexuality. This is insufficient. I would argue that the relationship between the 'dispositifs of alliance and of sexuality' (Foucault) still has to be developed for social theory. The concept of society and the understanding of societalisation can be productively expanded by recourse to Foucault and to his attention to dispositifs of knowledge/power and his concepts of biopolitics and governance (Bublitz 2001).

Moreover, even a superficial glance shows that the problematics of class, gender/sexuality, race, ethnicity, and nationality are included very differently in the complex relationship between 'forms of economic subsistence' and 'population strategy'. Against the background of the emphatic concept of societalisation in modern capitalist societies, it becomes clear that an intersectional analysis of the historical constitution of this form of sociability/societalisation ('before any particular stratification' [Adorno]) is bound to clarify the specific weight with which the different factors come into play in its genesis. Here we enter a central 'construction site' in the field of social theory. Due to the large number of open research questions and problems in terms of theory architecture, it cannot be anticipated whether a more complex, new theory of society can be developed at all, or whether the systematic claims of a theory of society will not have to be trimmed back to a certain degree in favour of more middle-range, constellative analyses. Thus, to name only one example, in historical research there is a dispute over which clusters of factors promoted the emergence of European societies into modernity, and in what sense and with respect to which periods of time one can even speak of 'European modernity' (Osterhammel 2009). From the perspective of global history, in the process of original accumulation, the historical 'take-off' of Occidental capitalism, the slave trade, and the systematic exploitation of slaves have played an important role. Yet the question of how their significance for the development of bourgeois capitalist society is to be translated and weighted in terms of specific countries or regions (Western, Northern, and Eastern Europe) has not been clarified. The problem becomes even more acute from the vantage point of a historical perspective on the development of modern societies on a global scale. From an intersectional sociotheoretical point of view, which presumes that race/ethnicity/nationality are central principles of separation, structuration and mediation in the historical formation process of modern European societies, this is a serious problem.

In relation to the question of the significance of gender relations in this context the situation looks somewhat more favourable, as on the whole there is a great deal of agreement. Even Weber argued that the historical separation of 'household' and 'business' (*Haushalt und Betrieb*), which both promoted and forced specialisation, was one of the historical conditions that enabled the capitalist logic of utilisation, with its form of rationality and time economy, to radicalise itself. Feminists have taken up this thought and elaborated on it. According to them, patriarchal pre-conditions and their modern re-articulation allowed capital to decrease its reproduction costs by sourcing important conditions of this reproduction out of the expanding market-mediating economy and – across all classes – delegating them to a gender group whose services were to henceforth be available as a 'natural resource'. The processes of the historical separation and hierarchisation of social spheres and the various inclusions of gender groups into the process of societal reproduction comprise one of the foci of feminist social analysis. However, the fact that the separation, hierarchisation, and disparate societalisation of the gender groups asserted itself across classes, yet was at the same time realised under class- and ethnicity-specific conditions, has not yet been sounded out and theorised in as much detail, at least not in German-language theory. The intersectionality discussion has given this a new impetus, in particular regarding questions of ethnicity and race.

To continue outlining the question of what intersectional invisibility may mean in a sociotheoretical horizon, I would like to address Becker-Schmidt's thoughts on the problem of the invisibility of mediations of domination. Explicitly taking up Marx's remarks on the forms of reversal in the relations between capital and labour, she investigates the chains of discrimination in women's lives by tracing 'false connections'. By 'false connections' she means, generally speaking, 'a social arrangement in which that which is otherwise separate is entangled in such a way that social discrepancies become invisible in the mode of their fusion, and the associated social impositions remain hidden' (Becker-Schmidt 2009: unpublished script). Becker-Schmidt understands 'fault connections' (Marx) in gender relations as the effect of the 'twofold societalisation' of members of the female gender group, that is, their historically predominant, simultaneous inclusion in two forms of social practice in European modernity. The combination of unpaid and paid work in the working ensemble of women is a 'false connection' whose historical and social conditions and costs can be denamed. Thus, what manifests the separation of the spheres of practice today in the so-called 'compatibility problem' or the 'work–life balance', but also in the 'care chain' (Lutz 2007), is an obstructed, unrecognised fundamental societal conflict: the incompatibility of the market-mediated and privately organised processes of reproduction in modern capitalist societies. This incompatibility points towards aspects of dominance both in the historical process of the differentiation of both sectors, in which historically antecedent forms of patriarchal domination modernised and amalgamated with capitalist interests and imperatives, and in the current form of their coaction. Thus what also remains unrecognised, not least due to its androcentric suppression in religion, science and politics, is that the 'false connection' of labour and capital Marx described gains particular relevance in women's working ensemble, where the fatal contradictoriness of the organisation of social processes of material and generative reproduction manifests itself. Last but not least, due to the separation of spheres and 'false connections', the power divide in the sectoral division of functions is also concealed, which has an impact on gender relations in the reinforcement of disparities. According to Becker-Schmidt, in a class- and ethnicity-specific way the chain of 'false connections' contributes to the outlining and aggravation of problem areas, but at the same time to their concealment (Becker-Schmidt 2007).

Outlook

When Adorno sees the task of de-reifying critique as tackling the 'irrevocability of things in being' by reading them '… as texts of their becoming', and when, in this context, he establishes that 'their becoming fades and dwells within the things; it can no more be stabilised in their concepts than it can be split off from its own results and forgotten' (Adorno 1966: 60), then one could translate intersectional invisibility in such a way that one reads it as a kind of disappearance of the relations constitutive of what has been constituted. With recourse to Adorno, one could then ask how antecedent forms of domination, differentiation, and inequalities that enabled and promoted the development of bourgeois capitalist modernity in the West still 'dwell within the things', where they can neither be stabilised in their concepts nor forgotten. And one could ask which factors and contemporary developments obscure insight into these interrelationships. From a feminist point of view, it then becomes a matter of how gender relations and their transformations are embedded in the historical constitution of this capitalist system of utilisation, which, as is generally known, feeds on resources that it does not itself produce. In her recent essay 'Feminism, Capitalism and the Cunning of History', Nancy Fraser pointed out the irritating possibility, which has also been part of the discussion on governance and new forms of subjectivation for some time, that the feminist project of emancipation is itself involved in the emergence of post-Fordist, neoliberal, and transnational capitalism (Fraser 2009). I believe that this kind of 'dialectics of feminist enlightenment' and the consequences that can be derived from it for feminist critique can only be understood in a sociotheoretical framework that has been extended by intersectional perspectives.

According to its self-claim, 'modern society' may not be based on relations that contradict its own concept. Thus, inequality in modern society is only acceptable if it can be meritocratically legitimised. In contrast, beyond a belief in equality and meritocracy, feminist social analyses make reference to mediations of dominance in the fundamental structures of modern society and to forms of their concealment. Up to now, the interrelationships between class and gender, and between capitalism and patriarchalism/andrarchism/androcentrism in their changing constellations, have been most extensively investigated in German-language feminist theory. Beyond that, and from the broader perspective of a critical archaeology of (European) modernity inspired by intersectionality, one must also ask what role the history of colonialism, slavery, and imperialism played in the constitution of this societal formation, and in what way its repercussions impact the present day. In the process, however, the focus on dominance and inequality cannot be allowed to become an absolute itself. The specific occurrences of dominance and inequality in modernity can only be made comprehensively accessible if the forms of institutional differentiation that have effectively been achieved are taken seriously and are not too strongly relativised in advance, whether this is due to the exclusive concentration on issues of dominance and inequality or to base–superstructure constructions.

In this context, the strengthening of a historical, time-diagnostic dimension would be necessary. I can only hint at this here. The forms of naturalisation, ontologisation, and reification treated above may continue to be primary factors in the production of social unconsciousness in the way they emerged in modern society. It is nevertheless obvious – and this leads to asynchronicities in the arrangement of socially structured forgetting, and thus in intersectional invisibility as well – that under the influence of new systems of governmentality and increasing mediatisation in the twenty-first century, older variants of ontologisation and naturalisation combine with novel forms and counteract, challenge, and in a paradoxical way reinforce them. Contemporary society's signature includes perhaps less than ever before the production of an appearance of immutability and constitutionality – although, on the one hand, these forms of ontologisation continue to exist, and, on the other, they were, upon closer inspection, also reworked even earlier within the framework of evolutionist and eugenic ideas and platforms at the turn of the twentieth century. With the transition to the twenty-first century, the associated ideology of feasibility was both radicalised and its sphere of influence expanded: the ontological appearance of the present feeds on the suggestion of the endless plasticity of the human and the unlimited flexibility and unconditionality of 'zero drag employees' (Hochschild 2002) to whose apron strings or trouser legs no one is tied.

Numerous challenges are associated with these questions. A central problematic under conditions of globalisation and transnationalisation concerns the space-related implications of intersecting forms of dominance, inequality and difference. What distinguishes from one another the spatial axioms that implicitly structure the perspective on class, gender, nation/ethnicity? Does the theorising of gender relations and forms of patriarchal dominance call other spatio-temporal frames into action, in addition to dealing with capitalism, class relations or nation-statehood and its associated systems of ethnic-racist inclusion and exclusion? And what kind of temporality emerges when we ask about intersections/intermediations? Are there intersectional path dependencies in different societies towards which comparative research should direct its attention (Gottschall 2009)? A spatial turn in the sense suggested would enrich the feminist discussion on intersectionality. This also applies to the question of the situatedness of knowledge production, one of the central questions for comparative or connective feminist research. We still know too little about the ways in which sociohistorical resonance spaces influence the resonant spaces of theory (Knapp 2008, 2009, Davis and Evans 2010). Moreover, a greater awareness of the historico-spatial implications of theory formation – and this is specifically applicable to the intersectional macro-perspective of social interrelationships and for time-diagnostic concepts – enables the emergence of a greater awareness of the limitations of the claims of validity which one can legitimately connect with one's own statements. This promises orientational knowledge for the tightrope walk between the Scylla of a formalisation of sociological theory in the service of a heightening of conceptual systematics, on the one hand, which are often paid for with a blind eye turned towards the particular, and the Charybdis of a particularistic contextual knowledge on the other hand, which is conceptually unable to apprehend that it itself is shaped by overarching societal constellations of differentiation, dominance, and inequality and the related forms of invisibility.

Bibliography

Adorno, T.W. 1966. *Negative Dialektik*. Frankfurt a.M.: Suhrkamp.

Adorno, T.W. 1990. Gesellschaft, in *Gesammelte Schriften 8, Soziologische Schriften 1*, Frankfurt a.M.: Suhrkamp, 9–20.

Becker-Schmidt, R. 1990. Vergesellschaftung – innere Vergesellschaftung. Individuum, Klasse, Geschlecht aus der Perspektive der Kritischen Theorie, in *Die Modernisierung moderner Gesellschaften. Verhandlungen des 25. Deutschen Soziologentages in Frankfurt a.M.*, edited by W. Zapf. Frankfurt a.M./New York: Campus, 383–95.

Becker-Schmidt, R. 1998. Trennung, Verknüpfung, Vermittlung: Zum feministischen Umgang mit Dichotomien, in *Kurskorrekturen. Feminismus zwischen Kritischer Theorie und Postmoderne*, edited by Knapp, G.-A. Frankfurt a.M. & New York: Campus, 84–126.

Becker-Schmidt, R. 2002. Theorizing Gender Arrangements, in *Gender and Work in Transition: Globalization in Western, Middle and Eastern Europe*, edited by Becker-Schmidt, R. Opladen: Leske und Budrich, 25–49.

Becker-Schmidt, R. 2007. 'Class', 'gender', 'ethnicity', 'race'; Logiken der Differenzsetzung, Verschränkungen von Ungleichheitslagen und gesellschaftliche Strukturierung, in *Achsen der Ungleichheit. Zum Verhältnis von Klasse, Geschlecht und Ethnizität*, edited by Klinger, C., Knapp, G.-A. and Sauer, B. Frankfurt a.M.: Campus, 56–84.

Becker-Schmidt, R. 2009. Unpublished lecture manuscript Kassel, November 2009.

Becker-Schmidt, R. and Krüger, H. 2009. Krisenherde in gegenwärtigen Sozialgefügen: Asymmetrische Arbeits- und Geschlechterverhältnisse – vernachlässigte Sphären gesellschaftlicher Reproduktion, in *Arbeit. Perspektiven und Diagnosen der Geschlechterforschung*, edited by Aulenbacher, B. and Wetterer, A. Münster: Westfälisches Dampfboot, 12–42.

Beer, U. 1990. *Geschlecht, Struktur, Geschichte. Soziale Konstituierung des Geschlechterverhältnisses*. Frankfurt a.M. & New York: Campus.

Benhabib, S. 1999. *Kulturelle Vielfalt und demokratische Gleichheit. Politische Partizipation im Zeitalter der Globalisierung*. Horkheimer–Vorlesungen. Frankfurt a.M.: Fischer.

Berger, P. and Luckmann, T. 1969. *Die gesellschaftliche Konstruktion der Wirklichkeit. Eine Theorie der Wissenssoziologie.* Frankfurt a.M.: Fischer.

Brubaker, R. 2007. *Ethnizität ohne Gruppen.* Hamburg: Hamburger Edition.

Bublitz, H. 2001. Geschlecht als historisch singuläres Ereignis: Foucaults poststrukturalistischer Beitrag zu einer Gesellschafts–Theorie der Geschlechterverhältnisse, in *Soziale Verortung der Geschlechter. Gesellschaftstheorie und feministische Kritik*, edited by Knapp, G.-A. and Wetterer, A. Münster: Westfälisches Dampfboot, 256–88.

Crenshaw, K. 2000. *The Intersection of Race and Gender Discrimination.* Background paper for the United Nations Regional Expert Group Meeting, Zagreb, Croatia, 21–24 November.

Davis, K. and Evans, M. 2010 (forthcoming). *Transatlantic Conversations.*

Douglas, M. 1991. *Wie Institutionen denken.* Frankfurt a.M.: Suhrkamp.

Doelling, I. 2003. Zwei Wege gesellschaftlicher Modernisierung. Geschlechtervertrag und Geschlechterarrangements in Ostdeutschland in gesellschafts-/modernisierungstheoretischer Perspektiven, in *Achsen der Differenz. Gesellschaftstheorie und feministische Kritik II*, edited by Knapp, G.-A. and Wetterer, A. Münster: Westfälisches Dampfboot, 73–101.

Fraser, N. 2009. Feminismus, Kapitalismus und die List der Geschichte. *Blätter für deutsche und internationale Politik*, 08/2009, 43–57.

Friedan, B. 1966. *Der Weiblichkeitswahn. Ein vehementer Protest gegen das Wunschbild von der Frau.* Reinbekbei Hamburg: Rowohlt.

Gottschall, K. 2009. Arbeitsmärkte und Geschlechterungleichheit – Forschungstraditionen und internationaler Vergleich, in *Arbeit. Perspektiven und Diagnosen der Geschlechterforschung*, edited by Aulenbacher, B. and Wetterer, A. Münster: Westfälisches Dampfboot, 120–38.

Hochschild, A.R. 2002. *Keine Zeit. Wenn die Firma zum Zuhause wird und zu Hause nur Arbeit wartet.* Wiesbaden: VS.

Knapp, G.-A. 1987. Arbeitsteilung und Sozialisation. Konstellationen von Arbeitsvermögen und Arbeitskraft im Lebenszusammenhang von Frauen, in *Klasse Geschlecht, Feministische Gesellschaftsanalyse und Wissenschaftskritik*, edited by Beer, U. Bielefeld: AJZ-Verlag/ FF1, 236–74.

Knapp, G.-A. 2008. Verhältnisbestimmungen: Geschlecht, Klasse, Ethnizität in gesellschaftstheoretischer Perspektive, in *ÜberKreuzungen. Fremdheit, Ungleichheit, Differenz*, edited by Klinger, C. and Knapp, G.-A. Münster: Westfälisches Dampfboot, 138–71.

Knapp, G.-A. 2009. Fort – Da. Geschlecht in ungleichzeitigen Konstellationen, in *Gender Scripts. Widerspenstige Aneignungen von Geschlechternormen*, edited by Binswanger, C., Bridges, M. and Schnegg, B. Frankfurt a.M./New York: Campus, 23–42.

Knorr-Cetina, K. 1989. Spielarten des Konstruktivismus. Einige Notizen und Anmerkungen. *Soziale Welt*, 40(1/2), 86–96.

Krüger, H. 2008. Lebenslauf: Dynamiken zwischen Biographie und Geschlechterverhältnis, in *Handbuch Frauen- und Geschlechterforschung.*

Theorie, Methoden, Empirie, edited by Becker, R. and Kortendiek, B. Wiesbaden: VS, 2nd ed., 212–21.

Küster, S. 2007. Staatsangehörigkeit in Deutschland: Historische Aspekte der Nationalisierung und Ethnisierung von 'Fremdheit', in *Achsen der Ungleichheit. Zum Verhältnis von Klasse, Geschlecht und Ethnizität*, edited by Klinger, C., Knapp, G.-A. and Sauer, B. Frankfurt a.M. & New York: Campus, 193–210.

Lutz, H. 2007. *Vom Weltmarkt in den Privathaushalt. Die neuen Dienstmädchen im Zeitalter der Globalisierung*. Opladen & Farmington Hills: Barbara Budrich.

Marx, K., MEW 23, Das Kapital. Kritik der politischen Ökonomie. Erster Band, in: Marx, K. and Engels, F.: Werke, Band 23, Berlin: Dietz Verlag.

Osterhammel, J. 2009. *Die Verwandlung der Welt. Eine Geschichte des 19. Jahrhunderts*. München: C.H: Beck.

Purdie-Vaughns, V. and Eibach, R.P. 2008. Intersectional Invisibility: The Distinctive Advantages and Disadvantages of Multiple Subordinate-Group Identities. *Sex Roles*, 59, 377–91.

Querelles-Net: Nr. 26. 2008. Dimensionen von Ungleichheit, Forumsdiskussion zu Tove Soiland: Die Verhältnisse gingen, die Kategorien kamen. Intersectionality oder Vom Unbehagen an der amerikanischen Theorie.

Rendtorff, B. 2008. Warum Geschlecht doch etwas 'Besonderes' ist, in *ÜberKreuzungen. Fremdheit, Ungleichheit, Differenz*, edited by Klinger, C. and Knapp, G.-A. Münster: Westfälisches Dampfboot, 68–87.

Sidanius, J. and Pratto, F. 1999. *Social Dominance: An intergroup theory of social hierarchy and oppression*. New York: Cambridge University Press.

Siems, S. 2007. *Die deutsche Karriere kollektiver Identität. Vom wissenschaftlichen Begriff zum massenmedialen Jargon*. Münster: Westfälisches Dampfboot.

Skeggs, B. 2004. *Class, Self, Culture*. London: Routledge.

Chapter 12

Intersectional Analysis: Black Box or Useful Critical Feminist Thinking Technology?

Nina Lykke

The concept of intersectionality has become popular among feminists. In recent years, an increasing number of special issues of journals, books, conferences, PhD courses and programmes have been devoted to intersectionality. The conference 'Celebrating Intersectionality?' which gave rise to this book was one of these events. The large number of participants and intensive discussions at the conference testified to the attractiveness of the concept. But different kinds of ambivalence and scepticism vis-à-vis the concept are also in circulation. The question mark, which was included in the conference title, was obviously inserted to indicate this.

Ambivalences and scepticisms take different forms. Is the metaphor of 'intersections', that is, roads crossing each other, helpful as a tool to rethink how power differentials, normativities and identity formations in terms of gender, race, class, sexuality, etc., are mutually co-constructed? Or does it rather create more analytical problems than it solves? Is it useful to think about developing a 'fully fledged' theory of intersectionality? And does this imply the need to define a fixed cluster of categories to be analysed as part of an intersectional analysis? Or should we, rather than trying to develop a 'fully fledged' theory with a fixed cluster of categories, opt for a definition of intersectionality as a nodal point,[1] an open-ended framework for comparing different feminist conceptualisations of intersecting power differentials, normativities and identity formations? These and many other critical questions are in circulation. I will address some of them in this chapter.

As an entrance point, I shall underline that I find it important to 'celebrate' intersectionality as a useful critical tool for feminist analysis. But I am also in agreement with those who inserted the question mark in the above-mentioned conference title. The concept of intersectionality deserves to be celebrated, but its use also needs to be critically reflected. My aim here is to carry out such a critical reflection.

The chapter is structured so that I first explain why I think it is useful to approach the concept of intersectionality as a nodal point for different feminist strands of theorising. Second, I argue that it is important to avoid black-boxing the concept

---

1   My use of the term 'nodal point' (cf. Laclau and Mouffe 1985: 112) serves to indicate my understanding of the feminist conceptual toolbox as 'temporary crystallizations in ongoing feminist negotiations of located theory making' (Lykke 2010: 49).

by always contextualising and situating it. But I also underline how its capacities for rhizomatic flight and for teasing out tensions and conflicts between different strands of feminist theory and politics might be used for posing new political questions and thinking through pressing theoretical issues. Third, I shall refer to a couple of examples from the history of feminist theorising, where political and theoretical struggles over intersections have come forcefully to the fore. I suggest that moments such as these can be re-read as moments of becoming of a kind of in-depth theoretical and passionate political intersectional analysis that I would like to see as an open-ended guideline.

Intersectionality as a Nodal Point

As many understandings of intersectionality are circulating in feminist theory today, I shall start by setting out how I use the term in my approach. First and foremost, I think that it is important, meta-theoretically, to define all concepts of the feminist toolbox, including this one, as nodal points (cf. note 1). This implies that I do not want to establish intersectionality as a concept with a once-and-for-all fixed definition. I find it more appropriate to handle the concept of intersectionality as a discursive site where different feminist positions are in critical dialogue or productive conflict with each other.

Against this background, I shall define intersectionality as a broad, open-ended and inclusive conceptual tool for feminist analysis. My aim is to sustain an understanding of intersectionality as a thinking technology that encompasses a multiplicity of ways in which the concept is used to analyse how power differentials, normativities and identity formations in terms of categorisations[2] such as gender, ethnicity, race, class, sexuality, age/generation, nationality, etc., co-produce in/exclusion, mis/recognition, dis/possession, re/distribution, majoritising/minoritising, etc.

As part of this general definition, it is also important to emphasise that the point is to analyse how categorisations are interweaved. Following the feminist theorist Karen Barad (2003: 815) and more elaborate arguments put forward in my recent book (Lykke 2010: 50–52), I shall, therefore, immediately revise my definition and replace 'interact' with the term '*intra-act*'. Barad stresses that interaction is something that takes place between bounded entities, clashing against each other but not generating mutual transformations. Conversely, intra-action refers to the interplay between non-bounded phenomena, which interpenetrate and mutually transform each other while interplaying. What is important for many feminists when they speak of intersectionalities between gender, race, ethnicity, etc., are

---

2   The German feminist scholar Antje Hornscheidt (2007: 67) has argued that the term 'categorisation' is more appropriate than 'category' when social and communicative processes of 'categorising' are to be emphasised; 'category' is associated with the reified and congealed results, while 'categorisation' captures the aspect of process better.

processes of co-production and mutual transformation. Therefore, I think that Barad's notion of intra-action is appropriate.

In order to take into account the meta-theoretical definition of intersectionality as a nodal point, I think it is important to reflect on the conceptual genealogies as well as the broader genealogies of feminist theorising of intersections. As I have argued in more detail elsewhere (Lykke 2010: 68–70), my point is to emphasise that the concept of intersectionality, when *explicitly* articulated by black US feminists in the late 1980s and 1990s (Crenshaw 1989, 1995), gave voice to theoretical endeavours that until then had been widespread and outspoken in feminist theorising but lacked the kind of joint nodal point that a shared concept can give. I have defined these wider endeavours as *implicit* theorising of intersectionalities. I have referred to such theoretical strands as feminist Marxisms, pre-Crenshaw anti-racist, black and post-colonial feminisms, various parts of psychoanalytic feminisms, queer feminisms, lesbian feminisms, and feminist youth culture studies. I have also presented some historical examples. I have followed bell hooks (1981) as well as Avtar Brah and Ann Phoenix (2004) in their references to the US anti-slavery movement spokeswoman Sojourner Truth's critical reflections on intersections of gender and race in her famous 'Ain't I a Woman?' speech at the Women's Rights Convention in Ohio in 1851 (Gates and McKay 1997). I have also referred to feminist socialists from the late nineteenth and early twentieth century such as Russian Bolshevik feminist Alexandra Kollontai and her critical discussions with the bourgeois women's movement on the issue of intersections of gender and class (Kollontai 1971: 34).

I think it is important to have a joint nodal point, that is, a shared framework for the negotiation of conceptualisations. Therefore, I find the concept of intersectionality productive. A conceptual nodal point facilitates the comparison of differences and similarities of related political, theoretical and analytical endeavours and can provide fertile soil for an analytical sophistication that can strengthen political solidarity and action. But as part of an exploration of genealogies, I think that it is important to acknowledge that intersectional thinking and analysis have been an integrated part of much feminist thought in a long-term historical perspective.

When the wider scope and genealogies of intersectional thought in different kinds of feminism are to be underlined, it is also important to mention that a range of other related concepts are in circulation in feminist theory, for example notions such as 'interlocking oppressions', as used in the classic black lesbian feminist manifesto by the US Combahee River Collective (1977/1982), 'inappropriate/d otherness' (Minh-ha 1986/87, 1989, Haraway 1992), 'interferences' (Moser 2006), 'differences among women' (Lauretis 1984, Braidotti 1994) and 'differential powers, politics and consciousness' (Sandoval 2000).

Feminist ideas about intersectionalities have come in different shapes. As a rough genealogical analysis (cf. Lykke 2010: 68–69), I have suggested a distinction between feminist intersectional analyses which:

- *explicitly* theorise intersections of gender, race, etc., via the concept of intersectionality
- *implicitly* theorise intersections of gender, race, etc., but without explicitly using the label 'intersectionality'
- use *other concepts and names* in order to refer to the phenomenon of intersections of gender, race, etc.

Black-boxing or Contextualising?

When critical feminist concepts such as intersectionality become popular, a black-boxing effect seems to be unavoidable. Black-boxing means that concepts turn into rhetorical devices, something that people refer to without reflecting on implications and contexts. As black boxes – and buzzwords – in this sense, concepts may also start functioning as markers of dis/agreement in an identity political sense. The bottom line is that people tend to use them in a decontextualised manner.[3] Taken out of the specific contexts that relate intersectionalities to various particular forms of mutually intra-acting power differentials, normativities and identity formations, the concept may end up as shorthand for multiple categorisations (gender, race, etc.) that oblige the analysts to reflect neither on their differences/samenesses nor on their status vis-à-vis each other. Precise distinctions between different kinds of categorisations may vanish, with the effect that the critical powers of intersectional analysis are reduced or disappear altogether.

The listing of intersecting categorisations (gender, class, race, sexuality, age, nationhood, dis/ability, etc.[4]) can be rhetorically seductive and generate a push towards making intersectionality an explanation in itself. If, for example, the analyst has explained something in terms of intersections between gender, class and race, everything seems to have been said about this particular phenomenon; the analytical endeavour stops and questions such as 'what is class?', 'what is race?', 'what is gender?', 'how do they intra-act on a micro- and a macrosocial level?' are left unexplored. Instead, the analyst may be carried away towards an open-ended line of other categorisations (sexuality, age, dis/ability, etc.) that need to be analysed. When this happens, intersectionality is reduced to a black box, a machine for throwing more and more new categories on the table.

To some analysts, a sensible counter-strategy to this machine-like performance would be to define a limited number of important intersections such as, for example, the classic triad of gender-race-class and then to scrutinise them on the basis of a coherent theoretical framework (for example a feminist neo-Marxist one) that will allow for in-depth analysis.

---

3   The notion of a black box effect is indeed narrowly related to Kathy Davis's buzzword effect (this volume 43f).

4   Judith Butler articulates the dilemmas related to the seductive lining up of categorisations as the 'embarrassed' etc. clause (Butler 1990: 143, Villa in this volume 171f).

Rhizomatics?

But is the demand for limited numbers of analytical categorisations and coherent theoretical frameworks that can be deemed suitable in advance for the analysis of a particular configuration of intersecting categorisations (for example, gender-race-class) the only answer to the black-boxing problem? Are there other possibilities than just declaring the machine-like and decontextualising performance of the black-boxing effect problematic and, against this background, trying to exorcise it from the analysis? Could it also be considered differently? My answer is yes. Let us see what happens if I shift the analytical perspective and, instead of a decontextualisation, reflect the black-boxing effect as a rhizomatic de-territorialisation in accordance with the concept of the French philosophers Gilles Deleuze and Félix Guattari (1992).

With a Deleuzian framework as my lens, the black-boxing effect may shift from a purely negative and problematic thing, which we as researchers should try to avoid and transcend, to something that can be considered as part of an analytical strategy with more positive and affirmative implications. In the philosophy of Deleuze and Guattari (1992), the botanical image of the rhizome (underground plant stems that move horizontally in all directions, and which bear both roots and shoots) is used to illustrate knowledge production that follows more associative 'lines of flight' or 'processes of de-territorialisation', that is, knowledge production that does not stick to one theoretical territory. Such knowledge-producing processes are contrasted with more traditional ones understood with the help of the image of a taproot growing deeper and deeper into the earth along a straight and predetermined line. Deleuze's reflections on rhizomatics are part of his work on redefining what it means to think, and as noted by feminist philosopher Rosi Braidotti, these endeavours 'to "image" the activity of thinking differently' (Braidotti 1994: 100) can be very useful for feminist theorists who share with Deleuze 'a concern for the urgency, the necessity to re-define, re-figure and re-invent theoretical practice' (Braidotti ibid.).

Like the plant stems that move horizontally in all directions, rhizomatics as an analytical practice means following theoretical lines of flight, and in so doing accepting non-hierarchical connections between heterogeneous and multiple phenomena touching each other in unexpected ways. Braidotti also describes theorising in a rhizomatical mode as a constant move between different theoretical positions – as a:

> going in between different discoursive fields, passing through diverse spheres of intellectual discourse. Theory today happens 'in transit', moving on, passing through, creating connections where things were previously disconnected or seemed unrelated, where there seemed to be 'nothing to see'. (Braidotti 2002: 173–174)

I agree with Leslie McCall that intersectionality is one of the 'most important theoretical contributions that Women's Studies, in conjunction with related fields, has made so far' (McCall 2005: 1771). For me this means we need to take seriously the metatheoretical potential of the concept of intersectionality to break up fixed theoretical frameworks, and in a positive rhizomatic sense to follow the non-hierarchical lines of flight within, between and across different social categorisations and intersections as the concept seems to ask us to do as analysts. More precisely, I find it challenging and productive to pursue questions such as these: What happens when we try to free the issue of co-produced power differentials, normativities and identity formations at stake in a certain analytical context from its link to a theoretical-political 'territory' (for example, theorisations of the intersections of gender-race-class within a feminist neo-Marxist frame)? What is the outcome if, for example, we try instead to tentatively locate the phenomenon under scrutiny in a framework of gender-sexuality-dis/ability discussions (that is, in fields with rather different theoretical and political traditions and ontologies)?

Seen with a rhizomatic de-territorialisation as an affirmative lens, the answer is that the process of shifting from one context to another may create open, new and important questions. When I shift the optics, the process that from another perspective may appear as a machine-like black-boxing that, in a negative sense, leads the analysis away from a thoroughly reflected context, can now be reconsidered. Intersectionality reappears as a 'shifter' that, in a positive sense, may facilitate the opening up of new analytical and political questions and generate a productive impetus to identify more interfering power differentials, normativities and identity markers than the ones that presented themselves to the analyst as the first 'evident' focus.

The critical race theory scholar Maria Matsuda articulated this positive potential of intersectional analysis to generate still new and unexpected questions and perspectives with elegant simplicity when she suggested the methodology of 'asking the other question':

> When I see something that looks racist, I ask, 'Where is the patriarchy in this?' When I see something that looks sexist, I ask, 'Where is the heterosexism in this?' When I see something that looks homophobic, I ask, 'Where is the class interest in this?' (Matsuda 1991: 1189)

To Combine Contextualising and Going with the Rhizomatic Flow...

In the two previous sections, I outlined two seemingly opposing ways of approaching intersectional analysis and two rather different reactions vis-à-vis the black-boxing effect that seems to accompany the growing popularity of the concept of intersectionality. One strategy is to oppose the black-boxing effect by giving priority to a meticulous theoretical contextualisation of specific intersections, limited in number and 'properly' defined within a certain theoretical framework. The second strategy urges the analyst to go with the machine-like flow of the black-boxing effect and to establish a rhizomatic and de-territorialising line of flight from intersection to intersection.

In addition to indicating some cross-cutting dilemmas of current discussions of intersectional analysis, I want to argue that a paradoxical combination of the two opposing strategies might bring interesting results. On the one hand, I agree with those who defend theoretical and political contextualisation as important for intersectional analysis. I, too, find it crucial not just to line up categorisations and intersections without reflecting, genealogically, on the theoretical and political traditions in which they are embedded, and which give them meaning as critical lenses for new ontologies. On the other hand, I think that one of the important strengths of intersectional analysis is precisely that it urges the analyst to 'go with the flow' – and to take up the challenges of this flowing mode, which include letting oneself be led towards unexpected, disturbing, messy, paradoxical and perhaps conflicting perspectives and questions.

Against this background, I opt for a strategy of contextualising *and* opening up cross-cutting dialogues on disturbing intersections and conflicting theoretical-political perspectives. To illustrate what I mean, I shall briefly refer to a couple of feminist theoretical-political debates that were not explicitly carried out under the banner of intersectional analysis but which, genealogically, could be read through this lens.

Judith Butler will be a protagonist in both examples, and intersections related to sex and sexuality will figure prominently. I could have chosen other examples, theorists and intersections. My particular choice is motivated in two ways. First, I think that Butler's very sophisticated theoretical contributions to the intersectionality debate are not taken into account sufficiently. Her work deserves more attention in relation to the emerging canon of texts on intersectionality. Secondly, I think that sex and sexuality lead a strange shadow-life on the margins of this canon; often, they appear as categorisations that, without specific reflections, sometimes are and sometimes are not added to the basic trinity of gender-race-class.

The Queer/Feminist Debate on Sex, Sexuality and Gender

As my first example, I shall refer to the debate on the relationship of sexuality, sex and gender that took place as part of the unfolding of queer theory. In a genealogical perspective, the debate between queer scholars such as Gayle Rubin and Eve Kosofsky Sedgwick, on the one hand, and queerfeminists such as Butler, on the other, begs to be read as a crucial moment in a process of becoming of a disturbing and transformative intersectional analysis that is firmly embedded in contextual theoretical reflections, but that at the same time passionately and rhizomatically moves out of the comfort zones provided by these contextualisations. To make my point, I shall briefly re-read the debate from this perspective.

The debate grew out the US feminist 'sex wars' (Duggan and Hunter 2006), that is, the political struggle that took place in the late 1970s and 1980s, where anti-pornography feminists and sex-positive feminists became entangled in major conflicts. In the wake of the 'sex wars', Rubin and Sedgwick articulated a strong critique of the status of the heterosexual couple as the hegemonic norm for all intimate life, claiming that the anti-pornography feminists reproduced this norm in their discourses. As part of the fight against what Rubin (1984) and Sedgwick (1990) saw as the heteronormativity of the anti-pornography feminists, they launched the idea that analyses of gender and analyses of sexuality ought to be separated. According to Rubin and Sedgwick, such a separation would make it possible to scrutinise sexual hierarchies, sexual diversity and sexual ambiguities without risking a constant destructive interference from an essentialist and normative two-gender model and from an anti-sex version of feminism. Queer theory was to be used as an analytical tool in the analysis of sexuality, while gender theory was appropriate for the analysis of gender – this, in brief, was the argument that constructed a neat separation.

The analytical separation of sexuality and gender has been celebrated, but also criticised from queerfeminist positions. According to queerfeminists such as Butler (1990, 1993), discourses on gender, sex and sexuality are so entangled in each other that separating them will lead to both analytical and political reductionism. Instead, queerfeminists argue that it is important to scrutinise the relationship between sex, sexuality and gender and to deconstruct the normalised and naturalised link between them. In order to avoid hegemonic discourses about two heteronormatively defined genders unreflectedly interfering with the queer theoretical analysis, Butler and other queer feminists argue that it is necessary to critically analyse how gendered and sexualised power differentials, normativities and identity formations are entangled in each other.

While Rubin and Sedgwick's position would lead in the direction of a simple additive kind of intersectional analysis – first we analyse gender, then we analyse sex/sexuality, or vice versa – Butler (1990, 1993) takes on the more complex task of reflecting in a meticulously contextualised way on the difficult questions posed by the open-ended flow/flight and displacing moves between sex, sexuality and gender: how would we carry out an intersectional analysis of the three categorisations in an intra-active sense? Read through the lens of intersectional analysis, what Butler does in *Gender Trouble* (1990) and in *Bodies that Matter* (1993) is to answer this complex question through a major genealogical thinking through intra-active links between constructions of gender, sex and sexuality. Her texts are good examples of the work to be carried out when one has committed oneself to the task of taking conflicted and disturbing intersections and cross-cutting lines seriously in a contextualised way.

Merely Cultural? Between Redistribution and Recognition

Another example of a feminist theory debate that begs to be read through the lens of intersectional analysis is the one between US political philosopher Nancy Fraser (1995) and Butler (1998) on redistribution and recognition as political strategies. This debate can be read as yet another moment of thoroughly contextualised feminist theorising of disturbing, conflicted and troubling intersections.

Let me briefly recapitulate the debate. Fraser (1995) wanted to insist on the importance of the debate on material inequality and the logic of unjust distribution of material wealth in a 'post-socialist' age, where issues of class struggle were in decline. But she also wanted to take into account the rise of the queer movement. In order to accomplish this dual task, she articulated a model for intersectional analysis that took into account the categorisations of class, race, gender and sexuality. Class and 'despised sexualities' (Fraser 1995: 74–76) were theorised as based on different, one-dimensional logics of inequality. Class was seen, along Marxist lines, as produced by a logic of unjust economic-political distribution, while despised sexualities were considered as produced by a logic of cultural misrecognition. By contrast, gender and race were analysed as what Fraser (1995: 78) called 'bivalent' categories, that is, related to two kinds of inequality. Both (like class) were seen as based on a logic of unjust economic-political distribution as well as being (like despised sexualities) based on a logic of cultural misrecognition (see also Yuval-Davis in this volume (155f)).

Butler (1998) criticised Fraser's aspirations towards a political unity on the Left that did not take into account political differences. In particular, she argued that Fraser's distinction between economic-political injustice, on the one hand, and cultural injustice, on the other, was theoretically unsustainable and generated the problematic effect that the issue of social stigmatisation of queers was relegated politically to the sphere of the 'merely cultural'. Butler argued that Fraser's model reproduced a simplistic and economistic Marxism's problematic, hierarchical division between an economic base and a cultural/ideological superstructure. Lining up with more complex readings of Marx, Butler emphasised how issues of culture, family and sexuality in Marxist theory are reflected as issues belonging to the political-economic base, or more precisely how, in these alternative Marxist traditions, they are seen as phenomena that demonstrate the reductionism of such a theoretical distinction.

If I read the debate between Fraser and Butler through the lens of intersectional analysis, it seems to me that Butler's arguments are sustained – both through the kind of complex readings of Marx that reject the simplistic base-superstructure model and through the demand for an intra-active understanding that is a crucial dimension of most feminist interpretations of intersectionality. Fraser wants to articulate a model for intersectional politics. But what she ends up with, when she insists on the analytical distinction between economic-political redistribution and cultural recognition, is a tool for repeating a simplistic additive approach that theoretically and analytically avoids entering the messy spaces that will emerge when feminist Marxist traditions of analysis of gender-race-class intersections are brought to intra-act with queer feminist, Foucauldian and deconstructive traditions of analysis of gender-sex-sexuality intersections.

As in the discussion with Rubin and Sedgwick on the intersections of gender, sex and sexuality, Butler again takes a different and more complex route than her dialogue partners. Instead of just insisting on a queer theoretical analysis as more comprehensive than what is suggested by Fraser, Butler challenges Fraser on Marxist grounds. She mobilises more sophisticated analyses of the place of family, culture and sexuality in Marxist theory than the simplistic base-superstructure model allows. But she does more interesting things than this.

As part of her move into feminist Marxist analysis, Butler also argues for a temporary leaving of the comfort zones of one's own established theoretical points of departure – in her case: a post-structuralist deconstructionist perspective. She defines her analytical move into Marxist arguments as a 'parodic identification' (Butler 1998: 34), stressing that parody is something that is different from a mere external kind of ridiculing. Parody implies a dimension of serious identification and intimacy, Butler argues. Without this serious commitment, the parody does not work:

> It is, I would argue, impossible to perform a convincing parody of an intellectual position without having a prior affiliation with what one parodies, without having and wanting an intimacy with the position one takes in or on as the object of parody. (Butler 1998: 34)

To characterise this element of serious try-out of arguments beyond the comfort zones of one's own well-rehearsed theoretical stances, Butler goes so far as to talk about generating an uncertainty about where one stands. She argues that this is necessary if one wants to perform a convincing parody:

> Parody requires a certain ability to identify, approximate, and draw near; it engages an intimacy with the position it appropriates that troubles the voice, the bearing, the performativity of the subject such that the audience or the reader does not quite know where it is you stand, whether you have gone over to the other side, whether you remain on your side, whether you can rehearse that other position without falling prey to it in the midst of the performance. (Butler 1998: 34–35)

Butler describes the uncertainty the parody must produce to be convincing as a 'wavering' (Butler 1998: 35), and her rhetorical and analytical strategy is to invite the readers into the parodic 'wavering' between a feminist Marxist and a queerfeminist deconstructive position. The purpose of this gesture is a reaching out for a more sophisticated discussion of solidarity on the Left across theoretical and political differences. Butler's point is that a 'synthesis of a set of [political and theoretical, NL] conflicts' (Butler 1998: 37) like the one Fraser tries to construct creates exclusions and new hierarchies (the relegating of queer politics to the sphere of the 'merely cultural' is a case in point). According to Butler, what is needed instead of the Fraserian synthesis is

> a mode of sustaining conflict in politically productive ways, a practice of contestation that demands that these movements [the more traditional socialist Left and queer movements, NL] articulate their goals under the pressure of each other without therefore exactly becoming each other. (Butler 1998: 37)

I think this gesture of parodic 'wavering' on Butler's part is interesting as an analytical and political strategy that fits well together with intersectional analysis and politics. A well-prepared and contextualising move beyond the comfort zones of one's theoretical stances – like the one to which Butler (1998) commits herself – is, I think, an important approach when it comes to addressing conflicted, disturbing and politically as well as theoretically troubling intersections without ending up in hegemonic and competitive theoretical claims as to which categorisations and intersections are the most politically pertinent.

I also think that there are interesting parallels between Butler's parodic 'wavering' and what Nira Yuval-Davis (1997, and this volume) has presented as 'transversal dialogue', that is, a methodology to approach 'truth' (cf. Yuval-Davis, this volume) and a political tool to produce solidarity in and between different social movements, based not on identity politics but on a politics of affiliation across differences and political boundaries. For Yuval-Davis, transversal dialogues are based on a combination of 'rooting' (reflectedly situating oneself) and 'shifting' (temporarily identifying with the perspective of other dialogue participants) (Yuval-Davis 1997). I think Butler's 'wavering' (1998: 35), seen within Yuval-Davis's theoretical framework, can be productively interpreted as such a temporary 'shifting' to a feminist Marxist position. But I also think that it can be productive to read Yuval-Davis through Butler's lens, and such a reading would emphasise that the 'shifting' does not necessarily imply a mere copying of the position of the other. While shifting to the Marxist feminist position, Butler complicates Fraser's position.

Conclusion: A Fully Fledged Theory of Intersectionality?

Intersectional analysis is born out of conflicts within and inbetween social movements struggling for social justice, cultural transformation and a difference- and diversity-sensitive, socially, culturally and ecologically sustainable democracy. Social movements need to keep moving, otherwise they die. For me this implies that intersectional analysis cannot be fixed *a priori* to a limited number of categories or frameworks without risking problematic exclusions and tunnel vision. But it is also my conviction that it is important to be specific about contexts, political genealogies, continuities and discontinuities within and inbetween different social movements. Therefore, I have argued for a type of intersectional analysis that should take into account a need for thorough contextualisation and reflection on political-theoretical genealogies of specific intersections, as well as an equally pressing need for openness to rhizomatic lines of flight towards new kinds of intersections.

I shall end by commenting on the question about the need for a 'fully fledged' theory of intersectionality. Do we (feminists committed to intersectional analysis) need such a theory or not? My answer is both yes and no, or perhaps a 'yes, on certain conditions'.

On the one hand, I think we need to scrutinise the genealogies of feminist intersectional analysis – and take better care to learn from previous ways of theorising intersections. We have just begun to do this. We have sophisticated theories about some kinds of intersections, but we certainly have done very little to theorise others. To take an example: Marxist feminists and Marxist-inspired post-colonial and anti-racist feminists have developed a lot of reflections on gender, race and class. Queer feminists have developed a lot of reflections on gender, sex and sexuality. But because the groups committed to Marxist-inspired frameworks, on the one hand, and queer, post-structuralist and deconstructionist frameworks, on the other, often have fought each other rather than trying to establish transversal dialogues beyond their respective comfort zones, we cannot connect the two kinds of intersectional analysis very well. So if developing a fully fledged theory on intersectionality means working along the lines of establishing more transversal dialogues between different branches of feminist theorising in order to get more sophisticated analytical tools, I am definitely 'in'.

If, on the other hand, developing a fully fledged theory means freezing a new theory, I am 'out'. I see feminist theorising as producing discourses of resistance in a constant process of negotiation with social movements, politics, science, etc. Against this background, I understand feminist theorising, including the construction of conceptual tools such as intersectionality, as non-fixable moments in time. But the non-fixable character of these moments does not exclude the possibility that we can learn from them, if we use them productively for as long as they survive as critical figures!

Bibliography

Barad, K. 2003. Posthumanist Performativity: Toward an Understanding of How Matter Comes to Matter. *Signs: Journal of Women in Culture and Society*, 28(3), 801–31.

Brah, A. and Phoenix, A. 2004. Ain't I A Woman? Revisiting Intersectionality. *Journal of International Women's Studies*, 5(3), 75–86.

Braidotti, R. 1994. *Nomadic Subjects: Embodiment and Sexual Difference in Contemporary Feminist Theory*. New York: Columbia University Press.

Braidotti, R. 2002. *Metamorphoses: Towards a Materialist Theory of Becoming.* Cambridge, UK: Polity.

Butler, J. 1990. *Gender Trouble: Feminism and the Subversion of Identity.* London, New York: Routledge.

Butler, J. 1993. *Bodies that Matter: On the Discursive Limits of 'Sex'.* London, New York: Routledge.

Butler, J. 1998. Merely Cultural? *New Left Review*, I(227), 33–44.

Combahee River Collective. 1977/1982. A Black Feminist Statement, in *All the Women Are White, All the Blacks Are Men, But Some of Us Are Brave. Black Women's Studies*, edited by Hull, G.T., Bell Scott, P. and Smith, B. New York: The Feminist Press at the City University of New York 1982 (reprint), 13–22.

Crenshaw, K.W. 1989. Demarginalizing the Intersection of Race and Sex: A Black Feminist Critique of Antidiscrimination Doctrine, Feminist Theory and Antiracist Politics. *University of Chicago Legal Forum*, 139–67.

Crenshaw, K.W. 1995. Mapping the Margins: Intersectionality, Identity Politics, and Violence Against Women of Color, in *Critical Race Theory. The Key Writings that Formed the Movement*, edited by K.W. Crenshaw et al. New York: The New Press, 357–84.

Deleuze, G. and Guattari, F. 1992. *A Thousand Plateaus: Capitalism and Schizophrenia.* London, New York: Continuum. Transl. Brian Massumi from *Mille Plateaux. Capitalisme et schizophrénie.* Paris: Minuit 1980.

Duggan, L. and Hunter, N.D. 2006. *Sex Wars: Sexual Dissent and Political Culture.* London, New York: Routledge.

Fraser, N. 1995. From Redistribution to Recognition? Dilemmas of justice in a 'post-socialist' age. *New Left Review*, I(212), 68–93.

Gates, H.L. and McKay, N. 1997. *The Norton Anthology of African American Literature.* New York: Norton.

Haraway, D. 1992. The Promises of Monsters: A Regenerative Politics for Inappropriate/ed Others, in *Cultural Studies*, edited by Grossberg, L., Nelson, C. and Treichler, P. London, New York: Routledge, 295–338.

hooks, bell. 1981. *Ain't I a Woman.* Boston: South End Press.

Hornscheidt, A. 2007. Sprachliche Kategorisierung als Grundlage und Problem des Redens über Interdependenzen. Aspekte sprachlicher Normalisierung und Priviligierung, in *Gender als interdependente Kategorie. Neue Perspektiven auf Intersektionalität, Diversität und Heterogenität*, edited by Walgenbach, K., Dietze, G., Hornscheidt, A. and Palm, K. Opladen and Farmington Hills: Verlag Barbara Budrich, 64–105.

Kollontai, A. 1971. *New Woman. The New Morality and the Working Class. The Autobiography of a Sexually Emancipated Communist Woman*, Herder and Herder. Transl. Salvator Attansio from *Novaya moral i rabochii klass*, Moscow 1918. Available at: http://www.marxists.org/archive/kollonta/1918/new-morality.htm [accessed: 21 June 2010].

Laclau, E. and Mouffe, C. 1985. *Hegemony and Socialist Strategy: Towards a Radical Democratic Politics.* London: Verso.

Lauretis, T. de. 1984. *Alice Doesn't: Feminism, Semiotics and Cinema*. London and Basingstoke: Macmillan.

Lykke, N. 2010. *Feminist Studies: A Guide to Intersectional Theory, Methodology and Writing*. New York, London: Routledge.

Matsuda, M. 1991. Beside My Sister, Facing the Enemy: Legal Theory out of Coalition. *Stanford Law Review*, 43(6), 1183–92.

McCall, L. 2005. The Complexity of Intersectionality. *Signs: Journal of Women in Culture and Society*, 30(3), 1771–1880.

Minh-ha, T. T. 1986/7. She, The Inappropriate/d Other. *Discourse*, 8.

Minh-ha, T.T. 1989. *Women, Native, Other: Writing Postcolonialism and Feminism*. Bloomington, Indianapolis: Indiana University Press.

Moser, I. 2006. Sociotechnical Practices and Difference: On the Interferences between Disability, Gender, and Class. *Science, Technology & Human Values*, 31(5), 537–64.

Rubin, G. 1984. Thinking Sex: Notes for a Radical Theory of the Politics of Sexuality, in *The Lesbian and Gay Studies Reader*, edited by Abelove, H., Barale, M.A. and Halperin, D.M. New York, London: Routledge, 3–45.

Sandoval, C. 2000. *Methodology of the Oppressed*. Minneapolis, London: University of Minnesota Press.

Sedgwick, E.K. 1990. *Epistemology of the Closet*. Berkeley, Los Angeles: University of California Press.

Yuval-Davis, N. 1997. *Gender & Nation*. London: Sage.

Postscript

Kimberlé Crenshaw

Introduction: 'Intersectionality Travels'

I was delighted to have been invited to participate in the January 2009 conference marking the twentieth anniversary of 'Demarginalising the Intersection of Race and Sex Discrimination: A Black Feminist Critique of Anti-Discrimination Doctrine, Feminist Theory and Anti-racist Politics.' This volume begins with a republication of 'Demarginalising' and I am honoured to have an opportunity to offer some reflections about the uptake and trajectory of that work herein.

This privilege is not without its challenges, however. As a mere observer to the unfolding debate about intersectionality in Europe and one of many theorists writing under that rubric, the effort to sort out how to speak and write into this particular moment is daunting. Indeed, there is a plethora of intersectional projects that are swept together under this rubric and it is not always clear whether the debate positions intersectionality in this generic sense versus the more specific articulation of it that appears in my work. While my default position has been to presume the former, the occasions where a rather surprising claim about intersectionality is specifically attached to my own work disrupts my studied observer status. Thus, my comments here reflect on the debate through the lens of intersectionality as I have conceptualised it in my own work, recognising of course that my own take on the concept reflects a set of sensibilities that may be disciplinary, political or temperamental.

Equally challenging in this regard is sorting out the actual parameters of the debate. As I noted in the closing plenary, the question posed by the conference title – 'Celebrating Intersectionality?' – seemed most appropriate for others to address. On the other hand, the specific queries put before the panellists, particularly questions about the context of 'intersectionality's' original articulation and the way the term has been imported, adapted and developed in 'Europe' offered a more concrete and substantive foundation from which to engage the dialogue. Yet even this perch proved somewhat elusive, as the debates seemed to be animated by propositions, expectations and claims about intersectionality that were neither articulated nor fully attributed. As a relative outsider in this European context, trying to map exactly what was at stake in these debates was occasionally mystifying.

Subsequently, I gained clarity when in preparing this volume, the editors posed the questions thusly:

- Can such an all-round, catch-it-all-concept possibly be more than a 'buzzword'?
- Can it be regarded as approximating an overarching theory of oppression and marginalisation at all?
- What are its geographical, topical and methodological limits?

In retrospect, this triad of questions amply framed the discursive politics conference. At the same time, they revealed a set of assertions and assumptions that reflected different sensibilities about the what, why and how of intersectionality. Indeed, the responses they anticipate – some definitive articulation of intersectionality's grand objectives, mechanisms, and trajectories – are quite foreign to my own sensibilities about intersectionality. My own take on how to know intersectionality has been to do intersectionality; to assess what intersectionality can produce is to canvass what scholars, activists and policymakers have done under its rubric. Thus, the invitation to measure and evaluate intersectionality as theory in the abstract has not drawn my engagement over the years. Indeed, in the 20 years since writing 'Demarginalising' I have had neither the occasion to debate whether intersectionality is 'an overarching theory of oppression' nor to proscribe or predict its limits. What I have done was to use intersectionality as a prism for examining a host of issues, conditions, policies and rhetorics. These projects have built on and have moved beyond the immediate interests that gave rise to 'Demarginalising', encompassing legal as well as social issues, engaging domestic as well as international discourses, producing cultural critique as well as policy analysis, addressing academic readers as well as lay audiences. Moreover, in the burgeoning literature that takes up the concept – including pieces in this volume– I've consistently learned more from what scholars and activists have done with intersectionality than from what others have speculated about its appeal.

This is not to say that there are not enormously valuable research questions pertaining to the possibilities and limits of intersectionality, especially pertaining to the conditions under which it can serve as a predicate for reconfiguring collectivities towards transformative action. These are empirical questions to be analysed by reference to what specific analytic functions intersectionality has served rather than categorical questions to be settled by pronouncements about what intersectionality is or isn't. I too approach the discourse around intersectionality's 'spectacular career' with some curiosity, but I am far more puzzled by the notion that scholars, activists and policymakers – those who have used intersectionality – have not already provided answers to the question of whether intersectionality is 'anything more' than a catch-it-all buzzword.

I am struck that within the conference debate and to a lesser extent within this text are some rather surprisingly familiar dualities. The various assertions about what intersectionality has been, currently is and has the potential to be have been framed through many of the same dualities that troubled the introduction of both gender and race studies into the academy. Between the lines and often inside the text are strains of particularism versus universalism, personal narrative versus grand theory, identity-based versus structural, static versus dynamic, parochial versus cosmopolitan, underdeveloped versus sophisticated, old versus new, race versus class, US versus Europe, and so on. Elsewhere I respond more fully to the rather curious ways that intersectionality has engendered some of the same disciplining moves among feminists that have also been deployed against feminism (Crenshaw, Forthcoming). Here I want to focus more closely on the ways in which some of the central questions posed in the debate might be better framed by reflecting on some of the generative dimensions of intersectionality's initial iteration and subsequent movement. Since this postscript provides the rare occasion to more fully situate the text that opens this volume, I want to highlight the temporal, political and institutional factors that created the conditions of its possibility. My purpose is not only to identify elements of intersectionality that have been lost in translation, but also to illustrate that the interpretive work that must be done to make ideas work in different contexts is a feature of the discursive environment through which ideas travel rather than a reflection of inherent deficiencies in ideas themselves.

It is quite clear that as an idea travels, the ways that it is re-articulated, sizedup, written down, adapted, disciplined and deployed all become part of its discursive history – its travel log as it were. As such, the debate that it engenders is not about the character of the 'traveller'*per se*, but about the nature of its movement across borders, how it is interrogated and categorised, whether it is contained or integrated, what parts are embargoed or assimilated, lopped off or transformed as it moves from site to site. How we view, interpret and articulate its movements is indeed a discussion that can provide interesting insights not only about intersectionality, but about academic performance and the patterns of dominance and difference that characterise relationships between academics, disciplines and the other constituencies of interest.

Reversing the trajectory of intersectionality's journey, I invoke somewhat schematically some of the issues that have been raised about or inferred from intersectionality that might be usefully engaged by revisiting its origins. One question that has been asked is whether intersectionality will develop 'a methodology'. I sometimes call this the 'will intersectionality settle down and get a real job?' question. Implicit in this query is the assumption that intersectionality as currently understood is a good candidate on paper but without a usable methodology it has no ready-to-work skills. Of course what this rap belies is that methodologies are specific to disciplines; a perfectly well-understood and rehearsed methodology in one discipline may be incomprehensible or even invisible to another. It is likely that traveling ideas are particularly vulnerable to claims that they could do better 'if only...' despite the fact that they may have enjoyed remarkable careers elsewhere.

Not only are methodologies of origin frequently invisible to receiving disciplines, the critical work necessary to translate, reshape and integrate ideas and sensibilities drawn from a variety of sources into a form of knowledge that is recognisable within an unfamiliar discipline seems difficult to discern. For example, intersectionality is sometimes framed as though the texts of black feminism were simply downloaded in a zip file and automatically converted to run on the law's operating system.

Both of these images of intersectionality's border crossings – its problematic entry into disciplinary arenas where its ability to do 'real' work is suspect, and the relatively effortless ability of black feminism to take up residence in the law – are framed as static features of ideas themselves rather than reflections of the dynamic role of discursive agents within the traversed territories. The interpretive, creative, highly contested and sometimes perilous work of integrating insurgent knowledge into established, often conservative discursive communities is an underexamined dimension of intersectionality's travels.

While black feminism figures as the widely acknowledged generative source of intersectionality, somewhat conversely, the role of black women has sometimes troubled those seeking to grow intersectionality beyond its discursive origins. The fact that questions about whether intersectionality is 'just' about black women are still voiced despite the contributions of many scholars represented in these pages and elsewhere who deploy intersectionality to analyse a plethora of issues, contexts and groups, seems to reflect a deeper anxiety about the constitutive role of race in intersectionality and of black women in particular. These concerns, somewhat ironically, parallel the very judicial anxieties that initially prompted American courts to reject black women's bid to serve as class representatives for all women. In the same way that courts saw the specific pleadings of black women as setting forth a particularity that disqualified them as representatives of the universal experience of sex discrimination, some theorists taking up intersectionality intimate a certain parochialism in its origins that compromises its theoretical comprehensiveness. There is a sense that efforts to repackage intersectionality for universal consumption require a re-marginalising of black women. This instinct reflects a fatal transmission error of 'Demarginalising's' central argument: that representations of gender that are 'race-less' are not by that fact alone more universal than those that are race-specific.

Often, it seems that the figure of the black woman at the centre of intersectionality, standing alone and absent contexualisation, links to other misreadings of 'Demarginalising'. Questions about whether intersectionality is simply a feature of identities or structures, whether it maps a static location of unchanging oppression or the dynamic interface of systems of power across a variety of institutions and contexts, suggests that the figurative role of black women has reified intersectionality against the more nuanced narrative that 'Demarginalising' endeavoured to tell. Indeed, if intersectionality is understood as simply a spasm of black feminist identity politics repackaged in a fancy new word, then perhaps intersectionality's appeal to a wide variety of discursive communities might be understandably puzzling. In fact, 'Demarginalising' was informed by and written to bridge a number of divisions and discursive traditions that made up critical legal studies (CLS) in the 1980s. In the richly diverse but highly contested space occupied by left-leaning law professors, debates among and between adherents of various intellectual traditions in all their classical, post and neo articulations were standard fare. CLS was a site where liberal feminists struggled and aligned with post-modernists and dominance feminists, where neo-Marxists and post-structuralists struggled between them and against liberal anti-racists, where liberal anti-racists took issue with radical black nationalists, who in turn struggled with queer and feminist anti-racists. 'Neo, post and critical' functioned to define different intellectual sensibilities and to carve out rhetorical space, yet at the same time, politicised identity discourses overlapped with, modified and sometimes superseded these loose intellectual affiliations. In this space, intellectual and political alliances were discernable but not static, structured in some ways by the historical markers that embodied power, yet sometimes disrupted and reconfigured by the debates immediately at hand. Feminists split by their intellectual allegiances to post-modernism or liberalism might converge to critique a specific expression of male power; critical race theorists who allied with FemCrits to wrest control from white males – themselves an aggregation of disparate intellectual adherents – would on another occasion, ally with liberal race theorists to critique the 'whiteness' of CLS. Navigating spaces constituted by such shifting dynamics and distinct discursive registers was art as much as politics. In fact, one might think of 'Demarginalising' as a performance piece, a transcription of a multi-layered engagement that was fully recognisable as legal method within the law and as insurgent practice within the established routines of CLS. Thus historicised, the fact that intersectionality continues to engage multiple discursive communities is nothing mysterious.

The unique configuration of race and gender power in this historical moment – in particular, the unravelling of the transformative promises of US anti-discrimination law and the emergence of critical projects seeking to interrogate and reveal its mere regulatory dimensions – reveals that intersectionality's emergence at that temporal moment was not a mere accident of intellectual history. Neither was the foregrounding of black women in intersectionality merely an epiphenomenal dimension of a dynamic that was infinitely present and readily cognisable. Intersectionality emerged at a specific historical juncture in the US, one in which the parallel legal projects of race and gender discrimination law were undergoing critical theorisation within liberal and left legal formations. Neither these critical projects nor the legal frameworks with which they were engaged were poised to respond to the very visible invisibility of women who were not white and blacks who were not men. African American women drew attention to this gaping hole in doctrine, in feminist jurisprudence and in emerging critical race theory (CRT), both figuratively and literally. Critical legal studies provided the discursive tools and the critical mass to frame such interventions as collective enterprises.

If the context of CLS sets the stage for understanding intersectionality's methodological and discursive articulation, then it is equally significant to acknowledge how the unusual level of race and gender integration within this formation – specifically the participation of previously excluded groups such as white women and people of colour – also served as a necessary condition of its possibility. This integration was not accidental but was a product of the specific reformist concessions that produced increasing numbers of men of colour and women gaining access to law schools and into the legal teaching profession itself. Certain race and gender-conscious reforms at the structural level helped constitute the very collective which, in turn, influenced and in some ways transformed the trajectory of the CLS project. The widespread critiques of the exclusionary practices that had created a virtually all-white and male professoriate prompted modest efforts of liberal administrators to introduce affirmative action policies to address these exclusions. These were all unique features of American social history. Were it not for these efforts, many of the debates that evolved into the feminist and critical race theorist would have been muted or non-existent.

'Demarginalising' was additionally influenced by several specific debates that emerged as white women and people of colour attained critical mass. As the feminist turn in CLS was nearing its apex and the pivot towards critical race theory was beginning to turn, feminist scholarship was coming under fire from multicultural feminist for its solipsisms. These critiques sometimes inadvertently became packaged together with the post-structuralist scepticism towards all grand theory, although in practice, there was a somewhat discernible tendency to tar certain feminisms with that brush rather than other theoretical paradigms. Within debates where race was foregrounded, often the mere assertion of difference between women was enough to stop conversation altogether. Similar critiques were beginning to be levelled against the race projects in CLS, although for the most part the criticisms against 'race essentialisms' were lobbed from outside that emerging formation rather than as a demand for recognition and inclusion with it.

Positioned as a black feminist in these debates, I had no doubt that some feminist projects were under-theorised and under-inclusive. Yet it also seemed to me that the demand for inclusion was weakened by the failure of some critics to articulate what difference our differences made in the specific projects at hand. Moreover, the mere assertion of difference, without more, not only failed to expand the narrow contours of anti-discrimination law, but also in some ways worked to reinforce the very sensibilities that dictated the suppression of claims like *DeGraffenreid*. On the other hand, the failure to attend to difference within constituent groups also undermined the ability of advocates to fashion interventions that anticipated the needs of differently situated members. These simultaneous critiques – one challenging feminism from within through an ill-defined assertion of difference – the other challenging CRT from without as a misbegotten project wholly defined by racial essentialism – highlighted the need for an analysis that acknowledged the ubiquitous nature of difference but insisted on articulating the differences that made a difference in the project at hand.

This work was not purely academic. 'Demarginalising' arose from concrete debates in which women of colour struggled among themselves to come to terms with our own responsibilities to theorise difference in the context of feminist jurisprudence. It was simultaneously a reflection of debates among and between emerging critical race theorists to articulate a non-essentialist understanding of the materiality of race. We insisted that the 'constructedness' of race did not defeat or render incoherent intellectual projects that sought to recognise, analyse and redress its active role in 'race-ing' the worlds in which we lived.

This effort to carve out such an understanding brought contestation around race directly into the centre of CLS, dramatically so in response to the critique of rights. Indeed, one of the most significant debates in critical legal studies revolved around the critique of rights discourse. Although there were nuances and different emphases, most broadly those identifying themselves as critics highlighted the indeterminacy of rights and their mystifying and co-opting effects. Rigorous trashing was the prescriptive cure for ridding proponents of change of the false imperatives and abstract representations of rights discourse. On the other side were those of us who weren't particularly shocked by the notion that law was an indeterminate and sometimes counterproductive tool in social struggle. Among early race critics was the belief that there was no meaningful space to contest racial power without engaging law. Because law both constituted and regulated the racial terrain, the choice was not whether to engage it but how. Much of my own early work as well as that of Pat Williams, Mari Matsuda and Charles Lawrence was about acknowledging that law was obviously a discourse of domination, but at the same time, it constituted an arena through which the rules of racial subordination might be engaged. Our work sought to lift up key doctrinal moments and their policy implications to show that there were other ways that these issues could be resolved, to reveal that the racial politics and policy choices in the law that helped constitute and rationalise racial power could go a different way. Moreover, in keeping with the tradition of interrogating power not only 'out there' in society but also inside the very formation we were in – namely CLS – rigorous debates about structural, interpersonal and group power within CLS were commonplace.

Intersectionality thus was made possible by a variety of discursive, political and institutional forces: the linking of anti-racism and feminism, their parallel articulations within the law and the progressive critiques they engendered; the formation of left-liberal institutional spaces that were increasingly populated by newcomers to the discipline, and finally by the flourishing and successive discursive turns – real-life arguments and internal struggles – that constituted CLS in the mid-1980s.

***

Owing to the unique history of the mutual construction of racism and patriarchy in the American state, the intertwining of both has been a profoundly salient feature of American life. Yet despite these structural features, the dynamic interface between these systems was rarely politicised or contested either within anti-discrimination law or within the political formations organised to contest patriarchy and racism. Black feminist theory and advocacy sought from its earliest iterations to draw attention to this interface, not simply as a demand for self-recognition, but as a critique of the limitations of feminism and anti-racism and as a demand for accountability. Black women's marginality in the rhetorical discourses that purported to include them was memorialised and made 'sticky' by the phrase, 'All the Blacks are Men and All the Women are White,' the title of the ground-breaking book that chronicles the voices of black women speaking into the void.

This phrase constitutes the opening sequence of 'Demarginalising', establishing the cartography of race and gender discourse that naturalises what is, in fact, a peculiar vision of social inclusion. The story that 'Demarginalising' goes on to tell explores how law helps ground this peculiarity while recruiting feminists and anti-racists to visions of social justice that are inadequate to their stated goals.

Law helped constitute what intersectionality came to be by establishing interpretative templates that any discrimination claim needed to engage in order to be cognisable. These templates – constructed to operationalise the vetting of claims against a standardised (and partial) narrative of what discrimination was – informed the arguments, pleadings, proofs and opinions of judges. Legal opinions function in some ways like magnetic resolution images, revealing the architecture of anti-discrimination law and the various preferences that are attendant to it. CLSers read these images to demonstrate how law concretised and naturalised power relationships that were in fact contingent and constructed. Engaging 'law' within this space was thus a multidimensional affair – CLS texts often walked the walk of doctrinal analysis and talked the talk of insurgent critique with withering accounts of law's mystifying and legitimising dimensions. Many projects conceived and executed within the context of CLS carried this dual purpose – that of engaging the discipline itself through doctrinal analysis while at the same time revealing the ways that law reified social relations and rationalised the power dynamics that shaped the social terrain.

'Demarginalising' performs both dimensions of CLS scholarship; it reads several decisions to show the specific, sometimes contradictory ways that claims of discrimination were disciplined and dismissed, unpacking the doctrine to show the underlying assumptions, the institutional values, the subjectivities and concrete particulars against which black women's claims were rendered illegible. It reads these cases in part to uncover the specific material consequences of raced and gendered workplaces that were all-to-often elided in conventional analysis. It seeks not only to put structural discrimination against African American women into the discourse but also to interrogate the ideological process by which their claims were quarantined. Piercing the rationalisations that the courts deployed to contain black women's claims, 'Demarginalising' revealed the underlying preference for conceptions of discrimination that both limited the laws' scope, and privileged white women and black men as its essential subjects. These cases, upon closer inspection, revealed that the troubling particularism that Pandora's Box was invoked to contain was not the limitless generation of new subjectivities, but the specifically embodied narratives of discrimination that had already slipped Pandora's grasp, narratives that were masquerading as universal in their conception.

The significance of this critique is often lost on readers who interpret 'Demarginalising' as simply an argument for the recognition of black women as a separate juridical category. This understanding not only belies the multifaceted discursive purposes 'Dermarginalising' served, it also resists the critique of the sameness and difference paradigm that 'Demarginalising' was making. The recognition of black women as a juridical category would have not constituted a meaningful solution to the broader principle that *DeGraffenreid* revealed – that black women were seen solely as a variation of the general. Nor would this move reveal the ways that the law tightly regulated the overall function of anti-discrimination law.

'Demarginalising' was not simply a descriptive account of the marginalisation of certain claims but a normative argument for reversing the dominant conceptions of discrimination – especially the paradigm of sameness and difference – that underwrites them. Setting forth this complex dynamic required an analysis that not only advanced a claim on behalf of the *DeGraffenreid* plaintiffs but also brought into plain view the violence that this narrow frame imposed upon the aspirations of other plaintiffs. Thus, *DeGraffenreid* presented only one way in which black women's particularities were constructed as something other than sex discrimination. The article also points out that even where black women were not formally prohibited from making claims on the basis of race and gender, they were denied the ability to represent all women (because as one court put it, the plaintiff was not making a claim as a woman, but *only* as a black woman) as well as the ability to represent African American men (such that even the plaintiffs' success in proving race discrimination put them at odds with black men who were also discriminated against). Ultimately, the picture that emerged was that even as law sought to provide narrowly framed interventions on behalf of some plaintiffs, it did so at the cost of re-inscribing the system for others who could not fit the law's narrow requirements of pleading.

To these courts, a woman who was black could only represent a smaller subset of all women in contrast to the white representative who has nothing else to complain about except for her gender. Similarly, to specify femaleness in the context of race was to make a narrower and thus under-inclusive claim of race discrimination. Thus the problem was not just that the doctrine as interpreted by the court forced black women to be the same as white women or black men to get their claim recognised. The problem was also that black women's difference was too great to permit them to represent all women or all men. Of course black women are as different from white women and black men as white women and black men are to them, yet their symmetrical difference did not defeat the curious claim that black men and white women could embody the universal, while black women could not. Thus, my argument was not simply that black women were harmed where they were different and the law required them to be the same; I also argued that they were harmed when their experience was treated as too different to be treated as the same. It was the need to re-present this apparent contradiction into a coherent framework capturing the multiple ways that power operated that gave rise to the image of the intersection. I was arguing for a certain understanding of the dynamic of discrimination and the structures that are created and ossified by that discrimination.

My challenge was then to figure out a way to draw attention to the dual dimension of this particular discrimination. First, it was necessary to foreground the structural dimensions of the workforce, but to do so in a way that linked the particular consequences of the racial identity of these women, women who were not black and blacks who were not women. Beyond the discrimination produced by these converging patterns of workforce stratification was the failure of anti-discrimination law to address the particular ways that workplace structures advantaged some and disadvantaged others. Intersectionality, quite frankly, came from an attempt to think about an easy way to capture these various dynamics. Intersectionality is simply the metaphor to capture both the structural and dynamic aspects of this discrimination.

It seemed to me that what was happening to these women was that they were overrun with currents of power and, that having been run over by these dynamics, they were seeking law's intervention to administer to and correct the situation. The law in return seemed to be saying that these women could not be indemnified against this particular kind of injury because it could not be identified with the clarity that the extant rules required. But given the terrain upon which the accident occurred, the women were placed in a particular intersection because they were on the subordinate side of both the race and gender divide. It was as if, in my mind, the ambulance was called to arrive at the scene of the collision and rather than picking up the plaintiffs, the drivers simply left them there because the cause of their injuries was unlike all the others they had been trained to treat. Namely, black women's marginalisation was the consequence of multiple collisions when the insurance indemnified only against one driver. Had the accident been clearly traced to the race divide, or across the gender divide, it would be clear where the responsibility rested.

***

The metaphor upon which intersectionality is scaffolded acknowledges a wide variety of encounters as well as relationships. In this sense, intersectionality applies to everyone – no one exists outside of the matrix of power, but the implications of this matrix – when certain features are activated and relevant and when they are not – are contextual. Intersectionality represents a structural and dynamic arrangement; power marks these relationships among and between categories of experience that vary in their complexity. To map intersectionality from instance to instance both confirms the relevance of categories, and provides the impetus for disrupting dominant discourses that regard these categories as fixed and mutually exclusive. Intersectionality then was an attempt to create a prism that revealed the confluence of structure and identity and to highlight vectors in which discrimination was rendered invisible by the prevailing frameworks that were deployed to identify and intervene against it. Intersectionality was not the only attempt to do so nor would it be the last. Indeed, as I have indicated before, intersectionalty is a provisional conceptualisation, a prism refracted to bring into view dynamics that were constitutive of power but obscured by certain discursive logics at play in that context. I made no attempt to articulate each and every intersection either specifically or generally, nor to foreclose or anticipate how intersectionality might unfold across time and space. To my mind 'Demarginalising' was less of a snapshot of a particular dynamic than it was a video clip, captioned as 'intersectionality' and offered up with the query: this is a piece that I can see. What other clips of social power might be part of this collection?

Conclusion

'Demarginalising' was not simply a brief for black women's rights, nor was its articulation so specific to the US configuration of race and gender power that its various implications could be embargoed and contained within the confines of US anti-discrimination law. As a legal scholar, my attention was focused on using intersectional analysis to advance an argument *within* law while at the same time interrogating certain dynamics *about* law and its relation to social power. Similarly, as intersectionality has travelled, those who have effectively deployed it have sought to adapt it to certain problems while challenging the disciplinary or rhetorical parameters that would otherwise render such projects unspeakable, unknowable or unmanageable.

The need to *work* intersectionality and to develop methods that are both recognisable and insurgent within different disciplines is part of intersectionality's travel log.

In this sense, the popular uptake of the term may in fact be misleading to casual observers unfamiliar with intersectionality's critical stance towards the dominant sensibilities in knowledge production and politics. Indeed, the term's evocative popularity exists in some tension with the critical task of rendering analysis that is simultaneously recognisable and disruptive within specific discursive communities. That it is easier to call for intersectional analysis rather than to perform it is not a failing of the concept but a recognition that performing intersectional analysis is neither a simplistic symbolic signifier nor is it a paint-by-numbers analytic enterprise.

Yet certain dimensions of the debate about what intersectionality is or can be made to do seem to be grounded in an inference that there is no 'there' there. For some critics the easy invocation of the term as a political signifier on the one hand, along with the challenges encountered by theorists attempting to discipline the concept on the other, suggests that intersectionality needs intervention. At least one response to intersectionality's supposed indeterminacy gravitates towards standardisation in order to shore up its theoretical bona fides, while a competing approach counsels acceptance of intersectionality's empty-suit character in light of its capacity to inspire analysts to essentially create the theory in attempts to understand it.

Although these gestures appear to underwrite competing orientations towards the intersectional project, they both proceed from a common sense about what real theory is. What this suggests is that some of the analytical frames put forward to 'measure' intersectionality seem to misapprehend its basic insights. In my view, intersectionality does not anticipate or call forth a listing of all differences nor does it offer a one-frame-fits-all theorisation of how power is dynamically constituted through structures and categories, either separately or constitutively.

Measuring intersectionality against such expectations seems far more consistent with the claims of grand theory, itself a dubious enterprise along with its accompanying industry of scientifically inflected authentication. That intersectionality doesn't meet the standards of something that it never claimed to be and, in fact, implicitly contests, justifies neither a call to celebrate its so-called 'incompleteness' nor a need to muscle it up to run with the big boys. In this respect, I have called intersectionality an analytical, a heuristic or hermeneutic tool –one designed to amplify and highlight specific problems. Intersectionality has been called a 'theory' of discrimination – that is to say the legal theory that describes why the plaintiffs in *DeGraffenreid* should have prevailed. It's even been called a Swiss army knife, but it has never been framed by me as a 'grand' theory.

Grand theories have totalising aspirations; they seek to capture and emphasise the general and the universal. While post-structuralism animates distrust for totalising theoretical meta-narratives, we need not give up on all efforts to comprehend the source of particular problems. In this sense, intersectionality more closely resembles Antonio Gramsci's mid-level theoretical framework, or what Louis Althusser calls descriptive theory – that is to say, the use of situated knowledge to construct understandings out of social contradictions.

For me what is valuable isn't the doing of theory *per se*, but determining whether the theory in question is useful in highlighting particular kinds of problems that are obscured by the toolset we normally deploy in our academic and political work. If a theory draws attention to dynamics that are constitutive but that are usually overlooked, I consider it useful not solely as an analytical tool but as a potential template for intervention. Indeed, one of the more contested dimensions of the debate is whether intersectionality is a project of the thinking professions, thus warranting a certain 'professionalisation', or whether its principal function is as a tool to develop better real-world interventions. Intersectionality of course traverses both the fields of thinking and acting; as such, drawing attention to the real-world consequences of non-intersectional interventions that are thought to be inclusive and universal is a project that is both academic and practical.

Thus, as the debate continues about what kind of theory intersectionality is, I gravitate towards thinking about intersectionality in relation to women whose stories appear in 'Mapping the Margins', women for whom even a minimalist approach to intersectional thinking in shaping the interventions that ultimately failed them might have made a difference in their lives. I think here about the woman who was desperately seeking shelter from a husband who had vowed to kill her yet was excluded from the local domestic violence shelters because their services were monolingual. I think about immigrant women entrapped in abusive relationships with citizen-spouses by fear of deportation, marginalised by immigration discourses that don't pay attention to gender and by feminist discourses that don't pay attention to immigration. I think about hundreds of thousands women who languish in prison, victims of a racialised public policy of mass incarceration and the gendered patterns of private violence, women who remain virtually erased by an anti-incarceration movement that sidelines women and an anti-violence movement that sidelines prisoners.

Intersectionality is of course contextual; as readers of this collection and the growing literature have learned, analysts and activists have fashioned intersectionality to unravel and intervene against the sometimes hidden or marginalised dynamics of power and exclusion across the social terrain. In this sense intersectionality is much more than a mere 'buzzword', which my dictionary defines as 'a vogueish word or phrase','an important-sounding usually technical word or phrase often of little meaning used chiefly to impress laymen'. It seems the term 'buzzword' does not do justice to the academics and activists who use intersectionality to illuminate and address discriminatory situations that would otherwise escape articulation. Moreover, the effort to reduce intersectionality to a prescribed set of analytical moves threatens to detain it within the professionalised boundaries of specific disciplines. This disciplinary impulse to measure intersectionality in the abstract rather than to build up from its many deployments across a range of contexts threatens to undermine rather than facilitate the knowledge that intersectionality might generate.

My own sense is that we should resist moves towards standardisation along with the contested scientific measures that would grade intersectionality as intellectually wanting due to its adaptability or its discursive signification or its resistance to plug and play theoretical modelling. Surely there will be uses of the concept in some quarters that will engender critique in others. Certainly various disciplines can and will develop a variety of analytic methods consistent with their established practices without any one of these being taken as the essential standard of intersectionality. Possibly an overarching consensus may emerge over time from a variety of the particular ways that intersectionality is undertaken. Indeed, there will likely be debates out of which dominant schools of thought might emerge only to be replaced by marginal ones that will become more persuasive over time. Without question intersectionality will take on different questions as the voices and sensibilities of organic intellectuals engage the debate, both within European/US borders and, importantly, from regions not represented in this book. Intersectional analysis may take us down many roads, but we will only discover what it is by using it.

Index

use of intersectionality 9

race/gender intersection
  discrimination against black women
    26–31, 28n10
  embracing, necessity of 40–1
  feminism and black women 32–6
  as process 56
  unrecognised by anti-discrimination
    framework 31
race/racism
  concept and study of in Germany
    10–13
  and emergence of intersectionality 224
  and gender, Islam, and sexuality
    114–16
  institutionalised rights discourses 61–2
  internal critiques in CLS 226–7
  as primary oppositional force 36,
    36n25, 36n26
  Rasse concept in Germany 10
  reforms in legal teaching 225–6
  See also migration/sexual orientation
    intersection; race/gender
    intersection
rape 34–5
Rasse concept in Germany 10
recognition/redistribution dichotomy
  Butler/Fraser debate 215–17
  characteristics of intersectionality
    157–60
  dilemma of 160–2
  and stratification 162–5
rhizomatics, intersectionality seen through
  211–12
rights
  discourses 59–60
  equal rights in US law 58–9
  institutionalised rights discourses 60–2
  stretching of discourses 61–2
Rubin, Gayle 213, 214

Saharso, Sawitri 5
Sedgwick, Eve K. 213, 214
sex trade 97–8
Sexton, Jared 108, 115
sexual orientation/migration intersection
  codings of same-sex desire 125–6

failures of research in 126–7
globalisation 129–30
heteronormative standards, regulation
  by 129
heteronormative/gendered assumptions
  127–8
intersections 131–3
state control of sexuality 128–31
Turks in Germany 122–4
work challenging heteronormativity
  130–1
sexual violence against men
  Abu Ghraib 108–9, 110–11
  and ethnicity 107, 109–10
  feminist reactions to 113–14
  heterosexuality, ethnicity and
    masculinity intersection 129
  and Islamophobia 115–16
  scholarship on 112–13
  visibility of perpetrators 110–11
  visibility of victims 110
  war in Yugoslavia 106–7, 107n2,
    109–10
sexuality
  and gender, Islam, and race 114–16
  and gender debate 213–14
  state control of 128–31
Snow, David A. 57, 60
social dynamics 157
social groups
  categorisation of people 193
  determining privilege of 75
  as diasporic 130
  etcetera problem 159–60
  formation of and hegemony 92
  men/women as 71, 79
social sciences, lack of dialogue with
  jurisprudence 7
social theory and intersectional invisibility
  194–200
Spain, current debates in 5, 5n8
specialists, appeal of intersectionality for
  49–50
Spivak, Gayatri C. 8, 93, 161
standpoints
  embodied 96
  epistemological 96
  feminist theory 156, 158